CHANGING CAMPAIGN TECHNIQUES:
Elections and Values in Contemporary Democracies

SAGE ELECTORAL STUDIES YEARBOOK

SAGE ELECTORAL STUDIES YEARBOOK

VOLUME II

Changing Campaign Techniques

Elections and Values in Contemporary Democracies

edited by

LOUIS MAISEL

SAGE Publications Beverly Hills / London

For information address:

SAGE PUBLICATIONS, INC.
275 South Beverly Drive
Beverly Hills, California 90212

SAGE PUBLICATIONS LTD
St George's House / 44 Hatton Garden
London EC1N 8ER

Printed in the United States of America

ISBN No. 0-8039-0683-8 (cloth)
ISBN No. 0-8039-0684-6 (paper)

Library of Congress Catalog Card No. 76-6311

FIRST PRINTING

To the memory of my father
Sidney B. Maisel

CONTENTS

CHANGING CAMPAIGN TECHNIQUES:
Elections and Values in Contemporary Democracies

INTRODUCTION

> Hell, make 'em cry, make 'em laugh, make 'em think you're their weak erring pal, or make 'em think you're God Almighty. . . . Tell 'em anything. But for Sweet Jesus' sake, don't try to improve their minds.
>
> Jack Burden to Willie Stark
> from Robert Penn Warren's
> *All the King's Men*

Perhaps a multidisciplinary volume on modern elections should have included a work of fiction. After all, the pictures our novelists paint are often very accurate reflections of the society in which we live. Warren's view, that the certain way to lose an election was to try to educate the public, is a common theme of literature. However, it is a view that I, as an editor, as a political scientist, as a citizen, reject. The essays in this book were collected out of a concern that elections in modern democracies were being fundamentally changed because of so-called advances in campaign techniques. Technological progress cannot and should not be retarded; however, as professionals concerned with the electoral process, we have, I feel, an obligation to examine the consequences of these changes.

Joe McGinniss's *The Selling of the President 1968* was most disturbing not because of the techniques that the Nixon campaign employed but because of the callous strategic reasoning behind those techniques that the book explicitly revealed. If today's professional politicians really believe that candidates can be packaged like laundry detergents and if those assumptions are proven correct by the electorate's decisions, then the values supposedly served by elections in contemporary democracies have been seriously undercut. However, if the "selling and buying" effect is more apparent than real, if what have changed are the techniques but not the functions of elections, then a clearer view of the effects of these techniques should be presented. The articles in this volume examine the effects of changing campaign techniques and comment on the consequences for democratic elections.

I

The goal of the Sage Electoral Studies Yearbooks is to draw together experts from various professional disciplines and in various countries to discuss problems of mutual interest. The question of changing campaign techniques is one for which this approach is particularly useful. Obviously the issue raised is a fundamental concern of political scientists. Through an expanded statement of the problem, it becomes apparent that many other professionals are equally interested.

The one single advance which has most affected campaigning has been the spread of television. Candidates now are able to speak to and be seen by millions of voters at one time, whereas once they could hope to contact only a fraction of that number during the course of a campaign. Television campaigning can take many forms, from long, well-developed issue statements through ten-second spot advertisements. Campaign managers make crucial decisions about how their candidates will come across best, about how much money can be spent on television, about when to spend the money.

However, the advertising of candidates is not the only way in which television affects campaigns. Much of the information which the voting public receives about an election comes from regular news broadcasts or from special coverage given an election contest. Television journalists are, therefore, an integral part of the dynamics of elections campaigns, even if news broadcasting is not precisely a "campaign technique." They too must ask questions about the effects of their performance, about the function which television coverage should play in the electoral process, about fairness, about the extent and timing of their coverage. Their involvement in the process is more central than was that of journalists in the past, and they need to explore the implications of their role.

Certainly all political information does not come from television. Daily newspapers, magazines, radio, and other forms of mass communication play important roles in informing the public. American politics has come a long way from the time when party newspapers were at the heart of elections. But, in the modern context, questions still must be asked about what role these media play. If television, and perhaps radio, give citizens a majority of their daily news, what functions do newspapers play in a political system? How concerned must we be about recent trends toward media monopolies in many areas? If one newspaper and perhaps one radio-television news service provide all the political information for the citizens of a certain area, how does this affect the political system?

Some are concerned that extensive use of new methods in political campaigns has resulted in a spiraling escalation of campaign costs, with the consequence that only those with access to massive amounts of money will be successful in future elections. Recent evidence from American elections certainly gives credence to this fear. Politicians in various countries have attempted to alleviate this problem through reforms in the electoral laws. Many countries, such as Sweden, Finland, and Germany, have turned to public financing of their election campaigns; others have placed limits on the amount of money which can be given to or spent on elections or have regulated broadcast campaigning. These laws have raised a series of practical as well as legal questions. Will the laws have their desired effect? Will they curtail civil liberties in unanticipated ways? Are they prejudicial to certain types of parties or candidates? Will they have latent consequences for the political systems, which were not foreseen? Those involved in writing these laws, in defending or challenging them, are thus involved in the debate over the effects of modern campaign techniques as well.

In addition, party officials question the impact which modern campaign techniques might have on party organization. Will candidate-centered campaigns, run by professional campaign managers using the latest techniques, make parties obsolete? Was the Committee to Re-elect the President an omen of things to come? And the list of those concerned could certainly be expanded.

II

The articles selected for inclusion in this volume center on a number of the themes mentioned. Four of the articles deal explicitly with the American system, and three of these with the debate over the Campaign Election Act Amendments of 1974, particularly the public financing provisions.[1] Joel L. Fleishman presents a cogent argument in favor of public financing. He feels that public financing overcomes most of the harmful effects of overreliance on private contributors. Looking at the recent American reforms from a lawyer's perspective, Fleishman concludes that some of the specific provisions in the current law might be defective but that the principle of public financing is one which can withstand the test of constitutionality. He suggests changes in specific sections of the law which could overcome possible Supreme Court objections. Jewel Bellush and William J.D. Boyd oppose public financing, fearing that reformers in their zeal to correct one flaw in the American system may well have generated new problems. They suggest a number of problem areas—the effect on civil liberties, the protection of incumbents and blocking of insurgents, the curbing of minor parties, and others—in a call for a further examination of the effects of subsidizing elections with public funds. In a commentary on these two articles, I have attempted to put the issue of public financing into the context of the 1976 election. Specifically, I feel that the effects of public financing on minor parties has been underplayed because it has been dealt with in the abstract and not in the context of the upcoming election. My analysis leads to the conclusion that public financing could lead to a situation in which electorally relevant minor parties would become a permanent feature of presidential campaigns.

The fourth article on American politics looks at the question of resource allocation during election campaigns. Paul A. Dawson and James E. Zinser, a political scientist and an economist respectively, present a model in which they explain resource allocation in terms of demographic variables. Specifically, they look at the statistical correlations between campaign expenditures and per capita income, income inequality, population mobility, age, and race, testing their model against the experience of the 1972 congressional elections. Their findings raise important questions about when modern techniques are likely to be applied in, and therefore be factors in, election campaigns.

Two of the other articles are concerned with news coverage. Alfred Grosser has examined the general problem of news dissemination in France. Starting from the premise that a democracy can only function if the citizenry is informed about what the government is doing and if the government knows of the citizens' feelings, Grosser discusses modern concerns: the problem, in France as elsewhere, of the concentration of media ownership; the problem of government domination; the problem of how the government informs itself. Grosser's analysis centers on whether a relatively closed system of news dissemination can serve the purposes of a democratic government.

Examining another aspect of news coverage, Anthony Smith has studied television coverage of the two 1974 elections in Great Britain. Smith emphasizes that the goal of the television industry was to present the elections in such a way that the people were informed without becoming bored, operating within the confines of fairness to all candidates. Apparently the coverage of the February 1974 election reached the point of boring the electorate; the amount of time allotted to the campaign in the early autumn was considerably reduced. Smith feels that television's responsibility is to arouse the electorate's interest in the campaign.

The remaining articles deal less with the modern techniques themselves and more with the effects they have had. Victor J. Hanby, in a study of the Scottish National Party (SNP), and Alastair Davidson, in his chapter on the Italian Communist Party (PCI), discuss how those running the campaigns of these parties have adjusted to a changing electoral environment. Hanby feels that the rebirth of the SNP is attributable to specific political factors and personalities. New techniques have been used, to good effect, but organizational and strategic developments have caused the most fundamental changes. Despite the differences in the parties examined, Davidson's conclusion is remarkably similar. He feels that recent PCI successes can be explained in terms of party strategy—an emphasis on regionalism and widespread participation; a stress on action to solve social and economic problems, not on ideology; a public commitment to working within the system, not to replacing it. The PCI has reacted to a changing political environment and has projected a new image; the willingness to compromise, not just the advantages of modern techniques, has been the key ingredient in its success.

E. J. Dionne's essay, which concludes this volume, deals explicitly with the fundamental theme. He claims that the nature of politics in Western democracies has not changed; only the methods have. And he further asserts that even the methods have not changed so radically as some contend. Dionne's study complements Smith's in that it looks at the two British elections of 1974, and complements Hanby's in that some of the constituencies that Dionne examines are central to Hanby's study of the SNP. However, this chapter stresses factors which have not changed, the conflicts of interest which persist between the parties, the importance of local factors. He admits that modern techniques might have an effect on swing voters in some areas, but feels that this line of argument can be extended too far and that the positive effects of improved information transmittal systems have not been probed sufficiently.

This volume hopes to present many of the important issues of concern raised by changing campaign techniques. There is one omission that is so glaring that it cannot be ignored. None of the articles deals explicitly with polling or with the use that parties have made of survey research data. One problem with dealing with modern elections is that events often move much faster than expected. I spent a recent leave of absence in Australia and noted the sophisticated operation through which the Australian Liberal Party sought to adjust its campaign themes, and particularly its image, to the wishes of the voters. Because their polling operation is as advanced as any of which I have knowledge, I asked a high-ranking party official if he would write an article for this book describing their procedure and discussing its implications for Australian politics. The Liberals had been planning for an election in mid-1976. When the Governor General removed Prime Minister Whitlam's commission and called an election for December 1975, no one was totally prepared. The Liberal Party official was obviously concerned with events much more pressing to him than his chapter for this book. Therefore, a gap exists. Perhaps it can be filled by a chapter in the third volume of this series, which will explore the impact of elections on subsequent party behavior and governmental policies.

III

The effects of modern campaign techniques on the values which elections serve in contemporary democracies cannot be summarized in a brief paragraph. Indeed, one common theme does not pervade this entire book. As E. J. Dionne reminds us, politics is about conflicts of interests, and those conflicts will continue to exist. The question is whether or not the method through which they are resolved has been changed in so fundamental a way as to alter the entire process. When we read *The Selling of the President,* we think it has; for the Nixon campaign strategy seems to represent an absolute perversion of what elections are supposed to mean. But perhaps it is only the forthright statement of what campaign managers think of the public which offends us. An undergraduate in one of my classes recently wrote a paper on the American presidential election of 1828. I was struck by some parallels. What is the essential difference between selling Old Hickory through a partisan press and selling the New Nixon on television? One man was said to be qualified for office because he led a successful army at the Battle of New Orleans; the other, because he promised to end the Vietnam War within a year. In each case, success depended on portraying a certain image to the electorate. But, of course, the entire process might be changed if the method of portraying that image is changed fundamentally or if other changes come about because people perceive that this has happened.

Certainly these are problems which should concern everyone who is engaged in, reports on, or analyzes political campaigns. This volume has achieved its goal if it has raised the level of dialogue about the nature of these issues.

ACKNOWLEDGEMENTS

Many people helped to make this book possible. Paul Sacks, who edited the first volume of this series with me, worked with me on developing the theme. Betsy Schmidt, our editor at Sage, was most understanding as I related the problems of compiling a book while moving from country to country. My friends on the Editorial Advisory Board seemed to take special care in assuring that this book was not lost among my moves. Beth Knight edited and typed a number of the chapters with speed and efficiency and a dedication for which I am most grateful. I told my wife that editing these books would not be terribly time-consuming, that it would not take me away from her and our children very often. Because I was wrong, I now want to thank Mary Lou and Dana and Joshua for their part in this book and promise more free evenings and weekends (until the next deadline approaches).

Finally, this book is dedicated to the memory of my father. He was very proud of his children, and we were devoted to him. But he never asked that we act in ways to please him, only that we see each task through to a conclusion that we were satisfied was the best we could achieve. I think of that often and try to live up to it, but mostly I hope that I—as a parent and as a teacher—can be as instrumental in helping others to achieve a sense of self-worth and to reach their potential as he was to me.

Louis Maisel
Waterville, Maine
December 1975

NOTE

1. The three articles dealing with public financing were prepared before the U.S. Supreme Court ruled in Buckley v. Valeo (1976) that certain provisions of the act were unconstitutional and before subsequent congressional action. The authors have had the opportunity to make only the most minor corrections; yet the theses of their arguments are still sound.

Chapter 1

PRIVATE MONEY AND PUBLIC ELECTIONS: ANOTHER AMERICAN DILEMMA

JOEL L. FLEISHMAN

> Who are to be the electors of the Federal Representatives? Not the rich more than the poor; not the learned more than the ignorant; nor the haughty heirs of distinguished names more than the humble sons of obscure and unpropitious fortune. The electors are to be the great body of the people of the United States.
>
> James Madison
> *The Federalist,*
> Number 57

I. INTRODUCTION

The point of democracy, after all, is to make men politically equal. Through free elections, citizens in a democracy select their leaders and, ultimately, the policies their government will pursue. Through the principle of universal suffrage, democracy seeks equal participation in those elections. Through the principles of majority rule and "one man-one vote," democracy seeks equal influence in its choices.

In today's America, money is the lifeblood of electoral politics. It is essential for every aspect of democratic choice—for candidates to communicate their positions, for officials to educate the public, for citizens to gain access to their leaders—and its growing importance poses a dilemma for American democracy. In our mass society, money is required for all forms of political communication, but that

AUTHOR'S NOTE: The author acknowledges his special gratitude to Arthur Aufses for his skillful and wise editing, to Daniel Wofford and David Isom for their generous aid in research, and to Janice Blinder for her speed and accuracy in preparing the manuscript.

dependence necessarily provides greater access to the wealthy than the poor. It threatens, therefore, to undermine the key democratic values of equality of participation and equality of influence.

The problem of political finance, then, is basic to democracy. Too little private spending may mean limited political communication. Too much private spending may mean political inequality and, ultimately, plutocracy. The task for government is clear, but tricky. It must steer a course which avoids these twin dangers. It must prevent political inequality without curtailing free speech; it must promote participation of the mass without discriminating against the elite; it must restrain manipulation without curbing all political communication. In the United States, these tensions have yet to be resolved.

For nearly 75 years, the federal government has regulated the financing of federal election campaigns. Yet, the spirit behind regulation has been grudging and the effort to secure compliance with the law only half-hearted. As a result, electoral law has become a leading example of dead-letter legislation—"more loophole than law," as President Lyndon Johnson described it (Drew, 1971:18). A decade of intensive and increasingly vocal efforts by public officials, journalists, scholars, and activists finally produced legislation in 1971. After many reports, hearings, and legislative battles, Congress enacted the Federal Election Campaign Act and the Revenue Act of 1971, embodying the Presidential Election Campaign Fund Act and Internal Revenue Code provisions for tax incentives for political contributions.

Whatever the constitutional defects and practical shortcomings of this legislation, there is little doubt of its significance. It marked the first major reform of federal election law in 50 years, and created, for the first time, both a statutory scheme containing teeth and an intention that it be enforced with bite, at least as applied to presidential campaigns. Its principal lasting provision was a well-designed, effective requirement for disclosing the identities of contributors to campaigns, the one form of campaign finance legislation on which all can agree. Had the Federal Election Campaign Act not been in force in 1972, the press, public, and Congress probably would not have learned the full facts of Watergate or uncovered the evidence which forced President Nixon's resignation. For that reason alone, all who seek honesty in government must be grateful. Moreover, the 1971 legislation provided the first federal subsidy for political campaigns—a limited tax deduction or credit for contributions by citizens directly to campaigns, and a tax-checkoff financed fund in the Treasury to be available, on an optional basis, for financing general election campaigns for the presidency.

By late 1974, Congress was ready to respond to Watergate by extending the 1971 acts in six important ways. First, it imposed ceilings on the amounts that donors might legally contribute to candidates for federal office. Second, it limited the overall amounts which such candidates might legally spend in their campaigns for office. Third, it revised the 1971 Presidential Election Campaign Fund Act so as to provide for full public funding of general election campaigns for the presidency, coupled with enforceable expenditure limitations. Fourth, in an important departure from previous practice, Congress enacted partial public financing of presidential primary elections, again with enforceable expenditure limitations. Fifth, in an equally significant innovation, it provided for public funding of party nominating conventions. Finally, Congress created, for the first time, a workable means of policing all federal election campaigns—the Federal Election Commission.

The 1971 and 1974 legislation was precedent-setting. Prior to it, the federal government had relied only on traditional, even if ineffective, means of constraining political activity—limiting the size and sources of contributions and the amounts candidates might spend and requiring public disclosure of the names of contributors. The new acts introduced public financing of elections at the federal level for the first time.

The use of public funds to defray campaign expenses is bound to have a great effect on American politics. At this time, it is impossible to predict those effects precisely. Nor can one be sure that the new provisions will survive constitutional attack in their present form, if indeed they survive it at all. Whatever the outcome of present litigation, or of subsequent legislative change, an important point has been made. Long after other Western countries, such as Germany, Finland, and Sweden (Leonard, 1975:10-28), had taken this step, the United States began subsidizing its political parties, adapting the approach to the nature of its own politics. The principle of partial public financing of federal elections has at last been implemented. Whether it survives will be determined, in part, by public understanding of what is at stake.

II. THE PROBLEM OF PRIVATE FINANCING

Political campaign expenditures have risen rapidly in the last 20 years (Alexander, 1972, 1975c). This is due mainly to the growing use of television as a political weapon and to the rise of professional campaign researchers and managers. It has been estimated that, in 1972, American politicians spent over $400 million in the pursuit of public office (Adamany, 1969:57-58; Heard, 1960:375-387; Penniman, 1971:8; Alexander, 1975c:126). Although some advocates contend that political expenditures should be reduced, most scholars agree that American elections are, in fact, underfinanced (Heard, 1960; Adamany, 1973; Winter, 1971). This conclusion is based largely on a comparison of American election spending with per vote expenditures in other Western democracies (Adamany, 1969:58).

This growth in campaign spending is bound to continue. Indeed, it *should* continue. Given the spiraling complexity of public issues and the growing diversity of political competition, the public's need for information is increasing all the time. To ensure effective communication and well-informed debate, political expenditures must keep pace. Moreover, even if it were desirable to reduce political spending, it would be practically and constitutionally difficult to design an equitable scheme for doing so (Fleishman, 1973a, 1975).

As a result, elections will inevitably cost more in the future. The money to fund them must somehow be raised. Two alternative sources of funding are available. The first is continued reliance on private financing. The weight of American tradition supports this approach. Yet this may succeed only in undermining democracy further. The other is a larger measure of public subsidization of elections, which, while marking a major departure in American politics, might nonetheless be the only way to approximate some greater measure of political equality in the United States.

A lively debate between the advocates of these two alternatives has already begun (Winter, 1973; Nicholson, 1974; Schwartz, 1975). It is the purpose of this article to contribute to that debate.

The problem of wealth in politics is crucial to American democracy, and this article will explore that problem in several ways. First, we shall study the impact of private financing on democracy. This analysis should document the need for reform. Second, we shall develop an argument for a system of partial public subsidies to federal elections, which will suggest that public financing is the most desirable of the available reform alternatives. Third, we shall examine several arguments which defend private financing and attack proposals for public subsidies. This critique should show that public financing is both supportable in theory and workable in practice. Finally, an analysis of existing law and litigation in the area of public financing will show the precise form which an equitable and constitutional reform must take.

American politics has staggered through 200 years. Some see this as a great success, reflecting the "genius" of American democracy. The arguments of those who advocate the status quo are appealing, but ultimately unconvincing. Attainment of the ideals of democracy demands political reform, of which an important next step toward political equality is greater public financing of elections.

III. THE IMPACT OF TOTALLY PRIVATE FINANCING

The net effect of private financing of elections is to weaken democracy. The consequences of private financing are, of course, unanticipated, but harmful nonetheless. In particular, private financing tends to deter able candidates from seeking office; promotes the political and economic interests of the wealthy; encourages bribery, extortion, and office buying; and erodes public confidence in government.

CANDIDATE DETERRENCE

Private financing of elections deters two different kinds of people—the poor and the meticulously independent—from seeking office; such double deterrence deprives the poor of representation and the nation of its full measure of deserved leadership. Qualified potential candidates who happen to be poor—who lack access to wealth—are obviously prevented from running for office. This impedes attempts to advance the interests of the poor. Although such exclusion primarily harms the poor, it also deprives the entire country of considerable potential leadership. Of greater effect upon the rest of us, however, is the tendency of private financing to discourage genuinely independent citizens, whether rich or poor, from running for office. One must assume that there are many concerned citizens around the country who have access to sources willing to finance a political campaign but who shrink from the idea of asking for, or accepting, such support. Such men and women, to whom being in political and financial debt is anathema, are precisely those whom we most need in politics. Yet their insistence on being independent prevents them from seeking office as long as private money alone is used. No doubt, there are many politicians today who feel similarly but who reluctantly choose to sacrifice their own peace of mind in order to pursue political office—and the public good. Were their campaigns financed in part with public funds, they would surely be freer to perform in office effectively.

SERVING THE INTERESTS OF THE UPPER CLASS

American elections unfold in three stages. First, potential candidates decide actually to seek office—to pursue a major party nomination or join the ballot via petitions. Second, party members—either through primaries, petitions, or caucuses—select nominees for general election. Finally, the voting public selects its officials from among the party nominees. Wealth exercises unfair influence at each of these stages.

As we have just seen, the need for great sums in campaigning deters potential, able candidates from seeking office. Only those with personal wealth—or with access to the wealth of others—can afford to compete. Wealth alone, then, helps to winnow out potential leaders. At the next two stages, wealth is again crucial. In primaries and general elections, active candidates need money for every aspect of campaigning—for recruiting expert assistance in developing programs, for hiring professional managers and pollsters, for communicating with the public. The wealthiest candidate does not, of course, always win (Fleishman, 1973a:460-461). Yet, in an era of increasingly sophistcated campaign practice, wealth clearly confers an advantage.

In the circumstances where wealth does confer an advantage—the close elections—the candidates most likely to win, then, are those who are favorable to, and favored by, established wealth. This increases the likelihood of continued benefits for the wealthy after the election. Specifically, it means that the policy preferences of campaign donors will be reflected in the actions of contribution recipients after they take office.[1] As the late Senator Richard Neuberger observed, "So long as private funding is permitted, officeholders will make policy decisions in accord with the views of contributors" (1956:105). What would therefore probably be illegal as a bribe if given *after* a candidate entered office is certainly legal if given during a political campaign.

It must be said that the relationship between contributions and policy is not clearly causal. Wealthy citizens have every right to contribute to candidates who have a preexisting stand in favor of their beliefs or interests. In that case, the contribution is regarded as made on the assumption that the candidate will vote in the future as he has in the past. Where the candidate has no preexisting stand on the issue or has a stand contrary to that of the donor, a contribution followed by a policy action favorable to the donor does smack of bribery. In fact, even in the former case, acceptance of a contribution may be regarded as reinforcing a candidate's position on a particular matter.

What about the politician who wishes to change his mind? Or the public figure who differs from his financial supporters on some issues? If he so free of concern about attracting funds for his next campaign that he will be willing to lose the favor of his financial supporters? Elizabeth Drew (1971:22) summed up the uncertainty nicely:

> The trouble with talking about [campaign financing] is that there is no way to measure the venality, if any, involved. And even politicians should be forgiven their friends—to a point. But anyone who supposes that various segments of society get an even chance at access to power in this democracy is blinking at the facts. As long as there is human nature, and at least part of it is greed, there is no way of legislating or enforcing ethics. But one thing that can be done is to break the power of money over those who would like not to be beholden to it.

By providing the capital needed for effective campaigning, the wealthy exercise political advantage. Through their influence over public policy, the wealthy are able to secure their economic advantage. Thus our reliance on private financing of elections contributes to the maintenance of economic inequality. It is surely not the only reason why our economic policies have tended to produce a stable pattern of concentrated wealth and enduring poverty, but it has, just as surely, helped to reinforce such patterns. It is almost trite to point out that, for four decades now, the wealthiest 5 percent of the population has maintained its 20 percent share of the national income, while the poorest 20 percent of the population has failed to increase its share of income above 5 percent, despite the redistributive intent of the graduated-income, inheritance, and gift taxes. One wonders whether the legislative resistance to tax reform and the consequent persistence of tax loopholes are not also related in some degree to total reliance on private political financing.

Another consequence of private financing is less significant, but associated. It discriminates against citizens without sufficient funds to spare for political contributions. When added to the positive influence with which the system of private financing endows those who do contribute, this denial of political influence operates doubly to disadvantage those without money.

EXTORTION BY OFFICEHOLDERS

Private financing exposes citizens to extortion by public officials. In the 1972 presidential campaign, Republican cabinet officers solicited sizable contributions from defense contractors and other corporations with interests in government proceedings. These brazenly illegal acts are only recent, notorious examples of a normally covert practice. Regulatory laws cannot prevent this kind of political extortion. The solution is obvious:

> But the real need is for Congress to make it impossible for companies like American Airlines to be put under the kind of pressures exerted on them last year; and, on the other hand, to make it impossible for companies or industries to grease Government palms with political contributions (as the dairymen did in 1971 and 1972) in hopes of favorable political decisions. The best way to do that is to provide an equitable means of Federal financing for Federal elections. [Wicker, 1973]

THE PURCHASE OF OFFICE

Private financing ensures that some key public offices will be bought with campaign contributions. It would be far better to have public positions awarded to those who either (a) agree with the policy preferences of appointing officials, (b) are old friends of appointing officials, (c) are campaign workers for appointing officials, (d) are distinguished experts, (e) are able managers, or (f) are widely respected for integrity and fairness, rather than to have them awarded to those who contribute money, whether or not they happen also to qualify as (a), (b), (c), (d), (e), or (f). One must also remember that the election of judges in campaigns financed by private wealth inherently violates the most cherished notions of every civilized legal and political tradition. How can such judges in fact pursue justice only, as the Bible commands, when their campaigns were financed largely by the lawyers who appear in court before them? And what kind of fairness is there in a legal system where some appointive judges obtain their offices through campaign contributions? For the sake of blind justice alone, we should be rid of exclusive reliance on private political financing.

ERODING CONFIDENCE IN GOVERNMENT

Finally, private financing erodes public confidence in the fairness and integrity of government. Not unreasonably, the public assumes that campaign contributors expect personal rewards. Carrying the logic another step, citizens begin to believe that government is for sale to those who contribute and that the only way to obtain governmental benefits is to buy them, whether one is entitled by right or is merely one competitor among many and whether one seeks action or inaction by an executive department, Congress, or the courts.

This is not to suggest that, by limiting the role of private finance in elections, we will solve all of the problems in our political system. It does imply, however, that shifting part of the burden of campaign finance from private to public sources is the critical first step. When it is accomplished in full, we can see whether or not other reforms are needed. Indeed, we may be surprised to discover how many of our socioeconomic problems were created by private financing of elections.

IV. POLITICAL CONTRIBUTIONS AND CITIZEN PARTICIPATION: AN ARGUMENT FOR PARTIAL PUBLIC SUBSIDY

Widespread citizen participation in politics—from voting to active campaigning—is essential to effective democracy. Indeed, it is the key constitutive element of democracy. Accordingly, any reasonable devices for encouraging such participation should be welcomed.

Political contributing is clearly a form of citizen participation. To proponents of private electoral financing, contributing is so basic an activity that it should not be curtailed. Contributing, they argue, both expresses and induces public involvement in politics. The big question is whether political contributing, in itself, is essential to

American democracy. If so, it would justify retaining private financing of elections. If not, it strengthens the argument for reform.

The appeal of private financing is persuasive. If one wishes to maximize participation in politics, *regardless of the quality and nature of that participation,* then political contributions (especially small ones) seem a harmless means to that end. A political contributor is certainly more likely to vote than a noncontributor. More importantly, the solicitation of campaign funds forces the voter to make an early choice of candidates. This may prompt him to take additional, more intensive steps in support of his favored candidate. The contributor may, for example, begin to advocate that candidate among his friends or devote substantial amounts of time and energy to the campaign or perhaps even make a public endorsement.

Political contributions, then, may have some beneficial effects. Yet, they are *not identical* with such effects. At best, they serve only as one means to desired ends. We have already seen the harmful consequences of the large contributions made by established wealth. We must consider, therefore, whether the beneficial effects of small contributions can be achieved by other means.

Why, for example, would a request for an expression of support, on a petition or a newspaper advertisement, not be just as effective in forcing an early choice among candidates, with all the desirable consequences that are thought to follow such a decision? One answer is that, when spending money, the citizen is forced to a more serious consideration of his choice. Moreover, a choice which costs money is much more likely to reflect an intention to make greater subsequent contributions to a compaign than a costless choice, which would in fact be quite unreliable. As any campaign manager can attest, contributing is normally the first step in a series of involvements with a campaign. Adult contributors of time and energy almost invariably make their entry into the campaign operation with a small contribution.

From the citizen's point of view, the case is even stronger. A citizen's money constitutes one of the resources which he or she is able to deploy as a means of expressing political preferences. To deny someone the opportunity to express that preference by making a small contribution to a political candidate is no different from denying him the opportunity to spend time or energy working in behalf of a candidate. Most citizens think that such a restriction violates their constitutional rights to free speech about political matters, and it is hard to disagree with them.

Table 1. PERCENTAGE OF TOTAL CAMPAIGN CONTRIBUTIONS OF $500 OR MORE[a]

	1952	*1956*	*1960*	*1964*	*1968*	*1972*
Democrats	63	43	59	69	61	
Republicans	68	72	58	28	47	
Wallace					6.8	13

a. Comparable figures are not available for 1972, but Alexander (1975c:640-641) suggests that the respective percentages are even higher.

SOURCES: Dunn, 1969:63; Alexander, 1971:169; Alexander, 1975c:290.

Political contributions, then, are a valid form of participation. Large contributions, as we have seen, distort democracy and thus are indefensible. Small contributions, however, seem a guaranteed form of political expression and may promote even deeper participation. Assuming that large contributions are made illegal, can American elections be financed solely by small private donors?

This issue must turn, finally, on a simple, practical concern. Assuming, for the reasons suggested above, that we rule out contributions to any candidate in an amount greater than, say, $100, there is no conceivable way in which federal campaigns could be financed without large public subsidies. Let us look at the facts. The greatest share of political contributions has come consistently from large gifts. With the exception of Governor Wallace's 1968 and 1972 campaigns and Senator Goldwater's 1964 campaign, contributions over $500 have provided around 50 percent or more of total expenditures in all recent presidential campaigns. (See Table 1.)

Moreover, the number of contributors to presidential campaigns has never been more than 12 percent of the adult population, and that peak was achieved largely as a result of Senator Goldwater's special appeal to certain small contributors. (The figures are shown in Table 2.)

Table 2. TOTAL CONTRIBUTORS TO NATIONAL LEVEL PRESIDENTIAL CAMPAIGNS

	Number (in millions)	*Percentage of Adult Population*
1952	3	4
1956	8	9
1960	10	10.5
1964	12	12
1968	8.7	8
1972	11.7	10

SOURCES: Alexander, 1971:143-144; Alexander, 1975c:631, 633.

Large contributors play an even more decisive role in congressional campaigns. In the 1972 elections (the only ones for which comparable data are available) 68 percent of the dollar value of all contributions to congressional candidates was in contributions of more than $100 (Common Cause, 1975).

One might well ask if these trends must continue. Perhaps the proportion of small political contributions could be significantly increased by strenuous efforts. While hope springs eternal, all the evidence is to the contrary. With the exception of highly ideological candidates like Goldwater, Wallace, and McGovern, no effort to develop a continuing broad-based small-contribution campaign has ever succeeded in this country. Both the Ruml plan and the Graham plan were failures (Heard, 1960:250-256, 456), and the British Labour Party and the German Christian Democrats have similarly failed in their attempts (Leonard, 1975:8). If no more than 23.6 percent of American taxpayers are willing to "check off" one dollar of their actual tax liability for payment into the presidential election campaign fund (" 'Yes' for a clean fight," 1975:30), a decision which is almost totally costless in effort and money, how can one challenge the assumption that past patterns of political giving will persist into the foreseeable future?

We assume, then, that it is small political contributions, the ones below $500, which are both essential to citizen participation and so small as to preclude serious postelection policy favors in a presidential race.[2] Yet we must ask how political campaigns could be financed if we relied solely on the present proportion of small contributions. The alternatives are clear: we can either halve the cost of politics or enact public financing. The former alternative is clearly undesirable. Both absolutely and in comparison with other industrialized nations, our political system is already underfinanced (Adamany, 1969:58; Penniman, 1971:8). Accordingly, assuming we limit the size of contributions to any reasonable level, our only real choice is to begin public subsidies.

V. THE DEFENSE OF PRIVATE FINANCING

In America, public financing of elections is a relatively new idea. As with any reform proposal, it has not been universally accepted. Proponents of private financing claim several theoretical and practical advantages for the present system. Private financing, they argue, is justified by American democratic theory. In addition, they claim it to be more workable, in practice, than the proposed alternative.

Obviously, no political reform, especially one dealing so centrally with the process of election, should be implemented hastily. Advocates of private financing have helped to force reformers to develop their alternatives thoughtfully. In the end, however, the defense of exclusively private political financing seems unconvincing. Its theoretical claims can be refuted; the genuine practical merits of the present system are outweighed by its defects.

PRIVATE FINANCING IN AMERICAN DEMOCRATIC THEORY

Defenders (e.g., Winter, 1971, 1973) of private financing draw from the pluralist theory of democracy in two ways. First, they argue that political success in the United States is determined not by a single factor such as wealth, but by a number of political resources, such as the candidate's intelligence, available time, personal contacts, issue associations, name recognition, reputation, past record, and political organization. Some people have more time, others more political skill, still others more political interest, and so on. According to this theory, each candidate seeks public office by designing a campaign strategy which reflects a mix of whatever resources he may have available. A lack in one resource can be offset by a surplus in others (Dahl, 1961:226). In this view, wealth is not the chief source of political success. Thus there is no reason to single it out for public regulation.

Wealth, however, is *not* like other political resources. Every other resource is, in a sense, *primary,* while wealth is *instrumental.* Because of its easy convertibility, money enables its possessors to purchase all other kinds of political resources, thus acquiring the power to corner the political market. While some of the other political resources have partial convertibility into wealth, none can produce as much wealth as wealth can produce of them.

Furthermore, the other political resources are either genetically distributed, environmentally determined, or accumulated over a long period of time. Indeed, those other characteristics of the politically active are highly pertinent to their fitness for office. What could more properly be criteria for citizen choice than candidates' comparative honesty, vision, intelligence, charisma, political skill, or networks of friends and acquaintances? Even if it were desirable to limit the influence of such characteristics in politics, it would be impossible to do so. The amount of wealth that one commands, however, is both not pertinent to a candidate's qualifications and yet entirely susceptible to legal regulation. In other words, other political resources cannot be equalized among candidates. Wealth, however, *can* be equalized.

Arguments from pluralist theory are used in a second way to buttress the case for private political financing. The pluralist sees American politics as a polyarchic system, in which many interest groups and power centers compete and cooperate in attempting to shape public policy toward their respective ends (Dahl and Lindblom, 1953). According to this analysis, wealth is as much a proper participant in political struggle as are labor, ethnic minorities, farmers, or teachers.

There is a basic problem with this account. Wealth is not an individual interest group; instead, wealth represents an end for all of the competing groups. To permit wealth full access to political competition is inevitably to load the policy dice in favor of the wealthiest of the competing interests. The ability to use private wealth politically, therefore, pyramids advantages already enjoyed by those interest groups with preexisting financial power.

Moreover, the currency of competition, as well as of discourse, among political contestants ought to be analysis of what is best for the most—of what is in the public interest. Even Adam Smith would probably have admitted that the resolution of competing private interests would inevitably be skewed if some private interests were permitted to employ, in addition to arguments of fairness and right, the added direct power of wealth.

This is not to deny wealthy interest groups and individuals the opportunity to express their views politically. Wealthy citizens should be allowed to contribute to political campaigns, but only in limited amounts. Even then, they will have far more means than other citizens to advance their policy preferences in public by purchasing advertisements, owning newspapers and other media, sponsoring scholarship, publishing books and journals, and hiring lobbyists and publicists. These means of protecting the interests of productive wealth should be more than sufficient to prevent its destruction or diminution by majority power. Restricting wealth's access to the political arena will simply deny contribution-induced influence. It should also force wealth to resort to more open means of public persuasion in its continuing attempts to influence policy.

THE PRESUMED PRACTICAL ADVANTAGES OF PRIVATE FINANCING

The advocates of private financing are more persuasive in pointing out the practical advantages of the present system. At present, a free market mechanism allocates campaign funds among potential candidates. This method, they argue, is both more efficient and less complex than any conceivable plan for public financing.

The Problem of Efficiency

If efficiency were the controlling factor in the decision to reform campaign finance, private financing would win out easily. This is so for several reasons. First, the private market in political money spends far less than would any method of public allocation. In a sense, it performs quite rationally, since ordinarily it gives funds only to those potential candidates who appear likely to win. In contrast, any scheme of public financing would be required, under the Constitution, to distribute its subsidies evenhandedly among all candidates who satisfy its eligibility criteria. Public financing could, of course, embody stringent eligibility requirements, which would actually reduce the number of candidates who manage to qualify and thus reduce the amount of money spent. Yet, it is an undeniable fact that any constitutional scheme of public financing will necessarily result in the spending of more money during political campaigns.

Simple saving of money, however, is not the only consideration. Public financing seeks to attain goals other than pure economic efficiency. Indeed, to the extent that a system of public subsidies provides funds for worthy candidates who cannot raise money under the "more efficient" private system, it is achieving one of its main aims. The purposes of public financing are broader than the private market's function of financing prospective winners only; they include, as well, opening election campaigns to a broader range of individuals and interests. In other words, public financing is a means of buying political participation. It sacrifices economic efficiency in order to achieve broader and more intensive mass participation in politics.

Moreover, the defense of private financing as more efficient than its alternatives misses a crucial point. Defenders of private financing assume that the market in political money is perfectly free—that the arena is completely open to new competition and that the only determinant of success is the likelihood of the new entrant's winning at the polls. This, of course, is false. The political money market is not free. It is not completely open; competition within it is imperfect. Indeed, all of the characteristics of imperfect competition which led first to regulation and then to subsidies in the private business sector have their equivalents in the political arena. As in monopolistic and oligopolistic private markets, unknown entrants to American politics can rarely gain an opportunity to compete. If they do compete at all, it is at a disadvantage with respect to their better endowed opponents. John Rawls (1971:226) makes this point well:

> Essentially the fault lies in the fact that the democratic political process is at best regulated rivalry; it does not even in theory have the desirable properties that price theory ascribes to truly competitive markets. Moreover, the effects of injustices in the political system are much more grave and long lasting than market imperfections. Political power rapidly accumulates and becomes unequal; and making use of the coercive apparatus of the state and its law, those who gain the advantage can often assure themselves of a favored position. Thus inequities in the economic and social system may soon undermine whatever political equality might have existed under fortunate historical conditions. Universal suffrage is an insufficient counterpoise; for when parties and elections are financed not by public funds but by private contributions, the political forum is so constrained by the wishes of the dominant interests that the basic measures needed to establish just constitutional rules are seldom seriously presented.

The Problem of Complexity

The other supposed practical advantage of private financing is more troublesome. By definition, private financing leaves entirely in the control of private citizens the decision of whom to support and with how much money. Any system of public financing implies continual monitoring by the government. The system will create a set of rules. A body of governmental officials—a bureaucracy—will be required to apply them. In short, under public financing, government will be entering still another sphere of social life. This concern has led many to believe that any system of public financing is inherently more complicated, and thus less desirable, than continued use of the private political market, even with all *its* faults.

No doubt, it *is* less complicated to limit government supervision to the kinds of law we have used in the past—that which constrains, but does not replace, private funding. Simply put, the question is whether we are willing to create another bureaucracy in the pursuit of basic values. The pursuit of economic equality has long justified extensive governmental regulation in the world of private business. The pursuit of political equality can as easily justify regulation of political financing. The present system of electoral finance has abused our most basic democratic ideals. Public financing offers a chance to eliminate these abuses. Greater government regulation seems a small price to pay for this end.

THE CRITIQUE OF PROPOSALS FOR PUBLIC FINANCING

As we have just seen, a number of writers have claimed certain theoretical and practical advantages for the present system of campaign finance. Others concentrate on attacking specific elements of reform proposals. The opponents of public financing have raised a number of legitimate questions (Alexander, 1975b; Pincus, 1973; Bellush and Boyd, 1974; Steiger, 1975). It is impossible in a short article to address all of the arguments about the dangers of public financing. Yet it is important to confront and discuss the more serious questions.

Are Election Costs a Proper Object for Public Expenditure?

It has been suggested that public financing of elections is not a valid governmental purpose under the Constitution (Buckley v. Valeo, Brief of the Plaintiff, 1975). This claim is false. Although there is a Massachusetts Supreme Court decision construing a Massachusetts constitutional provision to the contrary (Opinion of the Justices, 1964), nowhere does the Constitution of the United States limit Congress to any "public purpose" in making expenditures. The "necessary and proper clause" and the "general welfare clause" assuredly provide adequate authority for congressional appropriation of tax funds to defray the costs of political campaigns. Moreover, the manifold direct subsidies to airlines, shipping companies, farmers, and railroads, among others, as well as indirect tax subsidies to nearly every kind of corporate enterprise, provide ample precedent for public financing of political campaigns for federal office. Surely these industries, however important, are no more deserving of public subsidy than politics itself—the means by which we govern ourselves and maintain a cooperative, orderly, social existence. If we were suddenly to cease subsidizing any of these enterprises, many of them would go bankrupt, and whole industries, such as passenger railroading, might even disappear. As regrettable as that might be, the nation would somehow survive. The Republic cannot endure, however, the bankruptcy of its politics. Yet that is the danger we risk if we impose ceilings on private contributions and fail to provide public funds to make up the difference.

Using Your Tax Funds to Support Candidates You Oppose

At first, one might be troubled by the fact that, under a system of public financing, part of one's taxes could be used to support the campaigns of candidates whom one vigorously opposed. That objection is not tenable. In fact, all the subsidies given to candidates and parties today are derived from the Presidential Election Campaign Fund, which receives all its revenues from funds specifically "checked off" for that purpose by taxpayers. Yet even if Congress had decided to use general tax revenues instead of specifically designated funds, such an arrangement would probably not violate the First Amendment. After all, elections are at least as much of a "public good" as public schools, public parks, and the national defense, and we assess all taxpayers for those costs whether or not they use the facilities and regardless of their opinion of the policies. In repeated holdings by the Supreme Court, it has been made clear that a citizen's obligation to support the government through taxes does not in any way carry with it a right to object to particular expenditures. It may well be, however, that politics is so sensitive an activity—since it involves the selection of the government itself—that the Court might someday feel compelled to apply a strict test of First Amendment constitutionality. That is an issue, however, which need not be faced at this time, since the operative public financing law does involve a choice by taxpayers to contribute funds with the full knowledge that those funds are going to be distributed according to certain formulas established in the enacting legislation. Under those circumstances, there is no serious First Amendment difficulty (Buckley v. Valeo, 1976).

Bellush and Boyd (1974:5) have offered a related criticism of public financing. Republican registration, they observe, is lower than Democratic; and Republicans, being higher-income taxpayers, pay more taxes than Democrats. Accordingly, it is unfair to force so many Republicans to support Democratic candidates. That logic rests on a misconception. While the value of Republican taxes paid may be a higher proportion of net tax proceeds (although even that is not clear), the *number* of Democratic taxpayers, given the registration figures and opinion polls, is much higher. If that is the case, and since the check-off funds are evenly divided between Republican and Democratic candidates, in fact more Democrats will be supporting Republican dandidates than vice versa.

A more serious criticism is that made by Congressman Steiger (1975). He notes that, because there are traditionally more candidates competing for the Democratic nomination for the presidency than for the Republican nomination, a larger share of the checkoff funds available to finance presidential primaries will go to Democratic candidates. That is undoubtedly true, but it results from the distribution of primary contests rather than the design of the subsidy itself. Given the availability of the subsidy in presidential primaries, it is entirely possible that the subsidy will operate to stimulate more primary contests in the Republican Party.

Public Subsidies as a Threat to Political Parties

One of the arguments most frequently advanced against public financing is that it would further diminish the roles of already weakened political parties (Alexander, 1975a; Bellush and Boyd, 1974). That concern is misplaced. The chief cause of decline in the importance of American political parties is the growing use of primaries to select candidates.[3] In other countries, where party organizations continue to select nominees, the role of parties in election campaigns remains strong.

Public subsidy of elections, far from being a nail in the coffin of the parties, can, if carefully designed, be used to reverse the trend of party decline. It can do so by funneling funds to parties for general elections and for conventions, as the current act does (Adamany, 1970). Moreover, since their demise as a means of nominating candidates, parties have played very little role in political fundraising except in machine-dominated states and cities. The principal fundraising burden has, for some time, rested squarely on the candidates and their managers, not on party bosses. To the extent that critics of public subsidy fear that public funds will replace party-raised funds, their concern is entirely misplaced.

Favoring the Major Parties

By far the greatest dilemma for subsidy proponents is how to subsidize the major parties—the candidates of one of which will, in fact, be elected in virtually every election—without discriminating against the candidates of minor parties, none of whose candidates is likely to win. The difficulty appears so great that some scholars express doubt as to the possibility of devising a constitutionally acceptable formula (Rosenthal, 1972:412). Unfortunately, much of the writing on the subject seems motivated more by antisubsidy animus than by a desire to clarify the issues in order to discover an acceptable solution (Sterling, 1971:158-159). This is all the more regrettable since the problem is technical, and will not be solved by polemic.

It is not clear from the one holding in point, Williams v. Rhodes (1968), whether it is only favoritism to two particular political parties that is forbidden, or also favoritism to the very idea of a two-party system. As justification for its scheme, Ohio urged the propriety of favoring a two-party system because of its politically stabilizing tendencies. The Supreme Court found that the Ohio system in fact favored not *a* two-party system but *the* two particular parties then in existence and tended overwhelmingly to perpetuate them. It then went on to add that "new parties struggling for their place must have the time and opportunity to organize in order to meet reasonable requirements for ballot position, just as the old parties have had in the past" (p. 32). On another occasion (Sweezy v. New Hampshire, 1957:250-251), when a different kind of discrimination was involved, the Court made clear the policy reasons for protecting minor parties:

> All political ideas cannot and should not be channeled into the programs of our two major parties. History has amply proved the virtue of political activity by minority, dissident groups, which innumerable times have been in the vanguard of democratic thought and whose programs were ultimately accepted. . . . The absence of such voices would be a symptom of grave illness in our society.

It would seem, then, that any subsidy plan which excluded minor parties entirely would be unconstitutional (Casper, 1969:284). That conclusion would continue to hold even though minor parties had the easiest possible access to the ballot. Once the government intervenes to affect the outcome of an election, it must do so fairly.

In this context, however, fairness does not mean giving the same number of subsidy dollars to the minor parties as are given to the major parties, regardless of the differences in votes among them. Presumably, only such a subsidy would be unquestionably equitable, but it would utterly violate common sense. No court would insist on supporting a group of citizens who organize themselves into a political party at the same level as the established parties, irrespective of their relative likelihood of attracting votes. In Jenness v. Fortson (1971), which sustained Georgia's burdening of smaller parties with a petition signature requirement not imposed on major parties, the Supreme Court noted that "there are obvious differences in kind between the needs and potentials of a political party with historically established broad support, on the one hand, and a new or small political organization on the other. . . ." and that "[s]ometimes the grossest discrimination can lie in treating things that are different as though they were exactly alike" (pp. 441-442).

As the Michigan Supreme Court had pointed out in another case, a "minority cannot have an equal right to govern" (Schweitzer v. Clerk for City of Plymouth, 1969). Rather, it must be afforded an opportunity to compete, to make its "appeal of new . . . voices" heard (Jenness, 1971:442).

This suggests, then, that unequal distributions of subsidies would not be unconstitutional in principle, especially in view of the purpose of the subsidy legislation. Professor Rosenthal (1972:416) has made the point well:

> This is not to say that no conceivable program of direct subsidies giving different amounts to major and minor parties could possibly be constitutional. There is a strong interest in freeing political campaigns from dependence upon private contributions which would have to be balanced against the unequal payments to minor parties. If the latter were treated generously even though not equally, it might be shown that they were in fact accorded a better chance to convey their views to the voters than if all parties were dependent solely on private contributions.

How can we determine equity of distribution? What would be an acceptable criterion? The Court has already pointed the way by observing in Bullock v. Carter (1972:145) that "the criterion for differing treatment must bear some relevance to the object of the legislation." The main objective of subsidies is to free those who actually have a chance of winning office from dependency on private money contributions. Just as resort was made to indications of public support in sorting out serious from frivolous candidates in the first place, it seems appropriate to look to indications of public support as a measure of likelihood of winning. The fact that a minor party is, in the end, minor and likely to remain so is a legitimate criterion for differing treatment, so long as the subsidy enables it to wage a campaign commensurate in size with the demonstrated numbers of its supporters. The Court implicitly sanctioned such a criterion when it observed in Williams v. Rhodes (1968:34) that "of course, the number of voters in favor of a party . . . is relevant in considering whether state laws violate the Equal Protection Clause." Thus, any distribution scheme which computes minor party subsidy entitlement on the basis of its support in either past or current elections must be presumed to be constitutional in principle.

Critics argue that vote-based distribution formulas inherently reinforce the political status quo (Sterling, 1971:150). Although this claim is true in principle, there would be much less reinforcement of the status quo under public financing than exists at present. Most minor parties can now obtain very little financial support. Any tendency to stasis could be further mitigated by permitting minor parties to raise and spend additional private money up to the level of public subsidy of major party candidates, which the present law permits. This would, in fact, put minor parties in a much more favorable situation than they are now. A distribution plan, then, which favors major parties by tying subsidy entitlement to popular vote attainment seems to be constitutional in principle, so long as entitlements for minor parties are sufficient to allow them to be heard, even if greatly overshadowed by the actual contenders for office—the major party giants (Buckley v. Valeo, 1976).

This discussion suggests that any attempts to discriminate against minor parties by establishing thresholds for subsidy entitlement, such as the 5 percent vote threshold in the 1974 amendments, would be unconstitutional. In addition, relying exclusively on a past election for the vote base would be unconstitutional since it would deprive minor parties formed since the last election of the chance to qualify for the subsidy. For this reason, minor party entitlement formulas should use both past and present election year alternatives as vote bases, with the distribution figured on the higher of the two.

The crucial determinant of the constitutionality of distribution formulas is obviously the relationship between major and minor party allocations. If minor party entitlement is determined by actual votes received, while major party entitlement is a function of the number of persons of voting age in a particular jurisdiction, major parties would receive disproportionately more than minor parties. To insure constitutionality, therefore, the minor party entitlement should not be computed as a direct function of the number of votes received by the minor party. It should be calculated instead as a ratio—in other words, as that proportion of the major party entitlement which the minor party vote bears to the average of the major party votes. That is the formula used in current law.

Such a ratio also ensures that as a minor party acquires more votes, its subsidy entitlement will not be markedly less than the major parties' entitlement at points just below the threshold for qualification as a major party. If, for example, a "major party" were defined as one receiving 25 percent or more of the votes in the preceding election, and a direct vote base were used for minor party entitlement, a minor party with 24 percent of the vote would receive considerably less than the major parties. A ratio formula avoids that discrimination.

The minor party floor is more troublesome than the ceiling. The Presidential Election Campaign Fund Act, for example, gives no subsidy at all to parties which receive fewer than 5 percent of the votes. Neither do most of the other subsidy plans thus far proposed. While there is some useful public purpose to be served in avoiding subsidies to fringe groups, the use of such a threshold of eligibility might be considered by the Court as a discriminatory factor in assessing the subsidy plan as a whole. Rather than jeopardize the plan, it would be preferable to waste that small amount of public money involved in supporting the Greenback or Prohibition party. Finally, it is the scheme as a whole that will determine the constitutionality of the plan, and not any particular component (Jenness v. Fortson, 1971:431; Williams v. Rhodes, 1968:23). The Supreme Court is not likely to invalidate a public subsidy statute because of minor discrimination against minor parties, so long as the intent, policy, and framework of the subsidy are unobjectionable.

The Risk of Using the Subsidy for Partisan Ends

Nearly all critics of public financing, citing the well-known examples of the Nixon administration, worry about the extent to which subsidies might be used to favor particular candidates or parties. Given recent examples of high-level manipulation of governmental agencies for political ends, one can easily imagine a variety of ways in which a federal election commission might use a public subsidy to partisan advantage. Any public system will require some body of governmental officials to administer it. No matter how carefully such an agency is guarded by express statutory language, how scrupulously manned, or how closely monitored by Congress or the courts, it will always have some potential for partisan use.

Yet, subsidy administration *can* be adequately protected from political manipulation much more easily than government policing of private political funding. By lodging power over the subsidy-distribution mechanism in a multipartisan independent agency composed of persons of unquestioned integrity selected by Congress, the risk of manipulation can be substantially reduced. At the very least, such an agency would be considerably less threatening than the partisan judgments of a political Department of Justice, which now has authority to prosecute election offenses.

Whenever government controls the means of its own selection, there will be potential for favoritism. Our government has been supervising its own elections for a century or more, simply because the public came to believe that those crucial choices could not safely be left in private hands. A properly designed system of public subsidies poses no greater threat to the fairness of elections than does the current means of governmental control.

In sum, we must conclude that the certainty of harm inherent in exclusively private political financing outweighs the possible dangers of public subsidization. Funding through the private market entrusts the wealthy with the crucial gate-keeping function in politics. First, their own votes, bolstered by financial contributions, count more heavily in behalf of the candidates whom they favor (Adamany, 1969:236). Second, their unwillingness to provide political venture capital to potential candidates inevitably narrows the range of choices available to other voters. In other words, under existing electoral laws, the wealthy not only cast their own weight in votes for some candidates, but also choose the alternatives open to other citizens by controlling the access of candidates to the ballot.

It may be that such choice by the wealthy is primarily a predictive exercise (Fleishman, 1973a:462) in which they make contributions to those prospective or declared candidates who seem most likely to attract the necessary nonfinancial political support and votes to win. Even if so, it is a choice with the most critical consequences in elections, and one must wonder if it should be entrusted to so subjective a determination by so self-interested a group. Clairvoyance is not a science, and public opinion research, as reliable as it seems to have become, is likely to be a poor substitute for some more objective gate-keeping mechanism. The public's political preferences before and during campaigns are too fluid and mercurial to justify allowing *anyone's* predictions to control access. The candidates preferred at nomination deadline time may not be so favored once the election campaign has begun. Given the availability of direct means of gauging public support, such as nominating petition signatures, the reliance on rumor or poll-informed plutocrats to control the starting gates is indefensible.

Certainly, there are dangers in substituting some governmental support for exclusively private financing, but they appear far less serious than those which public subsidization aims at eliminating. Furthermore, such risks as do exist can be minimized, if not eliminated, by care and ingenuity in the design of the intervention mechanism.

VI. PRACTICAL SOLUTIONS TO REAL PROBLEMS

Public subsidies are clearly an attractive alernative to continued, exclusive reliance on private financing of elections. Difficult problems, however, remain to be solved. What kinds of eligibility criteria would be practical and constitutionally permissible in primary elections? What alternatives are preferable for distributing subsidy funds to those candidates who qualify? Although these questions are perplexing, they can be answered satisfactorily.

MONEY AS AN ELIGIBILITY-DETERMINING CRITERION

At first the idea of using a prospective candidate's capacity to raise money privately as the means of qualifying for presidential primary campaign subsidies is attractive. Like alternative qualifying devices, its purpose is to establish the bona fides of a particular candidacy—the seriousness and extent of the support which the candidate has. Surely the willingness of supporters to donate funds is a better test of their commitment to a candidate than their willingness to sign a petition in his behalf. Moreover, the satisfaction of the qualifying test—which, in the 1974 amendments, consists of raising $100,000 in contributions of $250 or less—is more easily determined and verified than the collection of a suitable number (probably a fairly large number) of voters' signatures, each of which would have to be checked for residency, registration, and any other conditions which might be attached. Varying state registration practices would complicate the verification process, making the petition signature alternative much more susceptible to fraud and manipulation.

Despite its simplicity and reliability, however, a monetary eligibility criterion has a serious constitutional flaw. Instead of demonstrating general public support for a contender, it reflects a candidate's support among those who can afford to spend discretionary income or capital on politics—a sizable, yet minority, proportion of the population. In view of the Court's holdings and language in the filing fee cases—Bullock v. Carter (1972) and Lubin v. Panish (1974)—it is difficult to see how an exclusively monetary criterion of eligibility could be sustained against an equal protection attack. In Bullock, the Court invalidated a Texas primary election filing fee system in which the charges could run as high as $8,900. In Lubin, the fee was only slightly more than $700, yet the Court held it unconstitutional. In both cases, the Court stressed the prospective candidates' inability to pay the filing fees, implying that mere unwillingness unaccompanied by inability would be insufficient to warrant a declaration of unconstitutionality (Bullock v. Carter, 1972:146; Lubin v. Panish, 1974:716-718).[4]

The problem, then, is not the existence of the money-eligibility criterion, but the fact that it is the exclusive mode of qualifying. For candidates with supporters who can afford to contribute, Court decisions suggest, it is a constitutionally acceptable means of determining seriousness. For candidates whose supporters are without the requisite funds, however, it is an insuperable barrier to actual candidacy and a denial of equal protection. It would seem impossible to distinguish persuasively between paying filing fees to qualify for a ballot position and raising private funds in order to qualify for a campaign subsidy. The purpose of the monetary-qualifying criterion is to ensure that only serious candidates—those who have a genuine chance to win—will be subsidized. The purpose of filing fees, as the Supreme Court has noted (Lubin v. Panish, 1974:709, 717-718; Bullock v. Carter, 1972:134, 145-146) is analogous—to ensure that only serious candidates will have their names printed on the ballot. The effects of both are similar too. Persons who cannot afford to pay filing fees are excluded from the ballot, whereas persons who cannot raise the requisite amount in private campaign contributions are denied public subsidy for their campaigns, preventing them either from running entirely or from campaigning effectively.

To be scrupulous, it should be noted that this point can be argued another way. Denial of access to the printed ballot is an ultimate sanction; it effectively prevents a candidacy, even if a write-in campaign is possible, rather than merely disadvantages it. In that sense, on an absolute scale, it is a more severe deprivation than denial of public subsidy.

Denial of campaign subsidy, however, while not as severe a sanction as denial of access to the printed ballot, is likely to be just as effective in destroying incipient candidacies.[5] With public "seed money," candidates who might never have been able to raise the funds necessary to run a campaign may gain sufficient attention to attract the necessary contributions. Denied such money, they are consigned to oblivion.

It might be argued that, since filing fees are usually paid by candidates, while the qualifying sum required by the subsidy plan is provided by a candidate's supporters, the analogy between the two is defective. Such a line of attack misses the point, however, because it was the interests of the voters who might choose to vote for the excluded candidate—and not the interests of the candidate himself—which the Court was explicit in protecting in Bullock v. Carter. In that decision, in language that seems tailor-made for the subsidy-qualifying issue, the Court remarked as follows (1972:134-144):

> Many potential office seekers lacking both personal wealth and affluent backers are in every practical sense precluded from seeking the nomination of their chosen party, no matter how qualified they might be, and no matter how broad or enthusiastic their popular support. The effect of this exclusionary mechanism on voters is neither incidental nor remote. Not only are voters substantially limited in their choice of candidates, but also there is the obvious likelihood that this limitation would fall more heavily on the less affluent segment of the community, whose favorites may be unable to pay the large costs required by the Texas system. To the extent that the system requires candidates to rely on contributions from voters in order to pay the assessments, a phenomenon that can hardly be rare in light of the size of the fees, it tends to deny some voters the opportunity to vote for a candidate of their choosing; at the same time it gives the affluent the power to place on the ballot their own names or the names of persons they favor. Appellants do not dispute that this is endemic to the system. This disparity in voting power based on wealth cannot be described by reference to discrete and precisely defined segments of the

> community as is typical of inequities challenged under the Equal Protection Clause, and there are doubtless some instances of candidates representing the views of voters of modest means who are able to pay the required fee. But we would ignore reality were we not to recognize that this system falls with unequal weight on voters, as well as candidates, according to their economic status.

The Court's heavy reliance on the interests of a candidate's prospective supporters and on their socioeconomic background is even more appropriate with respect to the subsidy-qualifying mechanism than it is to filing fees. To qualify for the subsidy, a candidate must raise the necessary funds from his supporters. If his supporters are without sufficient means to contribute, it is *their* indigency which is being discriminated against in the political arena, not *his.*

Perhaps the most persuasive factor is that public subsidy of election campaigns, quite unlike the passive character of regulation of access to printed ballots, is an enormous governmental intervention into politics. When the government chooses to act so influentially and decisively, it cannot do so in a discriminatory manner.

For this reason, what is involved in denying or granting a subsidy has consequences for voters which are at least as grave as the results of denying or granting ballot access. It is difficult to imagine, therefore, that the Court would choose to rest its decision on an extremely narrow and formalistic distinction between ballot access and public subsidy of campaigns.

Assuming this to be correct, what the Court said in Lubin v. Panish about filing fees would seem applicable to an exclusively monetary criterion of eligibility for subsidies (1974:718):

> The absence of any alternative means of gaining access to the ballot inevitably renders the California system exclusionary as to some aspirants. As we have noted, the payment of a fee is an absolute, not an alternative, condition, and failure to meet it is a disqualification from running for office. Thus, California has chosen to achieve the important and legitimate interest of maintaining the integrity of elections by means which can operate to exclude some potentially serious candidates from the ballot without providing them with any alternative means of coming before the voters. Selection of candidates solely on the basis of ability to pay a fixed fee without providing any alternative means is not reasonably necessary to the accomplishment of the State's legitimate election interests. Accord-

ingly, we hold that in the absence of reasonable alternative means of ballot access, a State may not, consistent with constitutional standards, require from an indigent candidate filing fees he cannot pay.

The Court's prescription for remedying the constitutional flaw in filing fees—the use of a reasonable petition signature alternative (Lubin v. Panish, 1974:718-719)—seems equally applicable to public campaign subsidy. Assuming a petition percentage requirement that is high enough to discourage frivolous candidates but sufficiently low to avoid unduly burdening serious contenders (Jenness v. Fortson, 1971:431; Williams v. Rhodes, 1968:23; American Party of Texas v. White, 1974:767; Fleishman, 1973b:391-395), petition signatures would seem to be the best cure for the most serious fault in the subsidy-qualifying mechanism. In the absence of such an alternative mode of qualifying, the presidential primary election subsidy must be regarded as unconstitutional as applied to indigent candidates.

AN EXCLUSIVELY MONETARY MEASURE FOR DISTRIBUTING SUBSIDY FUNDS

Under the 1974 amendments, the amount of subsidy to which qualified candidates are entitled is determined by the amount of private funds each candidate raises. Under the particular matching system of allocation incorporated in the Presidential Primary Matching Payment Account, a dollar of subsidy is paid for each dollar privately raised, up to an aggregate ceiling of $250 from any one contributor. Basing entitlement to public funds on the amount of private funds available to a candidate obviously poses the same kinds of questions raised by an exclusively monetary qualification criterion discussed above (Fleishman, 1975; "Developments in the law—elections," 1975:1269-1270). The issues are sufficiently different, however, to warrant a slight reworking of the analysis.

Matching is undeniably attractive as a method of primary subsidy allocation, and is therefore much more defensible constitutionally than an exclusively monetary qualification criterion. Its virtues are best seen through comparison with several alternative schemes.

The most obvious allocation principle is one which subsidizes equally all those candidates who satisfy the qualification criterion. Such a principle rests on the assumption that all candidates who succeed in passing through the eligibility gate are entitled to a chance to compete in the primary on an equal basis insofar as publicly provided monetary resources are concerned. Moreover, the logic of an equality allocation principle is consonant with, if not dictated by, the principal objective of public financing of primaries—the reduction of contribution-derived disparities between candidates competing for the same office. Unfortunately, two factors undermine the theoretical appeal of an equality principle. First it forces one to subsidize equally all candidates of widely varying degrees of seriousness, treating identically both those candidates who are genuine contenders for office and those who stand no chance at all. If the equal protection clause permitted a fairly high qualification threshold, it would be possible to screen out frivolous candidates at the outset. A difficult qualification test is not constitutionally possible, however (Fleishman, 1975:885-893), which means that an equal-allocation formula will necessarily "waste" a sizable amount of subsidy funds on candidates who have no conceivable prospect of winning office.[6]

Related to this is a second defect—what one might call the "candidate inducement" problem. That is, such a subsidy will not only have to support those candidates who would have run even without public funds, but will also encourage even more candidates to run *because* of the availability of such funds. Unfortunately, not all of the candidates so encouraged will be honest. Indeed, the specter of candidates running simply to acquire a share of the public subsidy for themselves and their friends loomed large in the congressional antipathy to an equal allocation principle.

If one is not to subsidize all qualified candidates equally, it is necessary to discover some constitutionally acceptable basis for discriminating among them. The most reasonable basis, and the one most likely to gain Court favor,[7] is one resting on the amount of preexisting support of candidacy. Two possibilities immediately suggest themselves—one based directly on the number of individual citizens who indicate their support of a candidacy by signing petitions, and the other based on the indirect manifestation of citizen support as reflected in campaign contributions.[8]

The former would clearly be preferable constitutionally, since it is completely unassociated with any wealth criterion. Unfortunately, it is not a reliable guide to the size of public support behind particular candidates, because, as the popular saying goes, "people will sign anything." Indeed, one guesses that many citizens, knowing that candidates' subsidy entitlements would be based on the number of petition signatories, would be inclined to sign every petition being circulated through the neighborhood, if only to get rid of a canvasser. While it is certainly feasible to prescribe that a citizen may sign only one candidate's petition, it is difficult to implement such a restriction. The checking of thousands of names to ensure that they are on the registration books and that there is no duplication would be costly. Moreover, no pure petition signature allocation measure is likely to be regarded by observers, or even by the signing parties, as anything more than a gratuitous accommodation. Because it is costless to the signer, its validity as a reliable indication of his candidate preferences is not strong.

There is one additional variant of this last allocation mechanism that deserves mention—a voucher system. The use of vouchers, the advantages of which have been ably demonstrated by David Adamany and George Agree (1975:189-192, 196-201),[9] would entirely finesse the need for a government agency to use any allocation principle at all. For example, if the agency devised a voucher redeemable for a stipulated sum and mailed it to each registered voter or to every person of voting age who has a Social Security number, citizen choice could operate directly to allocate the available subsidy funds. Moreover, such allocation decisions are not costless, because a citizen has only one voucher to give. But a voucher system has certain problems, which discourage its use. For example, a voucher system is quite costly to administer, with estimates as high as $50 million for administration expenses alone (Adamany and Agree, 1975:201). It also favors candidates who are friendly to the interests of huge groups, whether organized or not, such as labor and students, which have ready manpower for collecting the vouchers. Moreover, it is easy to imagine that a market in vouchers might develop, with politically active citizens collecting or buying the vouchers of friends or with apolitical citizens selling their vouchers to candidates at a discount price.

Against the background of these alternatives, the simplicity of an exclusively matching allocation principle is indeed appealing. By shifting to individual contributors the burden of making the crucial decision of how much subsidy a candidate is to receive, matching allocation avoids the need for any governmental allocation rules or decision.

But is it constitutional? In light of the discussion above, one must conclude that it should not be. Making the amount of private funds raised the *sole* determinant of the amount of public funds to be received frustrates attainment of the primary goal of subsidies

—reducing the dependence of political candidacy upon access to private wealth. To the extent that subsidy entitlement is determined by matching, candidates without access to private funds will continue to be discouraged from running at all, and candidates with access to only limited private funds will continue to be at a disadvantage in competition with their well-heeled rivals. It should be recalled that these are two of the three principal governmental interests which are offered as justification for most campaign finance reform, including public financing, and against which all attempts to achieve them must be measured. Consequently, any subsidy plan which frustrates them must raise serious constitutional questions.

The matching formula in existing law is pernicious, in addition, because of the comparatively high level of its matching ceiling. A $250 matching ceiling favors large contributors and uses public funds to reinforce their candidate choices. A plan which uses large contributions of money both as the exclusive means of determining eligibility in the first place and of allocating subsidy entitlement to those who qualify must fail doubly.

This does not mean, however, that a matching allocation principle cannot be used at all, but only that it should not be used exclusively. As was the case with the eligibility-determining mechanism, the allocation mechanism could be substantially cured by the addition of an equally distributed subsidy in a small amount to all candidates who pass the qualification hurdle. Such a subsidy—at perhaps the level of one-half cent per person of voting age, which would amount to $700,000 for each qualifying candidate in the 1976 presidential election—would be sufficient to enable a qualifying candidate to get his campaign off the ground and permit him to acquire sufficient public exposure to generate the additional private contributions needed to run an adequate campaign. By providing such a floor to all qualifying candidates, a small subsidy would make it possible both to diminish candidate deterrence and to alleviate somewhat the most severe disparities arising out of differential candidate access to private funds.

Moreover, the cost of supplementing matching with an equally distributed low-level subsidy could be substantially recovered by lowering the size of private contributions which would be matched. If, for example, only the first $125 of any individual's aggregate contribution were matched, the cost of the matching component could be cut by between one-quarter and two-fifths, depending on the size distribution of all contributions to be matched.[10]

By itself, a reduction in the matching ceiling would alleviate the equal protection concern over public subsidies to candidates of wealthy contributors. A lower ceiling would not be as objectionable in principle and, on balance, might even save the use of matching from invalidation. Taking both these steps—adding an equally distributed subsidy and reducing the level of the matching ceiling—would greatly increase the likelihood that the plan would be found constitutional. In addition, if the maximum size of individual qualifying contributions were similarly reduced,[11] if the minimum number of required contributors were correspondingly increased,[12] and if a petition signature alternative were added as suggested above,[13] the constitutionality of a presidential primary election subsidy could be assured.

VII. CONCLUSION

Public financing of elections marks an attempt to break the dependency of political participation on access to large amounts of money. The particular public subsidy plan now in effect for presidential elections is, with several minor exceptions (Fleishman, 1975), a reasonable way of defraying election costs so as to achieve that end. In combination with public disclosure of, and reasonable contribution ceilings on, private contributions to political campaigns, our current public subsidy of elections is a practical solution to a long-standing American dilemma. It promises greater political opportunity to Americans of all economic stations, and it offers the public a government much less subject to the influence of special interest. Perhaps most important, it offers some hope that the profession of politics may once again attain something of the honorable status it enjoyed when the Republic was younger. That alone would be sufficient to justify the bold departure we have now taken.

NOTES

1. Domhoff (1972:11-22) argues that the reliance of both major political parties on wealthy contributors has effectively erased the policy differences between the two. The result, he contends, borrowing a term from Ferdinand Lundberg, is "One Big Property Party." The motives of contributing "fat cats" are varied. Some seek pure financial self-interest—government contracts or foreign policies favorable to corporate expansion.

Others are not self-seeking, however. Some "want to turn their money into status and prestige"; still others "want to see a more humane society which usually means in practice some expansion of civil rights and more reliable welfare measures for the bottom layers of society" (p. 17).

2. The figure of $500 is, of course, arbitrary. It is used here primarily for the purposes of illustration, since the data in the tables being used are based on a ceiling on contributions of $500. A ceiling on contributions of $100 would have even greater impact. In the 1968 presidential campaign, the Republicans received 55 percent of their individual contributions in amounts of over $100. At the same time, the Democrats received 74 percent of their total contributions in sums greater than $100, while George Wallace received 16 percent of his total contributions in such sums (Alexander, 1971:159, 164-165). Thus to maintain existing levels of political spending with a ceiling on contributions of $100, the government would have to provide even greater subsidies to the parties.

3. Indeed, direct primaries were designed and introduced in the Progressive Era for the specific purpose of weakening party organizations (Ranney, 1954). V.O. Key (1954) has examined the impact of direct primaries on parties and found "indirect evidence" to suggest that the use of direct primaries weakens party cliques, thus leading to a decline in party cohesion and "organizational atrophy."

4. See, also, Adams v. Askew (1975), in which candidates who paid filing fees were denied reimbursement on the theory that filing fees are unconstitutional only as applied to those who cannot afford to pay them.

5. In this regard, it is interesting to note the extent to which the news media have seized upon the failure of candidates to qualify for the presidential primary subsidy as a principal indicator of a candidate's lack of promise.

6. The word *waste* is in quotation marks to emphasize that it is used with some qualifications. While subsidizing candidates who are simply seeking publicity is clearly wasteful, supporting the candidacies of ideological minorities can enliven and refresh political debate in a variety of ways. The latter is surely not waste.

7. There is language scattered through Williams v. Rhodes (1968) and Jenness v. Fortson (1971) which approves preexisting support as a basis for access to the ballot. There is no reason to think that a distribution principle which is acceptable for so sensitive a function would be unacceptable as a guide for subsidy allocation.

8. It would be entirely possible, of course, to use other measures of citizen support. A less troublesome version of a measure based on contributions would use the number of contributors rather than the amount they had contributed.

9. This has been embodied in legislation by Senator Lee Metcalf: S. 1390, 90th Congress, 1st Session (1967). See 113 Congressional Record 8006 (1967).

10. This is merely a guess, since it is not yet known to what extent the availability of matching funds is going to induce private citizens to contribute more than they would have without the enticement of the subsidy. If all the contributions of a presidential candidate were at the matching ceiling of $250, a reduction of the ceiling to $125 would obviously cut the costs of matching by half. Yet not all contributions will be at the level of $250.

11. Other than pure symmetry, there is no particular need to equate the qualifying contribution ceiling and the matching ceiling. One could easily keep the former at $250, while reducing the latter to $125, which would simply mean that only half the qualifying contribution would be matched by public funds.

12. Increasing the number of required contributors would probably help allay the fears of "candidate inducement" created by the addition of an equally distributed subsidy component.

13. The addition of a petition signature alternative as a means of qualifying for the subsidy would, by itself, be enough to save the present mechanism for determining eligibility, regardless of the amount of the ceiling on qualifying contributions. The amount of that ceiling, however, would undoubtedly bear strongly on the Court's examination of

the subsidy plan as a whole (see Williams v. Rhodes, 1968), especially when the raising of money through large contributions plays such an important part throughout. A reduction in the ceiling on qualifying contributions, therefore, might well help to sustain the constitutionality of a principle of matching allocations.

REFERENCES

Articles and Books

ADAMANY, D. (1969). Financing politics. Madison: University of Wisconsin Press.

——— (1973). "Public financing: A cure for the curse of slush funds." Progressive, 37(October):38-42.

ADAMANY, D., and AGREE, G. (1975). Money and politics: Campaign finance in the United States. Baltimore: Johns Hopkins Press.

ALEXANDER, H.E. (1971). Financing the 1968 election. Lexington, Mass.: D.C. Heath.

——— (1972). Money in politics. Washington, D.C.: Public Affairs Press.

——— (1973). "Impact of new federal election laws in the United States" (mimeo). Princeton, N.J.: Citizens' Research Foundation.

——— (1975a). "Democratic values in election reform." National Civic Review, 64(June): 290-295.

——— (1975b). "The impact of election reform legislation on the political party system." Paper delivered to the American Political Science Association.

——— (forthcoming). Financing the 1972 election.

BELLUSH, J., and BOYD, W. (1974). "Subsidizing campaigns: Dangers to the democratic process" (mimeo). New York: Hunter College Center for Policy Through Participation.

CASPER, G. (1969). "*Williams v. Rhodes* and public financing of political parties under the American and German Constitutions." Supreme Court Review, pp. 271-302.

Common Cause (1975). "Summary of key findings by the Common Cause Campaign Finance Monitoring Project for 1972 and 1974 federal elections" (mimeo). April 24. Washington, D.C.: Author.

DAHL, R.A. (1961). Who governs? New Haven, Conn.: Yale University Press.

DAHL, R.A., and LINDBLOM, C.E. (1953). Politics, economics, and welfare. New York: Harper and Row.

"Developments in the law—elections." (1975). Harvard Law Review, 88(April):1111-1339.

DOMHOFF, G.W. (1972). Fat cats and democrats. Englewood Cliffs, N.J.: Prentice-Hall.

DREW, E. (1971). "Washington." Atlantic, 227(March):18-26.

DUNN, D. (1969). Financing presidential campaigns. Washington, D.C.: Brookings Institution.

FLEISHMAN, J.L. (1973a). "Freedom of speech and equality of political opportunity: The constitutionality of the Federal Election Campaign Act of 1971." North Carolina Law Review, 51(January):389-483.

——— (1973b). "Public financing of election campaigns: Constitutional constraints on steps toward equality of political influence of citizens." North Carolina Law Review, 52(December):349-416.

——— (1975). "The 1974 Federal Election Act amendments: The shortcomings of good intentions." Duke Law Journal, (September):851-899.

HEARD, A. (1960). The costs of democracy. Chapel Hill: University of North Carolina Press.

KEY, V.O. (1954). "The direct primary and party structure: A study of state legislative nominations." American Political Science Review, 48(March):1-26.

LEONARD, D. (1975). Paying for party politics. London: PEP.

NEUBERGER, R.L. (1956). "Federal funds for party coffers." Christian Century, 73(January 25):105-107.

NICHOLSON, M. (1974). "Campaign financing and equal protection." Stanford Law Review, 26(April):815-854.

PENNIMAN, H.R. (1971). "Financing campaigns in the public interest." Pp. 1-41 in H.R. Penniman and R.K. Winter, Jr. (eds.), Campaign finances: Two views of the political and constitutional implications. Washington, D.C.: American Enterprise Institute for Public Policy Research.

PINCUS, W. (1973). "Campaign financing: Let's look before we leap." New Republic, 169(October 27):16-19.

RANNEY, A. (1954). The doctrine of responsible party government. Urbana: University of Illinois Press.

RAWLS, J. (1971). A theory of justice. Cambridge, Mass.: Harvard University Press.

ROSENTHAL, A.J. (1972). "Campaign financing and the Constitution." Harvard Journal of Legislation, 9(March):359-423.

SCHWARTZ, J. (1975). Public financing of elections: A constitutional division of the wealth. Chicago: American Bar Association.

STEIGER, W. (1975). "Dollar check-off is faring well, but is it fair?" Congressional Record, (March 18):H1921-1922.

STERLING‘ C.W. (1971). "Federal regulation of political party finances: A study in public policy." PUblic Policy, 19(Winter):143-165.

WICKER, T. (1973). "Strong arm and red hand." New York Times, 122(July 10):41.

WINTER, R.K., Jr. (1971). "Money, politics, and the First Amendment." Pp. 45-83 in H.R. Penniman and R.K. Winter, Jr. (eds.), Campaign finances: Two views of the political and constitutional implications. Washington, D.C.: American Enterprise Institute for Public Policy Research.

——— (1973). Campaign financing and political freedom. Washington, D.C.: American Enterprise Institute for Public Policy Research.

" 'Yes' for a clean fight" (1975). New York Times, 125(March 22):30.

Cases

Adams v. Askew (1975). 511 F.2nd. 700 (5th Circuit).

American Party of Texas v. White (1974). 415 U.S. 767.

Buckley v. Valeo (1976). 96 S.Ct. 612.

Bullock v. Carter (1972). 405 U.S. 134.

Jenness v. Fortson (1971). 403 U.S. 431.

Lubin v. Panish (1974). 415 U.S. 709.

Opinion of the Justices (1964). 347 Mass. 797, 197 N.E.2nd. 691.

Schweitzer v. Clerk for City of Plymouth (1969). 381 Mich. 485, 164 N.W.2nd. 35.

Sweezy v. New Hampshire (1957). 354 U.S. 234.

Williams v. Rhodes (1968). 393 U.S. 23.

Statutes

Federal Election Campaign Act of 1971, Public Law No. 92-225, 86 stat. 3 (cited as the 1971 Campaign Act).

Revenue Act of 1971, Public Law No. 92-178, tit. VII-VIII, 85 stat. 560-574 (cited as the Revenue Act).

Act of October 15, 1974, Public Law No. 93-443, 88 stat. 1263 (amending the Federal Election Campaign Act of 1971, cited as the 1974 amendments).

Chapter 2

SUBSIDIES FOR CAMPAIGN TIME: SOME CAVEATS

JEWEL BELLUSH
WILLIAM J. D. BOYD

He who accounts all things easy will have many difficulties.

Lao-tzu

Traditionally, Americans have held the political game in low esteem. In a system based on a good deal of political action and widespread citizen participation, this view flies in the face of the fundamentals of our style of democracy and electoral process. To a large extent, this antagonism toward playing politics has been fed by the recurring pattern of corruption in the system. More recently, the revelations of Watergate have fed this distrust, dismay, and distaste for politics. Professor Richard Neustadt has described the current period as one of "antipolitical politics." Public disillusionment is so widespread and the mood so cynical that it will probably take us years to recapture many of the positive qualities of citizen response to the political system.

One of the responses to this Watergate imbroglio, however, comes onto the scene as a mixed blessing. There is a surge for reform. And a host of civic organizations and excited good government types are rushing forth with a wide array of nostrums: the moment of solution

AUTHORS' NOTE: We would like to extend special appreciation to Helen Ferrante, an undergraduate student at Hunter College who helped with research and who served as a gadfly, always challenging assumptions. We would also like to express our thanks to Lorraine West for smooth mechanics. The viewpoints expressed in this paper are those of the authors and in no way reflect the opinions of either Hunter College or the National Municipal League.

is at hand. Suggestions for change include: limitations on campaign chests, free TV, tighter disclosure regulations, disallowance of large contributions and rules restraining business and labor in the electoral processes.

Under the impetus of Watergate there is an anxious spirit for change. But quick responses to complex problems may produce half-baked, if not dangerous, solutions. In this paper we set out some of our anxieties about subsidizing the ballot box. While all the evidence is not yet in, nor have a large number of states acted,[1] we feel it is time to underscore some of the key problems these reforms are raising.

Our concern here is with one reform which has been gaining popularity but which has received little care or detailed examination. It is public subsidization of political campaigns. Thus, we suggest a beginning for such an analysis by considering the following problems which subsidies seem to generate: interferring with civil liberties, protecting incumbents and blocking insurgents, encouraging anti-party politics, inducing the phony campaign, curbing the minor party challenge, linking expenditures and electoral success, inflating the price tage, and generating false expectations.

While our focus will be on subsidizing campaigns, at times we will have to touch on other reforms, since many of the regulations concerned with subsidies involve limits on contributions, restrictions on spending, and more detailed disclosure.

Without question, the expense of running for office should concern Americans, for costs have skyrocketed over the years. While research findings may vary on detail, those familiar with the data would agree that lots of money is spent on political campaigns. (This should not be overemphasized, however, for the nation's biggest advertiser, General Foods, spends more in its ad campaigns than the total spent in all election campaigns in any single year.)

Some argue that the way to "solve" this growing financial burden on potential candidates is to subsidize campaigns from the public treasury. Several bills have been introduced that would provide help for federal office, and in many states proposals have been recommended for state and local campaigns. Little or no attention has been paid to what impact these proposals will have for the American party process and, more importantly, for the constitutional liberties of citizens. We are typically an impatient people, often seeking simple solutions to our complex problems. It is one of the ironies of American political life that the reforms of today usually necessitate repealing the "reforms" of yesterday. This country has recently undergone the greatest rush of state constitutional rewriting in history. The only period that rivals it is the post-Civil War era, when we put into our constitutions various provisions regarding the financing of education, earmarking of state revenues, imposing limits on the length of legislative sessions, and curtailing the powers of the legislative branch. Removal of these provisions is today among the major reforms being sought.

These "reforms" of the past did much to contribute to the erosion of state vitality and the resultant growth in federal power. What those reformers of the past did was slowly but fundamentally to change the political structure of the nation. We could be doing the same thing with our political parties and the candidates they produce—and accomplish exactly the opposite of what we seek to do. Instead of making parties more responsible and insurgency more possible, we may crush the parties and enshrine the incumbents.

While admittedly the authors have shared, at times, the sense of frustration with reforming our electoral system (legislative apportionment, permanent registration, the 18-year-old vote, etc.) here is a reform which should be more carefully screened. Its proponents have made several assumptions that have yet to be challenged. Has anyone really considered the cost of subsidies? What about its fairness? How is this program to be administered and enforced? Will subsidies make a difference in the outcome of elections? Is money the only factor that guarantees success?

We raise these questions in order to open the debate which has yet to begin in the public arena. Too many aspects of public subsidization simply remain foggy generalizations, yet how we answer these questions specifically will indicate whether or not we can have a more democratic electoral system through subsidies.

I. CIVIL LIBERTIES

To begin with, we have found too few among the advocates who have even considered the possible impact that civil liberties would have on aspects of public campaign subsidization. One of the early experiments in public subsidization has been the dollar checkoff in presidential campaigns. This is linked to the tax system. While admittedly this reform requires the approval of the individual taxpayer who decides to make the contribution in this fashion, is there not an aspect of discrimination in allowing people to check off only the Democratic and Republican parties? What happens to those taxpayers advocating the Socialist Workers party, the Communist party, the Socialist Labor party or the American Independent party? Furthermore, a good many people are not anxious to give money until they know who the candidate will be. It was no accident that throughout the country the United States Senate and the gubernatorial races outpolled the vote for the President in 1972. This is the first time that this has happened on such a grand scale. Clearly the American people were saying, "a plague on both your houses." Immediately after this experience, are we now going to say, "Tough. We are going to make you pay for it out of your tax dollar!"

The proposal which passed Congress and which is suggested in most state laws expects the Congress and the state legislatures to vote supplemental funds if the tax checkoff does not produce enough revenue.[2] Is this not a clear violation of much of what the public wants? If people decline to make the checkoff, it means they do not want their tax money spent in this manner. But legislative bodies are nevertheless going to make them spend it that way.

Subsidization forces citizens, whether they like it or not, to funnel their money into political campaigning, including the campaigning of party and candidates that they may oppose but over which they have really lost control. Just think about this from the perspective of the citizen: the government, through handouts, compels you to allow your money to publicize the candidacy of someone you find objectionable. But you have absolutely no say about it. More often, if you are a member or an advocate of some minor party, you probably will not have even an opportunity to vote for your choice.

While we are most anxious to encourage citizen participation, this does not justify creation of an involuntary system of political involvement. Subsidization really helps stuff the ballot box in the name of expanding the democratic electorate but will, in effect, operate to the advantage of established political party groups beyond the citizen's control. Is this not an invasion of an individual's civil liberty, in that it calls for forced subsidies to one's political "enemies"?

Compelling candidates to operate within the context of a government-designed campaign subsidy system is a clear violation of civil liberties. Just imagine the kind of "guidelines," "strings," or "requirements" that the government can impose upon candidates and parties to fulfill the "intent" of the law. If this appears too alarmist or an exaggeration, take a closer look at Stanley Pottinger's guidelines on affirmative action for hiring policies at universities receiving federal money. Already, there is evidence of undesirable "strings" in some of the legislation. Missouri's reform law requires that income and gifts of $100 or more to a candidate, as well as fees and salaries paid for services of more than $500 for the previous year, have to be reported. A lawyer or doctor running for office would thus have to violate confidential relationships with clients and probably discourage them and other allied professionals from entering a political race. In Jackson County, Kansas, a financial disclosure ordinance applies to all political clubs that endorse candidates for county office but does not apply to Democratic or Republican county committees because they are created by state law and do not exist solely to support candidates.

Let us also look at this whole matter in terms of the real world of partisan politics. Everyone knows that the Republican party has been declining in registration. However, the one category in which it has managed to do best is with those people earning $15,000 or more a year. On the basis of 1971 data, those in the $15,000 and above category composed 18.3 percent of all taxpayers. However, they contributed almost 58.6 percent of all income taxes. A very large percentage of these people has consistently voted Republican in both national and state elections outside the South. The new campaign proposals are now saying two things to these people: (1) you can only give so much money to any one candidate or group of candidates and (2) your tax dollars are going to be given in equal amounts to both the person you favor and the person you dislike. Maybe the first act is fair and a just protection to the system, but it is hard to see how it is fair to make so many Republicans automatically support Democrats. That, in terms of real politics, is what these laws are doing.

Furthermore, the universal claim made by reformers who advocate subsidization is that it will bring greater equity to the electoral process. Senator Edward Kennedy made this very argument in defense of the new congressional Campaign Act which provides for federal matching grants for candidates for presidential nominations. Each private donation of up to $250 will be matched by an equal amount from Uncle Sam. While this is intended to reduce dependence on rich donors, note that a contribution of $250 brings 250 times as much public money as a contributor who gives but a dollar.

Equalizing campaign costs may sound democratic and just, but achieving it is another matter. Putting a lid on those who opt for public funding does not quite guarantee equity. For example, Candidate A may have the support of a Jane Fonda or Ronald Reagan (when he was an actor), who helps him get extensive and free publicity. Why can't Candidate B's pal, Joe Smith, balance the effect by a newspaper advertisement? This, however, would have to come out of the candidate's campaign chest, which has a specific limit.

In the process of supporting subsidies, one bright, radical graduate student urged people not to worry about the content of these laws impinging on civil liberties since all encroachments have their "kinks" and can be ironed out by the courts. The judges, it is suggested, will guarantee that the legislation will not conflict with the First Amendment. While this dependence on the courts makes one a bit nervous, this strategy does work at times. For example, a near violation of civil liberties was this time fortunately nipped in the bud by the Supreme Court. A legitimate citizens' group was refused advertising space in a noted newspaper on grounds that prior approval by a candidate, who was at the time running for office, was necessary. According to a 1971 federal law, a candidate had to acknowledge activity "on his behalf," and it was to be billed as his personal expense. But the group had nothing to do with the campaign or the candidate. The Court found this a violation of the First Amendment. More important, however, the federal official responsible for administering the law later reprimanded both the group and the newspaper for bringing the suit, suggesting that they could have obtained the same result by seeking *his* consent or that of the Justice Department. Indeed! Is it therefore so unreasonable to suggest that through the administration of subsidies for campaigns we will be delegating tremendous authority to bureaucrats and extending their opportunities to censure political opinions and programs of candidates, political parties, and interest groups? If we heed the student's advice, we had better create some bill-watchers for bringing suits to the courts!

Another civil liberties question concerns disclosure. Reform groups have been pressuring for publication of the names of contributors. For those of us with memories of recent history—particularly of congressional committees authorized to subpoena lists of contributors to left-wing groups and of federal agencies permitted to keep lists of "subversive" organizations and individuals—the disclosure route invites serious issues of the First Amendment. The subsidy system will invariably necessitate keeping a goodly number of lists and considerable information about campaigns which may, in turn, impinge on our fundamental democratic rights. For example, the state of Washington requires detailed listing of every donation over $5, including name, address, and date. The lobbyists must name the legislators they entertain, and every expense above $15 must be itemized. Lawyers in public office and part-timers on school boards must list their clients and those of partners. Young Americans for Freedom refused to publish its membership list and won its case with the help of the American Civil Liberties Union.

Under the federal disclosure law reports are required from any political committee that handles more than $1,000 a year, including names and address of all person who contribute more than $100. The American Civil Liberties Union now has a lawsuit on behalf of the Socialist Workers party, charging that the law "will deter and intimidate persons from associating with, contributing to and supporting its political campaigns and candidates." In our desire to regulate the "selling of an election" to the fat cats, we may, in the process, overextend ourselves and violate basic freedoms. In exchange for deceiving ourselves on the possibility of eliminating corruption by money, we may be opening the political process to government snooping.

II. PROTECTING INCUMBENTS AND BLOCKING INSURGENTS

While most reformers see subsidization as broadening the opportunities for more candidates, a number of party regulars see the money as enriching the organization's coffers. To avoid too many candidates, suggested reforms utilize party mechanisms to control the operation. If the handout is made to the party, however, this too invites difficulties and serious consequences for the very character of national political gaming—which may not be desirable for reformers themselves. If the subsidies are funneled through the national committees (for the president) and through congressional campaign committees (for legislators), we are shifting part of the locus of power in our federal system. Do we mean to do that? American parties are loose confederations of state and local organizations, and congressmen and senators (with exceptions) usually depend on the money and support that they can assemble back home. With national agencies given a larger financial role, the character of both governmental and party federalism may be significantly altered. Each national committee would have the responsibility for allocating subsidies to each of the states and congressional districts. What tremendous power! For example, try to imagine how the national party would write a formula for distribution of funds around the country. Who would Congress use to monitor this system? It would probably emerge as a typical congressional committee, attracting to itself powerful congressional chairmen, those with seniority (hence the more conservative, those from generally one-party states or districts). It would invite a highly partisan administrative system. Indeed, what we would be creating is a new form of delegated power to nongovernmental agencies. In this case, the congressional and presidential party leaders, not those at the constituency level, would be strengthened. Some reformers may want to augment the power of party control in Washington. However, let us understand what we are doing. This shift in authority may mean that newcomers, challengers, and, among them, new politics people may be cut off from some of the public funding because the national leadership may find them unacceptable, if not disagreeable. It depends upon who is in control of the party mechanisms.

Most subsidy proposals require that a certain "threshold" amount of money first be raised before matching government funds become available. At the same time, these measures place limits upon the amount of money that a candidate and his family may give and limits upon the amount that any other individual can contribute. Fine, this is going to stop the role of "dirty" money. It is also supposed to help finance the less well-to-do and to help insurgency. But will it? The incumbent will have at his ready disposal a sufficient number of contributors to reach the threshold level immediately. (Let us be realistic, there is a reverse element to campaign financing that is little short of an incumbent extorting contributions from a variety of constituents and from interests not in his district but over whom—in his committee roles—he has great power.) The incumbent will almost always start to receive matching public funds well before an opponent has reached the threshold. The incumbent will virtually *never* fail to raise the necessary funds to reach the total limit set on expenditures. The generally less well-known challenger may be trapped into a situation in which he must spend much, if not most, of his time and energies raising money from many small contributors before he can effectively launch the campaign. The present-day value of incumbency for a congressman has been variously estimated as between $300,000 and $600,000 (a safe district may be much less).

In a recent article, a former legislative assistant in the Senate acknowledged that an incumbent has *each year* almost a quarter of a million dollars in public funds for staff and office expenses. An incumbent's resources include status of office, the frank, the government library of photographs, recordings, and film, physical space, newsletters, free weekly columns in a local newspaper back home, and free time on a radio or TV station. The Radio-TV Galleries of Congress estimate that 352 members of the House used their facilities during 1974. Along with senators, congressmen engage the studios for periodic TV and radio reports that are sent home to local stations and carried as a public service. While legislators pay for these services, the rates are nominal. A public subsidy system may well increase these advantages, not decrease them. Then certainly it will help a good many individuals to enter the political arena who otherwise might not have done so. But while this very fact may insure several challengers to the incumbent in the primary, the incumbent will generally be assured victory by a plurality, if nothing else.

Except in rare instances—where the party wants to eliminate an independent character—the money given the congressional and senatorial campaign committees will be spent for the incumbents. Would these contributions count toward their threshold requirements and thus get more public funds? This becomes a vicious circle, doesn't it?

While we want to preserve the constructive, democratic, and stable qualities of party life, we also need the freshness and challenge of newcomers. Many reformers supporting subsidies believe that the key factor discouraging new candidates from playing the party game is money. If this is true (and we have some reservations about this claim), the current legislation is not encouraging. In part, this is due to the very nature and character of our present party system and the rules governing party organizations. The recent federal law (S.3044) provides for a limit on individual contributions to $1,000 each for the primaries and the runoff and general elections, with an aggregate contribution of $25,000 for all federal candidates annually. However, the $5,000 limit placed on each organization, political committee, and national and state party organization (i.e., for primaries and the runoff and general elections) has no aggregate limit on the amount that individual organizations can contribute to the party organizations supporting federal candidates.

Why limit individuals and not organizations? In fact, a good many campaigns run by challengers, both inside the party by insurgents and on behalf of some minor party, have been made possible by what reformers admit to be the "fat cat" individuals or "sugar daddies and mommies." The point is that these rich individuals are "ours"– those with a civic conscience (like Stewart Mott) who are outside the party organizational circles. Our hunch is that insurgency often needs an individual's money to make a challenge since the organizational route may be closed off. McGovern's presidential bid had a substantial fiscal base among wealthy individuals. Of course, individual subsidies have their dangerous aspects too. The important point being made here, as elsewhere in this paper, is that whatever reform is proposed, some win, some lose, some benefit, some are disadvantaged. And we had better understand who indeed we want to help and who we wish to limit. The electoral process is important to our democratic system. Let us be as clear as possible as to what we are doing to it. Cutting individuals out of contributing to campaigns may also harm the adherents of reform among the new politics people. With public subsidies there is a parallel strategy to make private giving more difficult. The candidate challenging an incumbent usually must spend more money than the so-called limits allow. Congresswoman Elizabeth Holtzman criticized the Common Cause-backed bill that failed this recent session of Congress because, she said, it set privately raised funds at a limit of $10,000, with an individual of $100, for any candidate who wanted to qualify for public subsidy. This would have not been adequate, she said, to challenge the incumbent in New York's 16th district. Several others in recent years who did defeat incumbents have likewise admitted that they needed more money than was provided for in the proposal. Republican David Treen of Louisiana spent $155,629 before the new legislative limits were set at $70,000 "without loopholes." (More of this later.) A few years ago, even President Ford, then a congressman running in a safe congressional district after 22 years of service and known nationally, admitted that he spent $87,000. According to a 1972 study of challengers by Common Cause, eight of the ten who defeated incumbent representatives outspent their opponents, as did three of the five who defeated incumbent senators.

III. THE RETURN OF ANTI-PARTY POLITICS

The plans for subsidization are sponsored by a goodly number of organizations and individuals holding a view similar to the rhetoric and thrust of the Progressive Era—which reflected a fear, if not outright disdain, of the political party system, American style. American politics is, to a large degree, oriented to candidates, and, consequently, subsidies are aimed to help democratize "the system" by opening it up to other candidates. And in places where there might be a one-party system, the wishful thinking of the current reformers is that subsidies will offer voters more candidates. Let us look at their arguments.

In the first place, fiscal support of the candidates will only exacerbate relationships between the party and the candidates. If the area or district is one-party dominated (and many are), the fiscal subsidy may have the effect of further fragmenting an already fragmented party system. It is a fact that in one-party districts a good number of races are carried on within a party's primaries. Where is the logic that more money to individuals will necessarily strengthen the opposition? Quite the opposite. How will this system control the number of candidates offering themselves on the opposition side and thus continue to have the effect of further fragmenting the party game?

Second, while this may not be the place for a defense of the party system, it is of critical importance to recognize some salient facts of American political life. Parties—though under pressure to change—still constitute the single most important institution for coherence and unity in a highly heterogeneous society. Furthermore, will it be in the interest of American democracy that we, through this subsidization process, finance further fragmentation of the districts and states from which senators and congressmen come? Let us not forget, particularly in this period of executive dominance, that we depend more than usual on congressional responsibility. Weak as that may be, imagine its character and thrust under a system of no-party politics. There is no alternative to checking power except with more power.

Under our present system it is bad enough that we can have a president elected with less than half the popular vote. What type of governmental chaos might ensue if a minority president sat in the White House and the Congress was composed of a majority of "independents." If we are going to shatter the parties and facilitate greater fragmentation of our system, we are asking for increased power in the presidency and a heightened role for well-organized and well-heeled pressure groups. The power vacuum is always filled by someone or some group.

IV. THE PHONY CAMPAIGN

A unique feature of the American political system is the primary. We are the only nation that uses it. Let us look at the primary in Southern states and the possible consequences there for public funding. Southern Democratic primaries may be hotly contested. But a word of caution, for this form of competition has proved to be less effective than a real two-party battle in stimulating interest and activity. Contrary to conventional wisdom, turnouts in the South, where the primary may be the real election, are no greater than the primary turnouts elsewhere in the nation (with but a handful of exceptions—the Mississippi gubernatorial race, for example). In fact, when candidates run without labels it is tougher to make a selection and the voter has a difficult time determining where his interest really belongs. The poorly educated, the "have-not" groups if you will, in the Southern electorate reap the least benefit from this sort of political game. Thus, public funding in Southern state primaries may only exacerbate what is already an unfair political condition. Furthermore, the problem in the primary is that we often do not know the candidates, and thus we are puzzled as to which among them should receive public funds. If we simply hand out dollar bills to all, we may be wasting much money. Some of the Southern primaries have been ridiculous multifactional affairs. In 1960, for example, Lyndon Johnson's senate seat was contested by some 73 candidates. Often, dozens enter Florida's state and local races due to its peculiar factional style of politics.

Most legislative districts—even a large percentage of the U.S. Senate seats—are one-party areas. Win the primary and, for all intents and purposes, one has won the election. Public subsidies cut two ways in this system. First, unless states change their laws and mandate runoff elections, the public subsidy feature may well lead to more and more candidates and hence a much greater chance for the primary victor to be the one with a plurality of the votes, not a majority. This is a built-in advantage to incumbents. If runoff elections become necessary, we are adding a tremendous cost to the entire electoral process. If runoff elections are not held, we are probably locking incumbents in for life.

What makes a district a "one-party" area? Is money the decisive factor? If it were, the Republican party could surely have done better than it has in recent years, since it has been traditionally the recipient of more funds than the Democrats (except in 1974). This is generally (but not always) true at the local level as well as in Northern and Western states. As a matter of fact, the safer the district, the less money the opposition party spends because they know it is useless. Money is not going to reverse the situation. An entire set of social, economic, ethnic, and psychological factors must change first. In such races today, if any candidate is put up at all, the opposition party names a party regular who conducts a low-key, inexpensive campaign just to keep the party's line on the ballot. Come matching campaign funds—particularly on the state level, where only petition signatures or a very low monetary threshold is established—and we are going to see increasingly expensive phony campaigns. (This is particularly true where states are not considering matching funds but subsidies of two, three, or four times as much public funds as private.) On the Lower East Side of heavily Democratic Manhattan, for example, some enterprising young Republican lawyer may go to a public relations man, a printer, a campaign button manufacturer, or whomever and solicit contributions of $500 each (or whatever the limit is). He then hires them to perform their respective campaign duties for him and pays them three or four times what they gave him. They make a good buck; he as a lawyer has received the type of exposure which the canons of the Bar Association prohibit in the way of advertising; and the public is out a healthy amount of money.

All of this would take place in a phony, hopeless campaign. Admittedly, in some places it might eventually help shift the district away from a one-party area. However, we would argue that money will be but a minor part of the change unless other more important conditions are present.

To avoid the phony candidates, reformers have proposed matching funds, as in the present federal law. Raising money serves as a test of whether or not the candidate really merits public funding. First, he raises up to $250 per contributor in presidential primaries or $100 in congressional primaries; then these private donations are matched by equal grants, but only *after* the total of donations crosses a certain "threshold." The key is what that threshold will be. If set too low, it will not serve as a damper on phony candidates attracted by free cash. However, if set too high, it will serve as an unfair handicap to the unknown candidate who has a difficult job raising seed money. In essence, whether you like this logic or not, matching funds can really have the effect of underscoring the vital import of private fund raising. To put it more concretely, candidate A raises $30,000 in small contributions and candidate B $15,000. Matching public money would give totals of $60,000 and $30,000 respectively—doubling the gap. The less well-known candidate is continually at a disadvantage, while the more prominent one continues to benefit from more and more public funding. Is not this the very result that reformers want to avoid?

Even if we accept the proposition that the objective of fiscal subsidies is to aid the serious candidates and that it is not to weaken the party or to encourage the seekers of publicity who may well use the system to build their business or clientele, there continues to be a serious problem of defining what we mean by a fair subsidy. This is not simply a semantic question. Given the complexity of the American political system, this is an almost insurmountable task. Few realize that what constitutes a political party in the United States varies from state to state.

While seeking to identify, within this complexity, who indeed is a serious candidate and who is taking the public for a ride, can the citizen be assured that equality of opportunity is being maintained? No matter what standards we finally select—whether by past vote, by fixed number of signatures on a petition, or whatever—each is arbitrary and, in effect, creates a different political result depending on the criteria selected. Furthermore, for a new candidate to get started in our system necessitates seed money and a goodly number of dedicated (and experienced) volunteers to get petitions signed correctly. In some districts with a strong incumbent, no system of subsidization will facilitate a breakthrough, because the preliminary politics essential for the challenging aspirant often require more than just money.

V. CURBING THE MINOR PARTY CHALLENGE

Minor parties have played an important role in America's traditional two-party system—injecting new issues, advancing innovative programs, and publicizing fresh personalities. Inevitably their destiny is to "come and go"—but "go" they must, only because their ideas have usually been adopted by one of the major parties. It is widely acknowledged, however, that minor parties have a trying time in many parts of the country due to difficult petition requirements, unfair electoral systems, expensive media costs, and local police regulations. Public financing offers the establishment another subtle opportunity to exacerbate the disadvantaged position of third parties. For example, to qualify for funds in presidential primaries, a party must first raise $100,000 in amounts of $5,000 in each of 20 states. Consequently, a regional party like States Rights and state-based parties such as the Liberals and Conservatives in New York would be disadvantaged. Another provision requires that to qualify as an organization, a party has to be in operation six months before the primaries.

Furthermore, there is a serious problem of *when* funding takes place for a minor party. Each major party, defined under the new federal law, is one which has garnered at least 25 percent of the vote in the last election. These will get funded at the start of the campaign. A minor party is often new to the political scene, and its leaders may change from one election to another. Thus, their circumstances vary considerably. But to qualify, minor parties must win 5 percent of the vote in the previous election. And a new minor party would have to muster 5 percent of the current election vote. Failing this, there is no public funding. Furthermore, unlike their major competitors, the minor parties will not be funded until after the ballots are cast. Where are they expected to find money before being reimbursed? Use a BankAmericard? Which bank or individual would provide a loan? And at the inflationary cost of interest these days! [3]

In addition, when competing for a House seat, a candidate is limited to $70,000. But the national committee and the state committee of his party can each give the candidate another $10,000–raising "the limit" (a misnomer) another $20,000. Thus a minority party or independent candidate without a national or state organization will be unable to use this loophole. It is another bonus to the major party candidates. Is this the kind of equity that reformers want in the system?

Finally, when carefully examined and fully understood, the new federal legislation will have the effect of changing our electoral system in ways we may find even more objectionable. If this legislation was in effect in the 19th century, the Republicans would have had difficulty benefiting from it, making it tough indeed for Lincoln to have been elected. The same may be said of the Bull Moosers who broke away from the Republican party in 1912. Senator Wayne Morse of Oregon may not have made it with this bill in 1952, nor Senator James Buckley of New York in 1970. In essence, the timing of funding is critically important to the lifeblood of minor and independent candidacies. Another unexpected consequence may result. Although George Wallace would not have benefited from the present legislation, his successor, four years later, would reap the rewards of Wallace's popularity. However, a good number of Wallace's followers would no longer be supportive of the party, missing the color and magnetism of their charismatic leader. Thus, the legislation will help perpetuate a minor party whose leaders and members may have disappeared or changed in the four-year interval.

VI. PRICE TAG UNCLEAR

Most of the subsidy reforms include paying for the electoral process as early as the primaries or preliminary to the conventions. While essential to the democratic process, picking up the tab early in the political game may be more expensive than one imagines. For example, the Charter Reform Commission of the Democratic Party and the subsequent miniconvention in Kansas City adopted a wide variety of proposals for restructuring the party organization in order to open the processes of decision making at the 1976 convention. Under most of the reforms, this will invite larger numbers of candidates to run as delegates. The cost of this newly built "grass roots" power base is impossible to calculate. In fact, it may be to the advantage of the Republicans in this instance to encourage the public subsidization of the forthcoming 1976 Democratic convention. This might well stimulate a massive participatory effort which would, in turn, create such conflict and dissension that agreement on a Democratic nominee or program would be most difficult to attain.

Under present federal legislation there is no assurance of adequate money in the fund. While the bill sets priorities, such as setting aside $2 million for each major party convention and providing a kitty for the nominees, will there be money left over for the primaries as well?

Another aspect of funding which invites a serious problem of equity is the situation in which losers get nothing and winners extra handouts. If, at the end of the election, money is left over (consider Senator McGovern's recent million dollar treasury) the official may use it to defray his costs of public office or to pay for anything else having "lawful purposes." Does this include a car, expansion of his home, and entertainment?

One of the largest expenditures for most candidates is TV and radio media. Some 60 percent of campaign budgets are said to go to this purpose. Obviously, much of the subsidy will be spent for 30- to 60-second spots. But do we want to encourage the selling of the candidate like a tube of toothpaste, with or without chlorophyll? If media is costly, and indeed it is, and if we want to help nominees get more public exposure, a better form of subsidy may be free time on TV or radio, in which the setting allows for mature discussion and development of the issues.

VII. RELATIONSHIP BETWEEN EXPENDITURES AND ELECTORAL OPPORTUNITY

The major thrust of those urging subsidization is based on an unproven assumption that there is a clear relationship between expenditures and electoral success. In the findings of the experts, this is simply not so, and at best rather ambiguous. Even if the "ideal" or "model" condition could be imaged—that each candidate in a particular election had the same amount of money to spend—the political game would still be unequal in critically important ways. Success in elections is a complex affair, and, while we do not mean to imply that money is unimportant, its dominant influence is highly questionable. Alexander Heard (1962), expert on this subject, has written:

> Money probably has its greatest impact . . . in the shadow land . . . where it is decided who will be a candidate . . . and who will not. The effect of money in politics is far more certain there (between primaries and other nominating steps) than in determining the outcome of elections.

There is little doubt that some public officials have been bought. Everyone knows that favors from government have been purchased. But what proof do we have that money has purchased the final election result? Was it money that defeated Goldwater in 1964? Did the Committee to Re-elect the President need to spend the money it did in 1972 to beat McGovern? If Arthur Goldberg had spent an amount equal to Rockefeller would the 1970 New York gubernatorial result have been any different? Who spent more money to win the 1964 California primary, Goldwater or Rockefeller?

Certainly there is a threshold level that must be expended to make a candidate known; the Metzenbaum campaign in the 1970 Democratic primary in Ohio showed the power of money to make an unknown a household word. But he outspent his Republican opponent in the final election too—and lost.

Furthermore, can equality or near equality be achieved by subsidization? Underlying the argument for public subsidization is a rather naive view as to when a campaign actually begins. Start-up costs for campaigns must be considered in discussions concerning subsidies. The head start that candidates have or can buy is often more crucial than the primary or election itself. Spending money early is one of the best ways to prevent opposition from developing. In 1970, Governor Marvin Mandel of Maryland showed such early strength that by June the sources of money for the other candidates had literally dried up, months before the campaign began.

In the pre-preprimary period of the 1974 gubernatorial election in New York state, the costs were substantial and critical. For example, it has been reported that Howard Samuels had to give the New York Telephone Company deposits of some $17,000 for installation of phones and as a guarantee that future bills would be paid. Queens Borough President Donald Manes spent at least $12,883 renovating and furnishing his campaign headquarters. Congressman Hugh Carey, who had not yet announced his candidacy in January, spent $1,695.20 for flowers, including green carnations for every woman at the Democratic State Committee meeting. Congressman Ogden Reid spent $4,333 for hospitality at the same event. Four months *before* the primaries, these four candidates had already spent at least $1.5 million.

In his 1974 inaugural address, Governor Brendon Byrne of New Jersey remarked, "If this administration is to be remembered for nothing else, I want it to be remembered as the last administration elected in the market place of private financial campaign contributions." But how can the "market" be eliminated at the "start-up" stage? In fact, in one of the legislative proposals in New Jersey, a candidate would not be eligible for subsidies unless he initially raised $40,000. Free market indeed!

There have even been campaigns where the polls indicated that the public began to resent the money being expended and that a candidate began to lose votes as he spent more. The direct cause-effect relationship between money and electoral success simply is not that well established.

Success for a candidate comes from a combination of factors. A few key variables will be noted to make the point. In the first place, the district (state or ward) in which the candidate runs is of considerable importance—relating to its size, the degree of party competitiveness, group pressures, and the availability of media to reach the local public. Second, the electoral processes operating in the district are important, relating to whether designation is by party caucus or petition, what number of petition signatures are required and what geographical distribution must be obtained, and whether it is a ward or an at-large base from which a candidate makes the run. Third, the candidate may or may not be the major factor, especially when the district or state is one-party dominated. On the other hand, personality, popularity, skills, and political influence are frequently paramount.

Finally, support in the form of the dollar sign may at times be second to support in the form of "in kind" or "freebies." The help that candidates get which may have monetary value but which is not within the purview of the law and its control include such key inputs as access to free printing presses (especially colored print and paper); free use of a staff; expertise from a friend's business or organization; labor, school, ethnic, or other interest groups; free use of a car or airplane and of telephones; and availability of "volunteers" from a friend's union or civic organization or business staff. Of course, there are many other features—the character of the opposition, the times, and other variables like a great depression or minirecession, or a president from whom one wishes to disassociate.

Since we are going to limit the influence of personal wealth, are we going to "clean up" the political scene so radically? What have been the pernicious influences upon our political system of John F. Kennedy, Nelson Rockefeller, Franklin D. Roosevelt, Barry Goldwater, Adlai Stevenson, Charles Percy, Averill Harriman, or William Scranton? All but Goldwater started their elective careers at the level of congressman, governor, or U.S. senator. Would any of these men have been so acceptable to their local political organizations had they not brought with them not only a prominent family name but also the wherewithal to pay for much of their own campaigns? Barry Goldwater began as a low-paid city councilman, because he could afford to do it and because Phoenix was desperately looking for men of unquestioned personal integrity for that office. He went immediately from that post to U.S. senator.

A good many prominent candidates are involved because they can afford to be and want to do something constructive. There is a great deal of "clean" money in politics just as there has been "dirty" money.

VIII. FALSE EXPECTATIONS: A MORALITY PLAY

A last and concluding caveat in public financing of the ballot box is the exaggerated hopes expressed in its behalf. In urging passage of the new federal law (S.3044), Senator Edward Kennedy insisted that it

> can spark a renaissance in American life, because public financing is the answer to many of the deepest problems facing the Nation, especially the lack of responsiveness of government to the people. Only when all the people pay for elections will all the people be truly represented in their government.
>
> At a single stroke, we can drive the money lenders out of the temple of politics. We can end the corrosive and corrupting influence of private money in public life.

These claims have been made by many adherents of the reform. The danger here is that we are offering the public a panacea which really cannot even begin to get at our difficulties. To root out the corrosive influence of money in American political life is a difficult and complex process. More importantly, it does not necessarily begin nor end with the election process. ITT, the Dairymen's League, and other manipulators have no difficulty in reaching Democrats or Republicans or the "civic-minded" between elections. Corruption reaches into the whole bloody system. At times its subtlety is what drives us to distraction, such as hoping that a reform like subsidization will make that bad thing go away "at a single stroke."

Public subsidies bring government into the electoral process on a scale which invites some serious potential for further erosion of the electoral system. Let us face the facts. Just imagine if President Nixon and his devoted (and we are not being sarcastic, they were devoted) aides had access to the public subsidization money. What would have prevented them from manipulating the funds, from controlling outlays, from applying the money to their own purposes? In his columns in the *New York Times,* John Herbers has written in detail how the president was able to move into each of the most important bureaucratic arms of government, placing his own trusted men in key posts of decision making. Despite Watergate, this process has not abated, particularly in the Office of Management and Budget under the direction of Roy L. Ash. Those of us who share a liberal outlook, who are adherents of the active or expansive role of the state in the economic arena, and who wish to extend the area of government to help open opportunities for the disadvantaged in our society need not be sucked into the same argument for expanding government's responsibility to make elections "more equal." The rationale for the former simply does not hold for the latter.

The potential for corruption is tremendous at all levels of government. Traditionally, in most stages—and that is where the big thrust of electoral power remains—election policy and administration are highly partisan affairs. The number of governors who have left office as rich men far exceeds the rate of retired millionaire presidents. While one can try to set up bipartisan commissions to oversee these funds, everyone has seen how this mechanism can be perverted. And what of the minor parties? Where are their protections and watchdogs? Granted, third parties have usually had only a transitory role to play on the American political stage, but many of them have provided a beneficial input into our system, and one of them, the Republican party, made it to the big time. Are we precluding any such future developments for all time by placing under the supervision of the incumbent parties (or worse, a single party) control over these funds? Many state laws would have the partisanly selected secretary of state and attorney general "watch-dogs" of these funds. Both are frequently the "tools" of the governor.

While an incumbent president (or governor) rarely has been denied his party's nomination (except for some governors in states having primaries), building up a war chest in the national (or state) committees makes certain that it will never happen. An incumbent president (or governor) is going to see to it that the national (or state) committee chairman of the party is his man or woman. With an initial war chest of several million dollars of public money guaranteed, the idea of a challenge to the incumbent within his own party becomes unthinkable.

Furthermore, the new bill (S.3044), in clear, bold print, puts a spending limit on a House nominee at $70,000. When the *Wall Street Journal* criticized this limit as too low, Senator Edward Kennedy responded by reprimanding the paper for missing "the mark in its uninformed discussion" of the limit. Admittedly, wrote the senator, one section of the bil does set $70,000 as a spending ceiling, but that is only the beginning of the analysis. Other sections of the bill operate to lift the $70,000 base in a number of important ways. The arithmetic goes like this:

> One section allows an extra 20 percent of the spending limit, or $14,000 to be used to offset fund-raising costs.
>
> Another section adds a cost-of-living escalator to deal with inflation.
>
> Still another section adds a so-called "meat and potatoes" exception, allowing any individual to spend up to $500 per election for invitations, food, and beverages for campaign functions at his residence.
>
> A fourth section allows a national committee and a state committee to spend an extra $10,000 each on an individual's campaign.
>
> Finally, certain other provisions include exemption for travel expenses paid out of one's own pocket by a volunteer, and the unlimited exemption for certain forms of nonmedia "slate card" advertising.

This list of loopholes is the very sort of thing which serves to deceive the public and which, when discovered, adds to the public's sense of disgust. A careful reading, as suggested by the senator, brings the real limit up to at least $125,000. Our own estimates are even higher, especially with the freebies.

CONCLUSION

Ironically, while the American people—primarily on a voluntary basis and only for the more prominent positions—spend entirely too much money on political campaigns, the public does not spend anywhere near enough on the running of elections themselves. There is a crying need to modernize our voter registration systems (such as statewide computer registration, as is now used in five states, most of them the "backward" Southern states) and greatly improved election administration. There have been major improvements in voting machines, but most jurisdictions are stuck with the same old ones. And some areas are still using the paper ballot. Only a handful of Western states (California, fortunately, is among them) provide voters with guides to candidates and issues on the ballots. Most citizens step into the voting booth on election day and, except for a handful of names at the top of the ballot, know virtually nothing about who the other candidates are (and generally do not understand the job they are running for). Most of the propositions on the ballot come as a complete surprise (the reaction, therefore, is generally to vote "no"). Here is where public financing should be put into play.

Certainly we should get good disclosure laws, possibly the courts will uphold expenditure and gift limits as constitutional. But let us move into the field of public subsidy slowly and with care. Put some other needed reforms through first. Wait to see what results they have, and then proceed to the next step. Right now we are being urged to alter fundamentally the whole set of ground rules for political campaigning and are doing so with a naive simplicity as to the possible results. Once we get public subsidy of political campaigns and if it does, as we fear, work greatly to the advantage of the incumbents, we will *never* be able to get rid of it. It is not one of those reforms one can take a step back from once it starts to be felt, because the incumbents will see to it that it goes on forever and ever.

NOTES

1. Maryland, New Jersey, and the Commonwealth of Puerto Rico all have such laws, and a public subsidy has been provided for the 1976 presidential campaign.

2. Since the federal legislation thus far enacted pertains only to the highly visible office of the presidency, the checkoff is expected to provide adequate funds. What if it is extended to the less visible 535 United States senators and representatives?

3. Many of the new campaign-financing reform bills also place severe limits on borrowing.

REFERENCES

ALEXANDER, H.E. (1964). Financing the 1960 election. Princeton, N.J.: Citizens' Research Foundation.

--- (1966). Financing the 1964 election. Princeton, N.J.: Citizens' Research Foundation.

--- (1972). Political financing. Minneapolis: Burgess.

BAKER, M.J. (1972). "A constitutional remedy for the high cost of broadcast and newspaper advertising in political campaigns." California Law Review, (September): 1371-1414.

Congressional Quarterly (1966). Weekly Report, January 21.

--- (1969). Weekly Report, December 5.

DUNN, D. (1972). Financing presidential campaigns. Washington, D.C.: Brookings Institution.

ERNST, H.W. (1962). The primary that made a president: West Virginia, 1960. New York: McGraw-Hill.

HEARD, A. (1962). The costs of democracy. Garden City, N.Y.: Doubleday.

KELLEY, S., Jr. (1956). Professional public relations and political power. Baltimore: Johns Hopkins University Press.

LEUTHOLD, D.A. (1968). Electioneering in a democracy. New York: John Wiley.

McGINNISS, J. (1970). The selling of the presidency, 1968. New York: Trident.

NIMMO, D. (1970). The political persuaders. Englewood Cliffs, N.J.: Prentice-Hall.

PINCUS, W. (1968). "Campaign spending: The public isn't let in on many secrets." Washington Post, December 9.

--- (1974). "Campaign kitties: Paying candidates' bills." New Republic, (March 16):15-17.

PLATTNER, M.F. (1974). "Campaign financing: The dilemmas of reform." Public Interest, (Winter):112-130.

President's Commission on Campaign Costs (1962). Financing presidential campaigns. Washington, D.C.: U.S. Government Printing Office.

ROSENTHAL, A.J. (1972). "Campaign financing and the Constitution." Harvard Journal on Legislation, (March):359-423.

SMOKLA, R. (1973). The costs of administering American elections. New York: National Municipal League.

Twentieth Century Fund Commission on Campaign Costs in the Electronic Era (1969). Voters' time. New York: Twentieth Century Fund.

"Tax-supported campaigns" (1973). New Republic, (December 22):5-7.

WHITE, T.H. (1961). The making of the president, 1960. New York: Atheneum.

Chapter 3

PUBLIC FINANCING AND THE TWO-PARTY SYSTEM: A COMMENTARY

LOUIS MAISEL

The effects of the Federal Election Campaign Act amendments of 1974 have been debated widely. One of the most controversial aspects of those amendments is the provision for public financing of presidential campaigns, from the primaries through the conventions and the general election. The preceding chapters—in which Joel L. Fleishman defends public financing while pointing to some potential constitutional problems with the current legislation and in which Jewel Bellush and William J.D. Boyd pose some of the difficult questions which are raised by the concept of public financing—contribute to the ongoing debate which has filled the pages of the nation's newspapers and magazines, political newsletters, and political science journals and law reviews.

A diverse coalition of liberals and conservatives—ranging from Senator James L. Buckley (Republican-Conservative, New York) to former Senator Eugene J. McCarthy, now an independent candidate for president, and including millionaire philanthropist Stewart Mott, the American Civil Liberties Union, and the Conservative party of New York—has formed to challenge the law in the courts. Those filing amicus briefs on each side cover an equally wide portion of the political spectrum. Arguing amidst an atmosphere of high drama, some of the country's most prominent lawyers and legal scholars debated the constitutionality of the law before the Supreme Court.

Harvard Law Professor Archibald Cox, whose government service includes terms as Solicitor General and Special Watergate Prosecutor; Deputy Solicitor General Daniel Friedman; University of Pennsylvania Law Professor Ralph Spitzer; and Washington lawyer Lloyd Cutler all defended the act. Yale Law Professor Ralph Winter; Joel Gora of the New York Civil Liberties Union; and Washington lawyer Brice McAdoo Claggett opposed it.

Such widespread concern is entirely appropriate, for proponents and opponents alike agree that the provisions in this act will have far-reaching effects on politics in the years ahead. All of those involved also agree that the motives behind the enactment of the law—halting "the arms race in political expenditures" (Cox's phrase used in his presentation before the Supreme Court) and decreasing the dependence on big money evident in the 1972 presidential campaigns—were pure. However, as the two preceding chapters ably demonstrate, considerable debate remains over whether the cure might not be worse than the disease.

I. THE EFFECT OF PUBLIC FINANCING ON MINOR PARTIES

In commenting on the chapter by Bellush and Boyd and that by Fleishman, I want to restrict myself to one aspect of the debate, the effect that the public financing provisions of the 1974 amendments might have on minor party candidacies. To extend the medical metaphor begun above, I plan to examine some of the latent effects that the cure applied might have on the body politic as a whole. In the debate over constitutionality and short-term consequences, I fear that important long-term effects may have been overlooked.

Senator Buckley, who won election as a Conservative party candidate in 1970, and Eugene McCarthy, who is currently running outside of the major parties, challenged the law for very pragmatic reasons. They felt that the public financing provisions, which call for proportional financing for minor party candidates (defined as those with from 5 to 25 percent of the vote in the preceding election) and for reimbursement only after demonstrating electoral strength for new parties, unduly favored the major party candidates. This affects McCarthy in an immediate way and would have hurt Buckley if the idea of extending this type of financing to senatorial and congressional campaigns, a provision which passed the Senate but which was beaten back by the strong opposition of Wayne Hays (Democrat,

Ohio) in the House, had been in effect in 1970. The nation's only non-major party governor, James Longley of Maine, filed a brief concurring in the opinion that these provisions were discriminatory.

Fleishman argues that it is possible to find a constitutional solution to the difficult problem of dealing with minor parties; he contends that the Court should look at the major goals to be achieved by the act and should not be distracted by the details of problems which are clearly tangential to the major fault in our system that the act seeks to correct. Bellush and Boyd expound on the fears of Buckley, McCarthy, Longley, and other minor party candidates; they also point out that the effects of the public financing provisions on minor parties can be argued both ways. Some critics are concerned that minor parties which appear for one election will be "rewarded" with money in the next, when their raison d'etre may well have disappeared. Bellush and Boyd and others point to the anomoly that in 1968 George Wallace would not have qualified for public financing until *after* he had polled nearly 10,000,000 votes, 13.5 percent of those cast, whereas his successor as 1972 American Independent Party candidate, former Congressman John Schmitz, who eventually polled only 1.4 percent of the vote, would have qualified for public funds because of Wallace's showing. Obviously such arguments suffer because "all things would not have been equal." They point to the conclusion that such arguments should not be stated in the abstract but rather should be examined in the light of the current political situation.

II. THE STATE OF THE AMERICAN PARTY SYSTEM

Political scientists are agreed that American parties have gone through a series of competitive two-party systems (Chambers and Burnham, 1975). Much of the historical analysis of American parties has been directed toward explaining the discontinuities in competitive two-party politics. While considerable debate rages over causality and precise lines of demarcation (see, for example, Burnham, 1974; Converse, 1974; Rusk, 1974), most observers agree that the coalitions which dominated American politics starting approximately with Franklin D. Roosevelt's first election represented the fifth such party system. There is much less agreement about current party alignments.

Electoral data and survey research material that were made

available after the 1964, 1968, and 1972 elections have led scholars to ask whether we might not be in another period of realignment and have led to the reexamination of commonly held views.[1] For example, recent research has led to a reassessment of some of the important conclusions developed from the early Survey Research Center studies. Angus Campbell and his associates, writing in 1960 in *The American Voter,* explained voter behavior largely in terms of partisan preferences. Voters were generally considered to be not very well informed on the issues and not ideologically motivated. More recent SRC data on presidential campaigns have raised serious questions about these findings. Mounting evidence points to the conclusion that voters are more concerned with pivotal issues and are considering these in their voting choices (Pomper, 1972; Miller et al., 1973; Nie, 1974) and that the major parties are now perceived in ideological terms (Pomper, 1972; Burnham, 1975:243). Misgivings about *The American Voter*'s view of the electorate are further fed by the evidence that an increasingly high percentage of voters no longer vote on party lines (DeVries and Tarrance, 1972). In addition, pollsters have noted a sharp decline in the number of voters associating with either of the major parties.

Some researchers have concentrated on isolating the sources of rising political independence (Schreiber, 1971; Glenn, 1972, 1973). Others, looking at the implications of these changes, have concluded either that America is entering a new two-party system (James, 1974:40-47) or, more radically, that the American polity is undergoing a "critical realignment to end all realignments" (Burnham, 1975:239). Still others feel that there has been an overreaction to these recent data, that the Michigan model has not been effectively challenged, and that what we are observing are short-term forces, not a major realignment (Rusk, 1974:1046-1047; Converse, 1972:322; Converse et al., 1965, 1969).

All these observers have debated the shape of American politics within a two-party framework. Rusk (1970, 1974) and Converse (1972) have argued that institutional and legal changes have had causal effects on party alignment, but they have not speculated that any such changes might threaten the existence of two-party politics. Analysts might be concerned that the major parties are losing their strength and must react in order to regain past allegiances (Broder, 1972; Saloma and Sontag, 1972), but third parties are dismissed now—as they have been since V.O. Key's classic description of them (1964, chapter 10)—as either ideological aberrations of a dedicated few or precursors of future realignment (James, 1974:57-58; Burnham, 1970:27-28; Sundquist, 1973:289-294).

All those writing in this field seem to accept Maurice Duverger's classic description of why two-party systems are maintained (1954:217):

> The influence of such national factors [historical dualism] is certainly very considerable; but we must not in their favour underestimate the importance of one general factor of a technical kind, the electoral system. Its effects can be expressed in the following formula: *the simple-majority single-ballot system favours the two-party system.* Of all the hypotheses that have been defined in this book, this approaches most nearly perhaps to a true sociological law. [Emphasis as in the original.]

Duverger may well have been correct in stressing the electoral system and Rusk and Converse in examining legal changes as causal influences, but attention needs to be directed at the financing of political campaigns as well as at the method of voting.

III. MINOR PARTIES IN THE 1970s

In analyzing the effect of the public financing provisions of the 1974 campaign reform act on minor parties' role in the American system, one must deal explicitly with the minor parties likely to be involved in the 1976 election. The starting point must be George Wallace's American Independent Party. Wallace's movement has been different in nature and impact from previous third-party movements. While it can be argued that Wallace's appeal was initially sectional and thus perhaps not different from Strom Thurmond's Dixiecrats of 1948, his appeal broadened and contributed to the dual trend of nationalizing Southern politics and Southernizing national politics (Burnham, 1970:189). Wallace in 1968 was clearly a national candidate running on what had previously been sectional appeals.[2] Not only was his a national effort, but it was distinguishable from previous third-party efforts. On the ballot in all 50 states, Wallace polled nearly 10 million votes, his popular total exceeding any previous third party's and his percentage ranking the highest since that of the Progressives of 1924. Wallace's 46 electoral votes exceeded the 1924 Progressives' 13 and the combined total of the Dixiecrats (39) and the Progressives (0) in 1948.

However, the single factor which most clearly distinguishes the Wallace movement from previous third-party movements which have had electoral significance has been its persistence. In 1964, the Alabama governor entered a series of Democratic presidential primaries and gave notice that his popularity could not be ignored in planning future political strategies. When he ran under the American Independent Party label in 1968, Wallace further demonstrated his appeal to the electorate with impressive national totals. In 1972, again running in Democratic presidential primaries, Wallace showed any doubters that many members of the traditional New Deal coalition now shared his policy views.[3] His health seemingly improved, Wallace has mounted an impressive organizational effort in preparation for the 1976 presidential campaign. In 1974, he raised over $1.7 million and spent over $1.6 million in setting up a sophisticated direct-mail, fund-raising organization, based on lists of people who had supported him in the past ("Wallace Far Ahead in Spending for 1976," 1975). Wallace has said that he wants to stay within the Democratic party in 1976, but Charles Snider, his national campaign director, has implied that his organization is prepared to mount another AIP campaign if the Democrats are not more receptive to the governor and his programs than they have been in the past. The national media continue to speculate about Wallace's possible moves should the Democrats ignore him in choosing their nominee and setting their platform (see, for example, Ayres, 1975). Thus, we must consider the serious possibility that the AIP will run a significant, national third-party campaign again and that, if it does, the AIP will surely qualify for public financing, not only under the "new party" provision in 1976 but in all probability under the proportional provision for minor parties in 1980.

Nor does Wallace stand alone as an extra-major-party candidate in 1976. Leading conservatives in the Republican party—perhaps best deemed economic conservatives in contrast to Wallace's social conservatism—organized in 1975 at a Conservative Political Action Conference. This group has explored the possibility of fielding its own candidate and has carefully studied the mechanism through which Wallace attained the ballot in all 50 states in 1968 (Apple, 1975). The most likely candidate from this group of economic conservatives is former California Governor Ronald Reagan. Reagan announced that he would challenge President Ford for the Republican nomination and would not run as a minor party candidate. Even before Reagan's formal announcement, the conservative threat was sufficient to force Vice President Nelson Rockefeller off the Ford ticket. This group may well decide not to field its own candidate, depending on the policies of the Ford Administration and the outcome of the Republican Convention. On the other hand, many well-placed economic conservatives, such as North Carolina Senator Jesse Helms or New Hampshire Governor Meldrin Thompson, are ready to make a stand of principle if the Republican party strays too far to the left.

The existence of an active conservative wing in each party has led some to speculate about the possibility of a new liberal-conservative realignment. William Rusher's *The Making of a New Majority Party* (1975) is typical of this view. Rusher calls for a conservative alliance combining Wallace's social conservatives with the Reagan-like economic conservatives. This party, according to Rusher's view, should field its own candidates because the Republican party has deserted its old conservative principles. Rusher predicts that this party would soon become the home for all conservatives (a majority of the nation in his view), that it would lead to the demise of the Republicans, and that it would stand as the majority party while the liberal Democrats would become a perpetual minority.

The idea of a coalition between Wallace's working-class, blue-collar conservatives and Reagan's corporate, white-collar conservatives strikes some as ludicrous on its face. However, it is worth noting that the idea has been raised not only by Republican conservatives but also by supporters of Governor Wallace (American Party, 1975). Should these forces field a candidate in 1976, they would certainly draw significant electoral support and qualify as a "new party" under the public financing provision.

At this time (December 1975) it is still too early to tell which, if any, of these minor parties will field a candidate in the 1976 presidential election. However, it is important to note that there is the potential for either one or two well-financed conservative alternatives to the major party candidates in 1976, the first election in which even marginally successful minor party candidates will receive public funds retroactively.[4] While it is true that these candidates will not receive public funds in advance of the elections and in that way will be disadvantaged by the new law, few doubt that either Wallace or a Republican conservative (or a "coalition conservative") could raise enough money to run an effective campaign, especially if contributors realize that they could well be reimbursed–if they so desired–once the votes were counted and the government had to repay the party proportionally to its success.

Where does this leave Eugene McCarthy? McCarthy's type of minor-party movement may well be just the kind which suffers most from the new law. Unlike in 1968, when the Vietnam War was the key issue, McCarthy now has no one issue which is attracting a large number of supporters zealously to his side. Because of the limitations on individual contributions, he cannot count on a few "fat cats" to finance the start-up costs of a new movement. Deprived of these two resources, the McCarthy candidacy, representing the furthest left alternative, seems doomed. However, it is a mistake to take McCarthy's fate to mean that the new public financing law dooms minor parties. It is perhaps most unfair to the political Don Quixotes of American politics, to those at the ideological fringes who choose to battle windmills in the electoral arena. However, while these parties perhaps serve an educational function, they have long been electorally irrelevant and have never been financed adequately. And Eugene McCarthy would have been electorally irrelevant and probably underfinanced in 1976 under any rules. As Fleishman pointed out in his chapter, the debate should not stray from the most important concerns because of those on the periphery of the political system. Their rights must be protected, but the system need not be designed to cater to them.

The point can be argued another way. Should the Democratic party choose to nominate Wallace or someone allied with him, then the liberal wing of that party would undoubtedly field a candidate, one much stronger than McCarthy, but perhaps utilizing the organization he has established. Such a candidate would quickly attract a following similar to McCarthy's in 1968 or McGovern's in 1972 and with that following would be able to raise enough money to wage an effective campaign despite the inherent unevenness of the public financing stipulations for minor parties.

Speculations about the course of minor party politics in 1976 are admittedly hazardous. However, these projections need not prove founded to sustain my argument. The public financing provisions of the campaign reform act do discriminate against minor parties and could prove extremely deleterious to some parties at the ideological extreme.[5] Despite this handicap, however, third-party movements with substantial popular followings should be able to raise enough money to wage effective campaigns. One or more such parties may well contest the 1976 election.

Once one of these minor parties achieves electoral success, the public financing provision clearly works in its favor. It will be guaranteed a financial base for the next election. Wallace in 1968 demonstrated that a minor party candidate can attain the ballot in all 50 states. Advanced campaign technology, particularly the emphasis on media-oriented campaigns, has eliminated the need for much of the nitty-gritty work which party organizations once performed. The electorate appears to have become more issue-oriented so that parties can direct their appeals quite precisely. The combination of these factors makes minor party candidacy appear as attractive to aspiring politicians frustrated within the major parties as it once was unattractive. Surely one lesson of George Wallace's career of the last 12 years has been that deserting the party—even in a losing cause—does not mean the end of one's power. That lesson has not been lost on politicians frustrated in their quest for power. Public financing, in combination with these other factors, may well guarantee that minor parties, once established, will persist and continue to contest elections with viable candidates. No more John Schmitzes will carry the AIP or like banners. I am certain I need not point out that if minor parties are once successful in denying the leading major party candidate a majority in the Electoral College, this will provide a major impetus for the proliferation of additional parties.

IV. CONCLUSIONS—A SIXTH PARTY SYSTEM?

Parts of this argument have been extremely—perhaps even wildly—speculative. However, I doubt that any will charge that the existence of minor parties in the 1976 campaign and their persistence thereafter goes beyond the realm of possibility; perhaps this scenario is even as likely as any of the others which have been painted. In this final section I would like to explore the implications of this discussion.

If this scenario or one like it eventuates, public financing, in combination with the other factors mentioned, could well mark the end of the fifth party system.[6] I do not see another two-party system replacing it; too much has changed. Nor do I see politics without parties (Burnham, 1975); too much remains the same. Too many Americans still feel traditional attachments to the major parties which have dominated the American political scene since before the Civil War (Converse, 1972). Too much in politics still depends on the presence of, if not a commitment to, enduring party organizations. Rather, I see a situation in which the major parties continue to dominate the political scene but in which minor parties—certainly one or two on the right, perhaps one on the left, some weak, some strong—become a permanent and influential feature, a two-plus-*n* party system. These parties will persist, they will have potential influence, they will be taken into consideration by the major parties in formulating strategies. Thus they will have to be included in a discussion of the American party system in a way third parties never before have.[7]

The critical feature of the system envisioned would be the continued existence within the major parties of ideological factions which are prepared to reject the major parties' nominees and field independent candidates. Ongoing, minor-party organizations, such as Wallace's in Montgomery, the Committee for Conservative Alternatives, or Rusher's Independence Party would guarantee that ideologues disappointed with the nominees of the major parties would have the capability of mounting national campaigns. These organizations would center around a corps of "extreme" ideologues; their strategy would be to provide a forum for nationally prominent figures, perhaps less "extreme" than they, but clearly of the same ideological bent, who were willing to desert the major parties. More prominent political figures may well be ready to chance a campaign under a minor-party label. The combination of ideological factions within the major parties (including their prominent leaders) and minor party organizations leads to the continuing existence of electorally relevant additional parties. The number of such parties actually fielding candidates in any one election would vary from year to year according to the actions of the major parties; hence a two-plus-*n* party system.[8]

With one crucial exception, the current political situation in New York State serves as a model for the national system described here. The Liberal and Conservative parties in New York play the same role as the hypothesized minor parties on the national level. These parties await clear indications of the types of candidates the major parties are likely to nominate. If the Republican party nominee is too liberal, the Conservative party will field a strong opponent against that candidate. Similarly, if the Democratic party nominee is not acceptable to the Liberal party, they will oppose him or her. The crucial difference from national politics is that New York State law permits a candidate to accept the nomination of more than one party and to aggregate votes received on different party lines. Thus the

Liberal and Conservative parties can endorse the major party nominees if they are acceptable; on occasion the "extra" votes that a candidate has received on the minor party ticket has been enough to put him or her into office, a situation which increases the influence of the minor parties.

The Liberal party's success in electing John Lindsay mayor of New York City under its label and the Conservative party's successful campaign for Senator Buckley prove exceptions to the rule that third-party candidates cannot win in a plurality-rule election and demonstrate how a system can be altered by the mere presence of a number of minor parties. However, the more common role played by these parties, that of influencing the major party nominations through threats of opposition, is of at least equal importance.[9] It is this role which I see as being duplicated on the national scene, with the additional factor that American national parties span ideologically wide spectrums and thus may spurn minor-party candidates from the left, if they go too far to the right, or from the right, if they go too far to the left–thus complicating the picture further.

Perhaps this speculation has progressed far enough. Its intention was merely to point out the far-reaching consequences for our party system that a change as fundamental as introducing public financing could induce. Bellush and Boyd are quite right to point out that reformers in their zeal to undo one evil may cause changes quite different from those they intended. Many of us favor the two-party system and look with alarm at anything that threatens it. The advantages of a two-party system are argued in terms of avoiding "frustration in government" (Broder, 1972:xvi; Burnham, 1975:269-273), of guaranteeing the representation of unorganized minorities (Burnham, 1970:132-134), of supporting the "popular consultation" and "majority rule" principles of democratic theorists (James, 1974:51-54; Saloma and Sontag, 1972:5-12). Yet we also view public financing as a way to correct serious flaws in the way our system is currently operating.

The question is then one of resolving conflicting values, weighing the likelihood of outcomes such as the one described here, and directing future strategies to achieve the system we envision. Public financing of presidential campaigns will go a long way toward ridding our system of the evils of excess so apparent in raising money for and conducting the 1972 presidential campaigns. However, the potential effects of public financing on the two-party system should be kept in mind as other legal and/or institutional changes are considered.

Public financing may well be proposed again for congressional campaigns; it has been and will continue to be proposed for state elections (Adamany and Agree, 1975:207). More fundamentally, calls for direct election of the president or at least for ending the unit rule in the Electoral College will certainly be heard again. Because of the changes which public financing of presidential elections might cause, these proposals should be reexamined, particularly in terms of their encouragement of minor parties. But these are questions for the future. For now it should suffice to say that public financing might well cause significant and fundamental changes in American campaigns and that the implications of these changes will surely create a full agenda for further research.

NOTES

1. Much of the following draws on and is more fully developed in Maisel, 1975.

2. Had Wallace split from the Democrats after his 1964 forays into presidential primaries, the analogy with the Dixiecrats would have been more apt. However, by 1968 he had shown his appeal to have wide acceptance in many sections of the country. His eventual percentage of the presidential vote was undoubtedly lower than the percentage of those who actually favored him. A September 1968 Gallup Poll showed him receiving over 21 percent of the vote, but this was not reflected in the final tabulation because of the extremely successful "But he can't win and you'll be wasting your vote" campaigns waged by both major parties.

3. After Wallace was shot, the AIP nominated former California Congressman John Schmitz as its presidential standard-bearer. It is unclear what course Wallace would have followed had he retained his health and not had more impact at the Democratic National Convention in Miami. Certainly the 1.4 percent of the vote polled by Schmitz did not accurately reflect the strength of the Wallace movement at the time. If he had run or, because Wallace was totally out of the picture, if another prominent figure had taken the lead of this political faction, the vote total would have been much higher. Wallace's temporary incapacity essentially meant that his movement was held in abeyance for the 1972 election.

4. It should also be noted that Maryland Senator Charles Mathias has announced that he would consider running as an independent if his Republican party strayed too far to the right. It is certainly possible that he would attract enough liberal Republican support to run a well-financed campaign as well.

5. If one assumes that these parties have never raised much money, even they could benefit because the major parties will spend less under the current limitations, and thus the ideological parties will be proportionately better off.

6. This is so at least in terms of national politics. For a discussion of the implications for state politics, examining the Longley phenomenon in Maine, see Maisel, 1975.

7. Chambers has provided the accepted definitions of competitive systems and of modern political parties. Parties of the type that I have described meet his definition for inclusion in a competitive system. See Chambers and Burnham, 1975:5-6, and Maisel, 1975.

8. If no prominent leader would accept the nomination of one of these parties, it is likely that they would run a stand-in candidate anyway; in this way they would retain the

ballot position in most states, even if they did not meet the minimal requirements for public financing.

9. In efforts to demonstrate political independence, these parties have occasionally nominated their candidates before the major parties have made their choices, perhaps trying to influence the major parties' choices by guaranteeing opposition if certain candidates were not nominated. Because major-party nominations are by direct primary, this strategy seems ill-advised as a means to maximize influence.

REFERENCES

ADAMANY, D., and AGREE, G. (1975). "Election campaign financing: The 1974 reforms." Political Science Quarterly, 90 (Summer):201-220.

American Party (1975). American Voice, 6(2). Pigeon Forge, Tenn.: Author.

APPLE, R.W., Jr. (1975). "The dilemma of the Republicans." New York Times, March 10.

AYRES, D. (1975). "Wallace linked to rightist ticket for '76." New York Times, June 22.

BRODER, D.S. (1972). The party's over. New York: Harper and Row.

BURNHAM, W.D. (1970). Critical elections and the mainsprings of American democracy. New York: Norton.

--- (1974). "Theory and voting research: Some reflections on Converse's 'Change in the American electorate.'" American Political Science Review, 68(December):1002-1023.

--- (1975). "American politics in the 1970's: Beyond party?" In L. Maisel and P.M. Sacks (eds.), The Future of Political Parties (Sage Electoral Studies Yearbook, vol. 1). Beverly Hills, Calif.: Sage.

CAMPBELL, A., et al. (1960). The American voter. New York: John Wiley.

CHAMBERS, W.N., and BURNHAM, W.D. (eds., 1975). The American party systems. New York: Oxford University Press.

CONVERSE, P.E. (1972). "Change in the American electorate." In A. Campbell and P.E. Converse (eds.), The Human Meaning of Social Change. New York: Russell Sage.

--- (1974). "Comment." American Political Science Review, 68(December):1024-1027.

CONVERSE, P.E., et al. (1965). "Electoral myth and reality: The 1964 election." American Political Science Review, 59:321-336.

--- (1969). "Continuity and change in American politics: Parties and issues in the 1968 election." American Political Science Review, 58:1083-1105.

DeVRIES, W., and TARRANCE, V.L. (1972). The ticket-splitters. Grand Rapids, Mich.: W.B. Eerdmans.

DUVERGER, M. (1954). Political parties. London: Methuen.

GLENN, N.D. (1972). "Sources of shift to political independence: Some evidence from a cohort analysis." Social Science Quarterly, 53.

--- (1973). "Class and party support in the United States: Recent and emerging trends." Public Opinion Quarterly, 37.

JAMES, J.L. (1974). American political parties in transition. New York: Harper and Row.

KEY, V.O., Jr. (1964). Politics, parties, and pressure groups (5th ed.). New York: Thomas Y. Crowell.

MAISEL, L. (1975). "The sixth American party system: Two plus n parties?" Melbourne Journal of Politics, 7.

MILLER, A.H., et al. (1973). "A majority party in disarray: Policy polarization in the 1972 election." Paper presented at the 1973 American Political Science Convention, New Orleans.

NIE, N.H., with ANDERSEN, K. (1974). "Mass belief systems revisited: Political change and attitude structure." Journal of Politics, 36.

POMPER, G.M. (1972). "From confusion to clarity: Issues and American voters, 1956-1968." American Political Science Review, 66.

RUSHER, W.A. (1975). The making of the new majority party. New York: Sheed and Ward.

RUSK, J.G. (1970). "The effects of the Australian ballot reform on split-ticket voting, 1876-1908." American Political Science Review, 64:1220-1238.

--- (1974). "Comment." American Political Science Review, 68(December):1028-1049.

SALOMA, J.S., and SONTAG, F. (1972). Parties: The real opportunity for effective citizen politics. New York: Alfred A. Knopf.

SCHREIBER, E.M. (1971). " 'Where the ducks are': Southern strategy versus fourth party." Public Opinion Quarterly, 35.

SUNDQUIST, J.L. (1973). Dynamics of the American party system. Washington, D.C.: Brookings Institution.

"Wallace Far Ahead in Spending for 1976" (1975). Congressional Quarterly Weekly Report, February 22.

Chapter 4

CHARACTERISTICS OF CAMPAIGN RESOURCE ALLOCATION IN THE 1972 CONGRESSIONAL ELECTIONS

PAUL A. DAWSON
JAMES E. ZINSER

I. INTRODUCTION

Campaign trails are well trodden but poorly mapped. It is perhaps surprising that election campaigns, for all the activity they generate, resources they consume, and attention they command, are so poorly understood. Despite advances in other fields of political science, election campaigns remain "the great Eleusinian mystery of the democratic state" (McCallum, 1955:509). We lack even the most basic information about campaign practices, such as good answers to the following questions: To what extent do candidates for particular offices spend similar amounts or employ similar strategies? Are there differences between Republicans and Democrats, incumbents and challengers, winners and losers, and between states and congressional districts with different demographic characteristics? On these questions, available literature is mostly silent.

AUTHORS' NOTE: Work on this study was partially financed by a grant from the Faculty Research and Development Committee, Oberlin College. Data originally published in the Congressional District Data Book was made available by the Inter-University Consortium for Political Research, Ann Arbor, Michigan. Martha Henderson and Thomas Kutzen provided valuable computational assistance. We wish to thank, for their constructive suggestions and encouragement, Hirschel Kasper, Robert Tufts, George Lanyi, David Segal, and Kurt Hausafus.

This study develops a model of rational campaign resource allocation in which candidates seek to maximize their share of the vote. Attempts to maximize vote pluralities are constrained by factors over which candidates have little control–for example, characteristics of the district and of the candidate. These characteristics may affect the supply of campaign resources, their allocation, and their productivity. In this initial effort, we examine empirical relationships between relatively fixed demographic characteristics of congressional districts and the supply and allocation of campaign financial resources. A forthcoming study investigates the effect of political characteristics on resource productivity.

Section II of this work summarizes difficulties which have thus far hindered serious and systematic study of political campaigning. Section III introduces the model of candidate behavior and outlines three broad categories of environmental conditions which affect electoral outcomes. They include political characteristics of districts, political characteristics of candidates, and demographic district characteristics. Section IV presents formal components of candidate campaign behavior. The context for this model is the 1972 congressional elections, and Section V includes a brief overview of expenditure patterns in both the Senate and House contests in that year. Empirical work, i.e., the statistical correlation between expenditures and demographic variables, is presented in Section VI. Finally, Section VII summarizes the major results.

II. DIFFICULTIES IN THE STUDY OF CAMPAIGN BEHAVIOR

Campaigns, by their very nature, are difficult to study. Within a particular campaign, events are ubiquitous, occurring in different places at the same time; fleeting, since most are of short duration and participants seldom linger; and fluid, in that sequences of events are neither fully set ahead of time nor inalterable in the course of a campaign. Moreover, campaigns for a particular office exhibit tremendous variety in the amount of effort exerted and money spent, in reliance on party organizations and auxiliary groups, in the use of professional consultants versus "friends and neighbors," and in devotion to some techniques and rejection of others. Diversity in campaign practices is illustrated by comments of congressmen who participated in a Brookings Round Table Conference. On "coffees":

"Think of all the thousands of women's clubs in your city district and all the coffees you can have. Even in a rural district like mine we tried the coffee break idea one time. We had about thirty in three days, and it worked beautifully." [Clapp, 1963:382-383]

"I find you waste a whole day. At the very most you might meet 75 ladies. It is far better to go down the streets where you can meet three to four hundred people in their places of business or on the street." [Clapp, 1963:383]

On debates with one's opponent:

"I challenge my opponent before he has a chance to challenge me, and we always wind up with a series of planned debates." [Clapp, 1963:387]

"I don't intend to go out and draw a crowd to come and hear what my opponent has to say against me." [Clapp, 1963:386]

On the use of television:

"TV is the very best of techniques." [Clapp, 1963:391]

"Television is virtually useless." [Clapp, 1963:391]

Apparently, variation in candidate preferences for some forms of campaigning over others is matched by the strength of these preferences.

A reasonable expectation is that campaign practices in the United States will differ widely. "National" party systems are highly fragmented, resulting in the sort of decentralized campaign management through which candidate tastes can easily affect campaign decision making. Districts vary in a number of respects, and candidates easily may feel a need to tailor their campaign to a particular environment. Finally, campaign practices differ across districts due to differences in the distribution of resources necessary for some forms of campaiging, e.g., the number of party faithful, the availability of campaign donations, the availability of adequate television or radio broadcasting facilities.

Preliminary efforts to analyze campaigns in general, supplemented by individual campaign case studies and conjectural views of campaigns, permit conceptualization about the nature of election campaigns.

III. THE NATURE OF ELECTION CAMPAIGNS

Campaigns possess one essential, underlying commonality: they attempt to convert political resources into preferred outcomes. In this vein, conceptualize the candidate as seeking to attain some preferred objective, such as, increased votes, an increased share of the vote, a maximum probability of winning, a "respectable" showing, or a host of alternatives.[1] Consider the case of increased votes. An efficient allocation of resources is one for which the maximum number of votes, given available resources, is attained. Formally, let v be the number of votes received by a candidate; e is a vector, elements of which include time spent campaigning, funds allocated to television announcements, radio broadcasts, outdoor advertising, etc. Candidate characteristics, c, include incumbency, party affiliation, tenure, age, etc. District characteristics—region, income, age, composition, and race—are denoted by d. The vectors c and d, unlike e, are fixed. Thus a candidate can increase v only by altering the size and composition of e. In general therefore, rational campaign behavior is constrained by the effects of (a) political characteristics of districts, (b) political characteristics of candidates, and (c) demographic characteristics on the supply of campaign resources and on the demand for particular resources. In addition, campaign behavior is constrained by (d) characteristics of resources that determine productivity. Each constraint is discussed below.

A. THE POLITICAL CHARACTERISTICS OF DISTRICTS

1. *Party Organizations.* In decentralized party systems, national-level party organizations perform vital functions. They actively provide information about campaign strategy useful to novices and specific information, such as an opponent's voting record (Clapp, 1963). Moreover, national committees make financial contributions to congressional races and target extra money and services to candidates in districts that are deemed vulnerable or capturable (Wasby, 1968). In general, however, the magnitude and productivity of these contributions, as compared with others, appears small (Bone, 1958; Cotter and Hennessy, 1964; Huckshorn and Spencer, 1971; Cottin et al., 1972; Glass, 1972). Fishel (1973:103-104) found that Republican congressional challengers in the period 1964-1972 seldom received more than one-sixth of their financial contributions

from national-level party committees. Nevertheless, evidence on the role of national party organizations is skimpy and could easily underestimate indirect contributions that national-level organizations make as political brokers between those with resources and those who need them.

Contributions of district and precinct organizations appear considerable. Local-level party organizations often supply information and manpower that can convert latent partisanship into votes; that is, they seem well equipped to turn out the faithful and thereby affect electoral margins (Cutright and Rossi, 1958; Katz and Eldersveld, 1961; Wolfinger, 1963; Crotty, 1968; Kramer, 1970). As Anderson (1970:x) has noted, old style political machines are well endowed with this capacity: "the machine's forte, in short, was not persuading the undecided but delivering the dependable." To the extent that they make this contribution, local political organizations increase candidate discretion. In fact, some critics believe that the efforts of local party organizations reduce total resource demand, thereby lowering total campaign costs, and these critics fear that the demise of such local organizations would cause increased spending (Clapp, 1963; American Institute for Political Communication, 1967; Saloma and Sontag, 1973). In addition, local party organizations are effective fund raisers (Key, 1964:490) and may have a direct hand in the shaping of campaign strategy (Clapp, 1963:380). Their involvement, however, may result in the use of antiquated, unproductive tactics, since "many campaign practices are determined by organizational precedent rather than by rational planning" (Kessel, 1966:301). Thus on balance there are no unambiguous grounds for expecting that local party effort is positively associated with decreased demand for dollar expenditures or with the efficient allocation of resources.

2. *District Competitiveness.* In contrast to the uncertainty about party organization, there is general agreement that the competitiveness of electoral districts increases the supply of various campaign resources and total spending (Heard, 1960:384; Key, 1964:490; Eulau et al., 1966:225-226; Leuthold, 1968:74-75, 80; Adamany, 1969:80, 1972:65-69). Moreover, evidence suggests that competition encourages particular campaign styles. To ensure maximum coverage, candidates in highly competitive districts rely on impersonal forms of campaigning—e.g., speaking to large audiences, printing cards or

posters, and using "untargeted" newspaper and television campaigns (Eulau et al., 1966:226-227; Leuthold, 1968:104)–and may find it necessary to make additional media expenditures if they lack strong newspaper backing (Jones, 1967:59). Minority party candidates in noncompetitive districts face a dilemma: on the one hand, they have an incentive to avoid communication with heterogeneous audiences and therefore will avoid use of broadcast and other forms of campaigning that cannot be targeted to particular audiences (Froman, 1966:14; MacNeil, 1972); on the other hand, they lack the organizational and manpower resources necessary for labor intensive campaigns and therefore show a greater reliance on impersonal, capital-intensive campaigns (Adamany, 1972:87-90; Black, 1975).

B. THE POLITICAL CHARACTERISTICS OF CANDIDATES

1. *Incumbency.* The effect of incumbency on total campaign expenditures and resource allocation follows several, often contradictory, threads of analysis. They include (1) the role of incumbency in attracting votes; (2) the relationship between incumbency and total resources; (3) voter awareness; (4) congressional office, committee participation, and voting records; and (5) the desire for higher office.

First, incumbency is an efficient, easily converted and productive resource for political candidates (Wolfinger and Heifetz, 1965; Leuthold, 1968; Hinckley, 1970; Erikson, 1971a, 1971b; Kostroski, 1973; Adamany, 1972). Moreover, in congressional races, "the overall electoral value of incumbency seems to have risen in the last decade" (Mayhew, 1974:36). The winner's incumbency is positively correlated with the margin of victory in elections for the U.S. House of Representatives (Dawson and Zinser, 1970:401) and in elections for the U.S. Senate as well (Hinckley, 1970). Thus it is not surprising that incumbency, by lowering the demand for resources, may reduce congressional expenditures, at least in House if not Senate races (Dawson and Zinser, 1970:401). Conversely, challengers "have to spend considerably more than the incumbent" (Jones, 1967:61). The size of a "considerable" amount however remains open to question; it is difficult to estimate precisely the size of the extra expenditure necessary to offset the electoral advantage of incumbency.

Second, with no apparent need, incumbents raise and presumably spend more money that their opponents. Incumbents start campaigns with more money (Fishel, 1973:98) and are more efficient fund raisers (Fishel, 1973:103).

Third, voter awareness of candidates and their positions shapes the role of incumbency in resource allocation, but there is little agreement that incumbency is associated with distinctive campaign styles. On the one hand, "small turnouts favor the incumbent" (Froman, 1966:12); thus incumbents may use more personal forms of campaigning which can be targeted efficiently to particular audiences. On the other hand, voter awareness of congressional contests is low and "even the incumbent has a problem of identifying himself to the voter" (Jones, 1966:28). This problem, given available financial resources, may induce incumbents to spend more than their opponents on untargeted media. This tendency, while slight, appears in data for San Francisco Bay area congressional contests (Leuthold, 1968:104). In addition, challengers spend more on salaries and expenses to counter the staff resources of incumbents (Adamany, 1972:111).

Although incumbents and nonincumbents may not differ in their reliance on mass media, length of incumbency may be associated with distinctive types of media appeal. For example, some incumbents prefer brief broadcast appeals while nonincumbents seek longer broadcast exposure: "One might expect a well-known incumbent to be satisfied merely to invoke his name frequently, whereas the challenger might feel some need to explain his views more fully" (Alexander, 1966:88).

Fourth, incumbency-related characteristics, such as office, committee appointments, and voting record, may influence campaign behavior. For example, unlike Senate counterparts, congressmen are able to frank mail to all mailing addresses in their districts; further, they show less use of other nonmedia forms of communication. Moreover, senators probably allocate a greater proportion of campaign expenditures to television (Heard, 1960:39).

Membership on particular legislative committees, legislative performance, and roll-call behavior may be associated with increased campaign resources. For example, membership on the House and Senate post office committees was traditionally associated with an increased supply of money and volunteer work (Mayhew: 1974:61). Membership on particular congressional committees may also be indicative of candidate campaign preferences. To illustrate, "in recent years Education and Labor has attracted media-conscious members such as Shirley Chisholm (D., N.Y.), Herman Badillo (D., N.Y.), and Louise Day Hicks (D., Mass.)" (Mayhew, 1974:87). Also, performance clearly affects electoral pluralities of some incumbents: "an unusually liberal Republican Representative gets at least 6 per cent of the two-party vote . . . than his extreme conservative counterpart would in the same district" (Erikson, 1971b:1023).

A related point is the effect of party loyalty; some forms may hurt reelection, as it did for incumbent Republican congressmen who signed a pledge of support for the presidential candidacy of Goldwater in 1964 (Schoenberger, 1969).

Finally, ambitions of Senate and especially House members for higher office prompt incumbents to maximize, for example, their margin of victory, instead of simply the probability of reelection. The result may be a substantial increase in total expenditures (Schlesinger, 1966; Mayhew, 1974).

2. *Other Characteristics of Candidates and Parties.* Democratic and Republican party organizations and candidates, at all levels, differ in their efficiency as fund raisers and in their preferences for campaign strategies. There is agreement that Republicans are more efficient fund raisers than Democrats, as measured by amounts of cash on hand at the beginning of the campaign and by contributions received during the campaign (Heard, 1960; Fishel, 1973).[2] In addition, older, traditional party organizations apparently spend more on organizational expenses than do newer, amateur style clubs (Adamany, 1972:119-120).

Heard (1960:391-392) found that Republicans and Democrats "at all levels . . . generally spend their moneis in about the same proportions for the same purposes." For the most part, this finding is well supported for broadcasting expenditures (Leuthold, 1968:104; Adamany, 1969:121), although Alexander's analysis of data (1966:86) collected by the Federal Communications Commission reveals that "Democrats spend considerably more on political broadcasting, over all, than do Republicans."

Other differences were observed by Leuthold (1968:106) in his study of San Francisco Bay area congressional candidates:

> Republicans spent a higher proportion of their funds for newspaper ads, signs and billboards, and . . . Republican workers were more likely than Democratic workers to arrange meetings at which their candidate spoke, or

to give speeches themselves. Democratic voters were more likely to be stimulated to vote only by some form of personal contact. As a result, Democratic candidates spent a higher proportion of funds for personnel and mailings, and asked a higher proportion of their workers to register voters, go door to door, telephone, and get out the vote on election day.

Finally, an interesting interaction between campaign patterns and district competitiveness was observed in one study of city councilmen: "Republicans in Democratic milieux are more likely to use door-to-door campaigning . . . –a technique favored by the Democrats–than are Republicans in Republican environments . . . or Republicans in competitive milieux" (Eulau et al., 1966:228).

C. THE DEMOGRAPHIC CHARACTERISTICS OF DISTRICTS

Several demographic characteristics of electoral districts affect the availability and allocation of campaign resources: district income, changes in other economic indicators, migration, population density, age, and region.

1. *Personal Income.* District per capita income is correlated with the supply of campaign resources, expenditures, and allocation. Heard (1960:82) presents indirect evidence of a positive correlation between family incomes and contributions. Moreover, "the level of campaign expenditures . . . depends in part on national prosperity" (Heard, 1960:386). Wealthy families are more able to contribute and apparently have a greater inclination to do so. The normal relationship between district income and contributions may be disrupted, however, in cases of campaigns that attract national attention and financing. The 1970 senatorial campaign in North Dakota seems to have been one example. It is estimated that 85-90 percent of expenditures by both candidates originated in out-of-state contributions (Stern, 1973:384).

Per capita income is also correlated with voter turnout. Here income serves as a proxy for voter education, interest in public affairs, involvement in politics, and other indicators of participatory democracy (Frey, 1971; Fraser, 1972).[3]

Distinctive campaign styles are also associated with differences in per capita income. For example, higher incomes generate campaigns that minimize expenditures on electronic media in that higher income families tend to be better informed and to receive political campaign information from printed rather than broadcast sources (Sheinkopf and O'Keefe, 1973).

2. *Other Economic Indicators.* Other economic indicators apparently influence expenditure patterns and electoral outcomes. For example, good or bad economic conditions are linked with the presidential party and "the national electorate rewards the congressional party of a president who reigns during economic prosperity and punishes the party of one who reigns during adversity" (Mayhew, 1974:29). Thus during times of economic adversity, some incumbents, those of the presidential party, may expect reduced contributions and little success in converting resources into votes through any campaign form. Mr. Dooley might have been considering running against an incumbent in such an electoral situation when he commented: "If I was runnin' f'r office, I'd change me name, an' have printed on me cards: 'Give him a chanst; he can't be worse' " (Hutchinson, 1963:19). Measures of economic activity include unemployment rates, inflation, and annual changes in income (Rees et al., 1962; Kramer, 1971; Kramer and Lepper, 1972; Stigler, 1973; McCracken, 1973; Okun, 1973; Tufte, 1975). Studies have found evidence that inflation affects outcomes and that increases in income benefit incumbents over nonincumbents. For example, Kramer and Lepper (1972:266) estimated that "a rise in income of 10 per cent would increase the incumbent party's vote share by almost 5 per cent, other things being equal." However, even these results are subject to some question; in Stigler's words (1973:160): "If this fact in fact a fact?" His work casts substantial doubt on Kramer's analysis. In addition, though candidates in districts with large pockets of unemployment expect reduced financial resources and resistance to traditionally successful campaigns, there is little tendency to "give the other fellow a chance" (Kramer and Lepper, 1972; Stigler, 1973).

3. *Mobility.* Immigrants from other districts or states tend to have lower turnout rates than those who have lived in the district longer (Sharp, 1955), and attempts to secure these votes are costly. Also, immigrants tend to have less stable candidate preferences.

4. *Other Demographic Characteristics.* Two additional characteristics have been mentioned in the literature: age and region. It

might be supposed that the percentage of younger voters in a district is associated with increased broadcast expenditures, but it does not appear that younger are more likely than older people to seek information from broadcast sources (Sheinkopf and O'Keefe, 1973:6). Similarly, it might be supposed that some regions of the country are not susceptible to newer and especially electronic media techniques—the South, for example. However, it also seems true that politics in the South is becoming increasingly similar to Northern politics and that a possible consequence will be "the emergence of officeholders—especially at the congressional level—more in style with their Northern counterparts." (Jennings and Zeigler, 1966:122).

D. CHARACTERISTICS OF CAMPAIGN RESOURCES

The *effectiveness* of resources depends on whether their use makes a difference to the realization of preferred outcomes. Most political resources probably have this minimal characteristic but differ widely in their relative effectiveness or, more precisely, in their *efficiency,* where efficiency is defined in terms of the rate at which units of the resource are converted into units of other resources or into units of the preferred outcome. In general, a particular campaign resource may be subject to increasing, constant, or decreasing marginal product. Moreover, it may be efficient for some purposes but not others. For example, enthusiasm of participants at a campaign rally may efficiently increase news coverage of that event but may not be at all efficient in increasing voter turnout. Success may thus depend on whether resources are *convertible.* While the enthusiasm of rally participants may not lead directly to increased voter turnout, it might stimulate campaign contributions that, in turn, could be used efficiently for the purpose of stimulating turnout. Finally, political resources differ in their *interchangeability,* that is, the extent to which they can be used in lieu of other, perhaps more efficient, resources which are unavailable to the candidate. For example, a nonincumbent may substitute an extensive media appeal for the advantages of incumbency.

IV. A MODEL OF RATIONAL CAMPAIGN BEHAVIOR

There are reasons to assume that rational candidates seek to maximize the margin of victory—if not the actual number of votes received. They compete in political environments that provide strong incentives to maximize. These incentives derive from the uncertainty of nomination and election contests (Kingdon, 1968:86-89; Mayhew, 1974:35), the actual and candidate-perceived variations in the vote which are attributable to local factors (Stokes, 1967, 1973; Katz, 1973; Mayhew, 1974:34), uncertainty about the rate at which slack resources might be deployed in an opponent's campaign (Mayhew, 1974:44), and the beliefs of candidates that campaign activities do make a difference on election outcomes (Kingdon, 1968). These incentives presumably encourage candidates to allocate resources in a manner that is most likely to ensure electoral success (Adamany, 1972:121). However, the supply and productivity of campaign resources may be constrained by factors that, for the most part, are not under the control of candidates, such as the relatively fixed demographic characteristics of electoral districts.

In this vein, the discussion and empirical analysis investigate the following question: To what extent do candidates change the levels and allocation of campaign resources in response to their demographic environment? To answer this question, our analysis centers on total campaign expenditures (and expenditures per eligible voter) and on two subcategories of expenditures: television and broadcasting. We test the extent to which these variables are statistically correlated with five demographic variables: per capita income, income inequality (the GINI coefficient), population mobility, age, and race.[4]

1. *Income.* Campaign financing does not appear to be a national phenomenon in which out-of-district money constitutes a substantial proportion of campaign budgets. Thus, within a district, per capita income should be positively correlated with the availability of campaign funds. Although candidates presumably can run more cheaply in high- as opposed to low-income districts since there is less need to allocate money for voter turnout, pressures to maximize electoral advantage should result in the expenditure of available funds. Thus we assume that per capita personal income is positively correlated with total campaign expenditures and with expenditures per eligible voter.

Relationships between per capita income and media campaigning might seem, at first glance, counterintuitive. It is likely that income serves as a proxy for voter education, interest, and involvement and is negatively correlated with electronic, especially television, campaign expenditures. That is, our knowledge of high-income voters suggests that, for them, electronic media are inefficient means of communication and therefore should not be used extensively. Nevertheless, pressures to maximize electoral advantage may dictate use of even inefficient appeals. In addition, income is positively related to leisure and therefore with media consumption. Finally, media expenditures can be made quickly and in large amounts, providing a ready outlet for the pressure to spend. For these reasons we hypothesize that per capita income is positively correlated with broadcast and television expenditures. However, voter demand for more personal forms of campaigning implies that income is negatively correlated with broadcast and television expenditures expressed as a proportion of the total campaign budget.

2. *Income Inequality.* Although not previously discussed in the literature, it is likely that income inequality significantly affects campaign behavior. First, inequality influences the supply of campaign revenues. A district's capacity to make contributions increases with the share of income in the upper brackets of the income distribution. This, coupled with pressures to spend available money, leads to the hypothesis that inequality is positively correlated with total campaign expenditures.

Second, districts with high levels of inequality are more diverse. The difficult task of communicating with diverse groupings is efficiently accomplished by untargeted media that span the electorate. Thus, by hypothesis, income inequality is positively correlated with levels of television and broadcast spending and with their importance in the campaign budget. In addition, inequality is assumed to be positively correlated with the fraction of broadcasting spent on television.

3. *Mobility.* Pressures to maximize electoral advantage will lead candidates to seek out recent residents who probably lack stable candidate preferences and who typically have a lower turnout rate; these attempts will increase campaign costs. Thus migration into a district is hypothesized to be positively correlated with total expenditures and with expenditures per eligible voter. In addition, the diversity of new residents should increase the use of those forms of campaigning which efficiently span a wide range of voters.

Migration is hypothesized to be positively related to the amount and relative importance of television and broadcasting expenditures.

4. *Age.* The effect of younger voters on the availability of resources and level of total expenditures is the product of conflicting pressures. On the one hand, younger voters probably contribute less than others; they also probably contribute more volunteer work and reduce the demand for expenditures that substitute for volunteer effort. On the other hand, it seems likely that competition for younger voters who have yet to form a highly stable partisan identification will increase total spending. The net effect is not clear. However, we assume that pressures for electoral advantage predominate; thus, by hypothesis, the fraction of young voters is positively associated with campaign expenditures.

Conventional folk wisdom about media consumption habits leads to the hypothesis that youth is also positively correlated with television and broadcast expenditures, and with their relative importance in the campaign budget.

5. *Race.* The racial composition of a district may have some effect on the supply of resources and on total expenditures. To the extent that racial differences are reflected in levels of system support, it might be expected that whites are more likely to make campaign contributions than nonwhites. However, the correlation is probably weak because of the role of income as a proxy; it picks up most of the differences typically associated with race.

The model assumes that demographic variables constrain campaign behavior irrespective of the office, party, candidate incumbency, or whether the candidate was running what turned out to be a winning or losing campaign. The model is tested within a particular context, the congressional elections of 1972. The following section describes this electoral context and, at an aggregate level, identifies the basic patterns of resource allocation.

V. THE PRACTICE OF THE ART: THE CONGRESSIONAL CAMPAIGN OF 1972

Every election has its own anomalies and salient features. The national elections of 1972 had plenty of both. For the first time, a party won the presidency by over 60 percent of the presidential vote and failed to pick up seats in both houses of Congress.[5] Republicans added 13 seats in the House but Democrats gained 2 seats in the Senate and added 1 to their lopsided advantage in governorships. President Nixon's coattails may have helped Republican challengers who captured a number of traditionally Democratic House seats in the South, but were not helpful in most House and Senate races. In the Senate, for example, Nixon outpolled 26 Republican senatorial candidates, running behind only 7. But Democratic senatorial challengers upset seemingly well-entrenched Republicans in Colorado, Delaware, Iowa, and Maine, despite an overwhelming Nixon vote in these states.

In general, however, incumbents fared well except where they had been redistricted or where they were forced to run against other incumbents. Other changes in the House were due to a rather large number (57) of openings created through retirement, primary defeat, or candidacy for higher office. The resulting 93rd Congress seemed more liberal and included the highest number of women since the 87th Congress and the first two blacks to represent Southern congressional districts in this century.

The 1972 national elections were conducted under new statutory constraints. Among its various effects, the Federal Election Campaign Act of 1971 set ceilings on certain expenditures and provided for public disclosure of contributions and expenditures.[6] Although the Campaign Act of 1971 did not become effective until April 7, 1972, good estimates of the cost of national campaigns are available: Common Cause (1974:vii), for example, has calculated that the 1,116 House and Senate candidates in the 1972 general election raised $69.7 million and spent $66.4 million. Nevertheless, in spite of these expenditures, national turnout of eligible voters fell to 55 percent—the lowest rate since 1948.

Against this general backdrop, we return to our initial descriptive concerns: At what levels and in what ways are financial resources allocated? Do Democrats differ from Republicans, incumbents from nonincumbents, winners from losers?

A. EXPENDITURES BY HOUSE CANDIDATES

In comparison with estimates of total expenditures from earlier years, the cost of campaigning for the U.S. House of Representatives has risen steeply. In 1972, House candidates spent, on the average, over $44,000 in primary and general elections. Incumbents spent slightly more than this, and nonincumbents spent slightly less (Table 1). Expenditures per eligible voter averaged $1.41 for all candidates, again somewhat more for incumbents. The presumed financial superiority of Republicans does emerge for Republican incumbents and especially for Republican winners. However, nonincumbents made up for a nearly 7 to 1 disadvantage in cash on hand and ended up spending only 8 percent less than incumbents. Differences between winning and losing candidates are quite substantial; winners spent approximately 62 percent more. Nevertheless, Will Rogers is still right: "It costs a lot of money to get beat these days."

Table 1. HOUSE OF REPRESENTATIVES: CAMPAIGN EXPENDITURES BY PARTY, INCUMBENCY, AND ELECTION RESULT

		Incumbency		*Election Result*	
Party	*Total*	*Incumbents*	*Nonincumbents*	*Winners*	*Losers*
Democrats					
TE[a]	45.37	43.83	46.80	49.55	39.91
BC[a]	6.96	5.67	8.32	7.03	6.86
TV[a]	4.03	3.09	5.02	4.09	3.96
TE/EV[b]	1.42	1.37	1.45	1.55	1.26
BC/EV[b]	0.22	0.18	0.26	0.22	0.22
TV/EV[b]	0.13	0.10	0.16	0.13	0.13
N	(435)	(224)	(211)	(242)	(193)
Republicans					
TE	44.42	50.89	40.80	62.75	29.77
BC	6.33	7.36	5.76	8.99	4.22
TV	3.74	4.26	3.45	5.18	2.60
TE/EV	1.40	1.58	1.30	1.97	0.94
BC/EV	0.20	0.23	0.19	0.28	0.13
TV/EV	0.12	0.13	0.18	0.16	0.08
N	(435)	(155)	(280)	(193)	(242)
Average					
TE	44.83	46.72	43.38	55.40	34.26
BC	6.64	6.36	6.86	7.90	5.39
TV	3.89	3.57	4.13	4.57	3.20
TE/EV	1.41	1.46	1.38	1.74	1.08
BC/EV	0.21	0.20	0.22	0.25	0.17
TV/EV	0.12	0.11	0.17	0.14	0.10
N	(870)	(379)	(491)	(435)	(435)

a. Expenditures in $1,000.

b. Expenditures divided by eligible voters in dollars.

SOURCES: See Appendix.

Substantial funds of House candidates went to broadcasting: $6,640, or $0.21 per eligible voter, on the average. For the most part, patterns observed for total expenditures also hold for broadcast campaigning and for television; that is, Democrats spend more on television and radio than Republicans, and winners spend substantially more than losers. However, two exceptions in broadcasting are of interest: in spite of their fewer resources, Republican challengers outspent Democratic incumbents, and nonincumbents outspent incumbents.

The relative importance of television and broadcast expenditures in total House campaign budgets is shown in Table 2. In general, House campaigns show little reliance on electronic campaign forms; radio and television allocations together amount to only 15 percent of total expenditures, and television alone amounted to only 7 percent of expenses. These figures compare with 20.4 percent and 14.4 percent, respectively, for Senate campaigns. Also, House campaign broadcasting emphasized radio more than television; only 30.5 percent of total broadcasting was allocated to television (69.5 percent to radio). Again, for comparison, Senate candidates allocated 63.2 percent of broadcasting to television (36.8 percent to radio).

Table 2. HOUSE OF REPRESENTATIVES: TELEVISION AND BROADCAST EXPENDITURES AS A FRACTION OF CAMPAIGN SPENDING BY PARTY, INCUMBENCY, AND ELECTION RESULT (%)

		Incumbency		*Election Result*	
Party	*Total*	*Incumbents*	*Nonincumbents*	*Winners*	*Losers*
BC/TE[a]					
Democrats	15.4	12.9	17.8	14.2	17.2
Republicans	14.3	14.5	14.1	14.3	14.2
Average	14.8	13.6	15.8	14.2	15.7
TV/TE[b]					
Democrats	8.0	6.6	9.4	7.4	8.8
Republicans	6.0	7.2	5.3	7.3	5.0
Average	7.0	6.8	7.1	7.4	6.7
TV/BC[c]					
Democrats	32.2	32.1	32.4	35.1	28.6
Republicans	28.8	35.0	25.3	35.4	23.5
Average	30.5	33.0	28.4	35.2	25.8

a. Broadcast expenditures divided by total expenditures (%).

b. Television expenditures divided by total expenditures (%).

c. Television expenditures divided by broadcast expenditures (%).

SOURCE: See Appendix.

Several interesting patterns emerge from the data in Table 2. First, Republican incumbents and nonincumbents allocate about the same fraction of total expenditures to broadcasting (14 percent). However, incumbents used relatively more television (35 percent of broadcasting, compared with 25 percent for nonincumbents). In contrast, Democrat incumbents and nonincumbents each allocated about 32 percent of broadcasting budgets to television, but nonincumbents had substantially more broadcasting, as a fraction of total expenditures. Also, winners had slightly less broadcasting as a fraction of total expenditures, but substantially more of their broadcasting went to television. The ratio of candidate television expenditures to total candidate expenditures (TV/TE) is slightly greater for winners than losers.

B. EXPENDITURES BY SENATE CANDIDATES

In general, Senate races were almost nine times more expensive than House contests. The average candidate spent almost $400,000, or $2.72 per eligible voter. For Senate races, party differences are in the expected direction; Republicans outspent Democrats by more than 36 percent. Further, this holds for every category of candidate, e.g., incumbents, nonincumbents, winners, and losers. The average Republican nonincumbent had greater expenditures than Democrat incumbents, although incumbents outspent nonincumbents: $2.86 per eligible voter to $2.63, respectively. Finally, winners outspent losers by almost 2 to 1.

In addition, Republicans outspent Democrats in most forms of broadcasting. On the average, a Republican candidate spent $86,600 on broadcasting, compared with $75,800 for Democrats. However, Democrats allocated a larger proportion of their budgets to broadcasting: 24 percent compared with 18 percent. Further, Republicans had much larger television budgets and relatively less use of radio.

Overall, incumbents had the larger broadcast budgets: $92,000, compared with $74,600 for nonincumbents. One exception: Republican nonincumbents spent about $0.33 on television per eligible voter, compared with $0.30 for Republican incumbents. In addition, nonincumbents allocated a greater fraction of total expenses to broadcasting. Winning Democrats and losing Democrats spent roughly the same amount on broadcast expenditures, $80,000 and $72,000, respectively; however, winning Republicans spent twice as

Table 3. SENATE: CAMPAIGN EXPENDITURES BY PARTY, INCUMBENCY, AND ELECTION RESULT

		Incumbency		*Election Result*	
Party	*Total*	*Incumbents*	*Nonincumbents*	*Winners*	*Losers*
Democrats					
TE[a]	320.26	381.08	297.44	380.94	263.15
BC[a]	75.78	81.39	73.68	79.91	71.90
TE/EV[b]	2.40	2.75	2.27	3.29	1.56
BC/EV[b]	0.43	0.51	0.39	0.54	0.32
TV/EV[b]	0.28	0.34	0.26	0.35	0.21
N	(33)	(9)	(24)	(16)	(17)
Republicans					
TE	476.16	559.74	397.50	644.65	297.16
BC	86.59	98.03	75.82	113.12	58.40
TE/EV	3.04	2.92	3.15	3.64	2.41
BC/EV	0.46	0.46	0.46	0.51	0.40
TV/EV	0.32	0.30	0.33	0.34	0.28
N	(33)	(16)	(17)	(17)	(16)
Average					
TE	398.21	495.42	338.94	516.79	279.64
BC	81.19	92.04	74.57	97.02	65.36
TE/EV	2.72	2.86	2.63	3.47	1.97
BC/EV	0.44	0.48	0.42	0.52	0.36
TV/EV	0.30	0.31	0.29	0.34	0.25
N	(66)	(25)	(41)	(33)	(33)

a. Expenditures in $1,000.

b. Expenditures divided by eligible voters in dollars.

SOURCES: See Appendix.

much as less fortunate Republicans. Losers allocated a larger fraction of their budgets to broadcasting and a larger fraction of total expenditures to elevision, but a preference for television over radio is clearly held by winning candidates, especially the Republican victors.

In general, findings on total expenditures are fairly clear cut. Broadcast and television expenditures reveal slight differences, but even these dispel some folk wisdom about campaign behavior. Many of the measures of resource allocation, however, when aggregated by party, incumbency, and election result either fail to show more than slight differences or show differences that do not suggest obvious explanations. To explore more systematically the causes of variation in the allocation of individual candidate expenditures, we return to the model of rational campaign behavior.

Table 4. SENATE: TELEVISION AND BROADCAST EXPENDITURES AS A FRACTION OF CAMPAIGN SPENDING BY PARTY, INCUMBENCY, AND ELECTION RESULT (%)

		Incumbency		*Election Result*	
Party	*Total*	*Incumbents*	*Nonincumbents*	*Winners*	*Losers*
BC/TE[a]					
Democrats	23.7	21.4	24.8	20.1	27.3
Republicans	18.2	17.5	19.1	17.6	19.6
Average	20.4	18.6	22.0	18.8	23.4
TV/TE[b]					
Democrats	16.1	14.1	16.8	13.9	18.1
Republicans	12.7	12.8	12.5	13.3	12.0
Average	14.4	13.3	15.0	13.6	15.1
TV/BC[c]					
Democrats	61.2	62.0	60.9	63.1	59.4
Republicans	65.2	64.8	65.6	69.5	60.7
Average	63.2	63.8	62.8	66.4	60.0

a. Broadcast expenditures divided by total expenditures (%).
b. Television expenditures divided by total expenditures (%).
c. Television expenditures divided by broadcast expenditures (%).
SOURCE: Appendix.

VI. EMPIRICAL RESULTS

Information reported in Tables 5 to 14 tests possible relationships between the size and allocation of campaign expenditures, on the one hand, and five demographic variables—income, income distribution, mobility, age, and race—on the other. For both the House and Senate we performed regressions on five sets of candidates: total expenditures (sum of the winning and best losing candidates), winning candidates, losing candidates, Democrats, and "Republicans."[7] These breakdowns permit direct comparison of the extent to which groups of candidates were either constrained by or cognizant of demographic conditions in their choice of expenditure levels and allocations. In addition, for four groups we included a dummy variable representing incumbency; it has the value of unity if the particular candidate was an incumbent and is zero otherwise.

In these tables statistical significance is indicated by either an * or a +, representing significance at the 0.01 and 0.05 level of confidence, respectively. Standard errors of the estimated regression coefficients are given in parentheses below the estimated coefficients.

A. HOUSE OF REPRESENTATIVES

Regressions for the House of Representatives are presented in Tables 5-9. Results suggest that demographic variables play an important role in expenditure allocations, but low R^2's indicate that other variables need be incorporated to explain fully candidate behavior. Specific results by independent variables are as follows:

1. *Income.* In the House, per capita income is significantly positively correlated with total campaign expenditures and with expenditures per eligible voter for all candidate categories. Either local resources are a significant constraint on spending, or conditions which lead to higher district incomes also lead to more costly races. Other things being equal, a one-dollar increase in per capita income would apparently generate an increase in total expenditures and expenditures per eligible voter of between one and two cents. However, income is not positively related to the expenditure components. Rather, for all candidate categories, an increase in per capita income is associated with statistically significant decreases in total television expenditures, the ratio of television to broadcast expenditures, television and broadcast expenditures per eligible voter, and the importance of television and broadcasting in the total budget. This result supports earlier contentions that higher levels of per capita income are associated with a more educated and well-informed population, reducing the need for broadcasting and, especially, television.

2. *Income Inequality.* Our measure of income inequality in the congressional districts is the most significant of all variables chosen for this survey. Further, signs of estimated regression coefficients are consistent with hypotheses formulated in Section IV. Specifically, income inequality, measured by the GINI coefficient, is positively correlated with an increase in total expenditures and with the broadcast components of total expenditures. Inequality increases the capacity for individual donations on the supply side and increases the need for total expenditures and those broadcast components that efficiently communicate with diverse income groups.

One interesting result is that estimated regression coefficients are positive but not statistically different from zero in only the following instances: TV, TV/EV, and TV/TE for winning candidates and TV,

Table 5. HOUSE OF REPRESENTATIVES: TOTAL EXPENDITURES

Variable	*Constant*	*Income*	*GINI*	*Mobility*	*Age*	*Race*	R^2
TE	−1432.0	2.17*	4485.0*	2068.0*	−1896.9	109.9	.106
		(0.65)	(1286.9)	(835.0)	(2948.5)	(333.9)	
TV	−149.0	− 0.22$^+$	540.2*	451.2*	309.6	31.2	.081
		(0.10)	(203.2)	(131.9)	(465.6)	(52.7)	
BC	− 217.2	− 0.19	787.7$^+$	696.2*	284.3	40.7	.090
		(0.14)	(264.4)	(174.1)	(615.0)	(69.6)	
TE/EV	− 3.190	0.0056*	12.481*	7.168*	− 5.572	−0.162	.089
		(0.0021)	(4.131)	(2.681)	(9.466)	(1.072)	
TV/EV	− 0.410	−0.0007*	1.682*	1.464*	1.056	0.043	.085
		(0.0003)	(0.653)	(0.424)	(1.495)	(0.169)	
BC/EV	− 0.524	−0.0007$^+$	2.350*	2.288*	0.982	0.032	.093
		(0.0004)	(0.865)	(0.561)	(1.982)	(0.224)	
TV/BC	− 0.144	−0.0007*	1.360*	0.750$^+$	1.401	0.050	.083
		(0.0003)	(0.508)	(0.330)	(1.164)	(0.132)	
TV/TE	− 0.112	−0.0003	0.355*	0.189$^+$	0.552$^+$	0.067$^+$	.120
		(0.0006)	(0.126)	(0.082)	(0.289)	(0.033)	
BC/TE	− 0.091	−0.0004*	0.499*	0.187	0.713	0.086*	.138
		(0.0001)	(0.161)	(0.105)	(0.370)	(0.042)	

SOURCE: See text.

Table 6. HOUSE OF REPRESENTATIVES: DEMOCRAT EXPENDITURES

Variable	*Constant*	*Income*	*GINI*	*Mobility*	*Age*	*Race*	*Incumbency*	R^2
TE	–253.2	0.913*	2001.7*	947.6$^+$	–1019.2	–293.0	–	.076
		(0.373)	(741.3)	(481.0)	(1698.6)	(192.4)	–	
TV	– 51.5	– 0.162*	366.2*	213.6*	143.4	– 17.0	– 19.7*	.108
		(0.059)	(116.7)	(75.9)	(267.4)	(30.9)	(7.9)	
BC	– 72.5	– 0.161$^+$	541.6*	327.8*	114.4	– 36.2	– 25.4*	.111
		(0.079)	(157.8)	(102.6)	(361.5)	(41.8)	(10.6)	
TE/EV	–0.129	0.0023$^+$	5.542$^+$	3.291$^+$	– 2.841	–1.204$^+$	–0.035	.070
		(0.0012)	(2.350)	(1.528)	(5.384)	(0.622)	(0.158)	
TV/EV	–0.128	–0.0005*	1.150*	0.677*	0.510	–0.085	–0.065*	.114
		(0.0002)	(0.372)	(0.242)	(0.852)	(0.099)	(0.025)	
BC/EV	–0.130	–0.0006*	1.632*	1.069*	0.440	–0.173	–0.085*	.118
		(0.0002)	(0.505)	(0.329)	(1.158)	(0.134)	(0.034)	
TV/BC	–0.234	–0.0007$^+$	1.263*	0.551	2.646$^+$	–	0.006	.092
		(0.0003)	(0.500)	(0.348)	(1.227)	–	(0.035)	
TV/TE	–0.139	–0.0003*	0.560$^+$	–	0.371	0.084	–0.032$^+$	.048
		(0.0001)	(0.233)	–	(0.514)	(0.063)	(0.016)	
BC/TE	–0.109	–0.0004*	0.842*	–0.071	0.398	0.093	–0.048*	.077
		(0.0001)	(0.280)	(0.182)	(0.640)	(0.074)	(0.019)	

SOURCE: See text.

Table 7. HOUSE OF REPRESENTATIVES: REPUBLICAN EXPENDITURES

Variable	*Constant*	*Income*	*GINI*	*Mobility*	*Age*	*Race*	*Incumbency*	R^2
TE	–1167.9	1.253*	2493.5*	1122.5*	– 912.9	384.8+	18.7	.107
		(0.373)	(743.2)	(481.9)	(1704.4)	(199.2)	(52.3)	
TV	– 72.6	– 0.055	184.9	224.4*	142.1	28.8	3.8	.046
		(0.057)	(114.4)	(74.2)	(262.4)	(30.7)	(8.0)	
BC	– 111.0	– 0.030	261.6	351.6*	133.7	49.3	7.6	.064
		(0.072)	(144.0)	(93.4)	(330.3)	(38.6)	(10.1)	
TE/EV	– 3.000	0.0034*	6.974*	3.856*	– 2.830	0.980	0.036	.088
		(0.0012)	(2.391)	(1.550)	(5.484)	(0.641)	(0.168)	
TV/EV	– 0.202	–0.0002	0.566	0.743*	0.475	0.068	0.008	.048
		(0.0002)	(0.367)	(0.238)	(0.842)	(0.098)	(0.026)	
BC/EV	– 0.285	–0.0001	0.765	1.163*	0.435	0.120	0.018	.063
		(0.0002)	(0.464)	(0.301)	(1.065)	(0.124)	(0.033)	
TV/BC	– 0.550	–0.0010*	1.758*	0.911*	0.949	0.364+	0.075+	.116
		(0.0003)	(0.519)	(0.337)	(1.191)	(0.139)	(0.036)	
TV/TE	– 0.122	–0.0002+	0.396*	0.172+	0.367	0.073	0.014	.081
		(0.0001)	(0.150)	(0.097)	(0.344)	(0.040)	(0.011)	
BC/TE	– 0.094	–0.0004*	0.406+	0.198	0.412	0.147*	0.021	.084
		(0.0001)	(0.203)	(0.131)	(0.465)	(0.054)	(0.014)	

SOURCE: See text.

Table 8. HOUSE OF REPRESENTATIVES: WINNING CANDIDATE EXPENDITURES

Variable	*Constant*	*Income*	*GINI*	*Mobility*	*Age*	*Race*	*Incumbency*	R^2
TE	−155.2	1.394*	1829.9*	705.3^{+}	–	66.4	−583.8*	.328
		(0.268)	(596.3)	(367.5)	–	(155.0)	(51.5)	
TV	− 16.4	− 0.055	162.2	193.2*	368.8	26.6	− 71.6*	.184
		(0.055)	(110.0)	(71.6)	(251.9)	(28.5)	(9.5)	
BC	− 38.5	− 0.019	274.8^{+}	301.3*	487.7	37.4	−104.9*	.246
		(0.067)	(134.2)	(87.3)	(307.4)	(34.8)	(11.6)	
TE/EV	0.337	0.004*	4.733*	2.502^{+}	–	−0.084	−1.875*	.328
		(0.001)	(1.862)	(1.148)	–	(0.484)	(0.161)	
TV/EV	−0.007	−0.0002	0.468	0.631*	1.178	0.056	−0.229*	.189
		(0.0002)	(0.346)	(0.225)	(0.793)	(0.090)	(0.030)	
BC/EV	−0.007	−0.0001	0.734^{+}	0.999*	1.565	0.065	−0.337*	.253
		(0.0002)	(0.423)	(0.275)	(0.970)	(0.110)	(0.036)	
TV/BC	−0.120	−0.0006^{+}	1.071^{+}	0.576	2.100^{+}	0.087	0.102^{+}	.077
		(0.0003)	(0.531)	(0.346)	(1.217)	(0.138)	(0.046)	
TV/TE	−0.063	−0.0002*	0.233	0.165^{+}	0.661^{+}	0.075^{+}	−0.038*	.112
		(0.0001)	(0.139)	(0.091)	(0.319)	(0.036)	(0.012)	
BC/TE	−0.076	−0.0003*	0.467^{+}	0.138	0.920^{+}	0.079	−0.030	.104
		(0.0001)	(0.195)	(0.127)	(0.446)	(0.051)	(0.016)	

SOURCE: See text.

Table 9. HOUSE OF REPRESENTATIVES: LOSING CANDIDATE EXPENDITURES

Variable	*Constant*	*Income*	*GINI*	*Mobility*	*Age*	*Race*	*Incumbency*	R^2
TE	–763.8	0.939*	2149.0*	1010.1*	–1128.8	86.1	417.2*	.097
		(0.377)	(752.8)	(487.2)	(1719.7)	(194.9)	(131.3)	
TV	– 65.5	– 0.145*	307.5*	217.4*	32.7	8.7	70.2*	.103
		(0.056)	(112.3)	(72.7)	(256.4)	(29.1)	(19.6)	
BC	– 82.5	– 0.145^{+}	414.6*	334.2*	– 70.3	10.0	91.7*	.098
		(0.076)	(152.2)	(98.5)	(347.8)	(39.0)	(26.6)	
TE/EV	–1.768	0.0024^{+}	6.065*	3.561^{+}	– 3.442	–	1.291*	.083
		(0.0012)	(2.258)	(1.576)	(5.564)	–	(0.425)	
TV/EV	–0.191	–0.0005*	0.994*	0.702*	0.170	–	0.212*	.103
		(0.0002)	(0.338)	(0.236)	(0.834)	–	(0.064)	
BC/EV	–0.225	–0.0005*	1.323*	1.091*	– 0.156	–	0.277*	.097
		(0.0002)	(0.461)	(0.321)	(1.135)	–	(0.087)	
TV/BC	–0.597	–0.0011*	1.785*	0.825*	1.772	0.350*	0.172^{+}	.137
		(0.0003)	(0.516)	(0.334)	(1.180)	(0.134)	(0.090)	
TV/TE	–0.203	–0.0003*	0.654*	0.016	0.173	0.121^{+}	0.055	.044
		(0.0001)	(0.244)	(0.158)	(0.558)	(0.063)	(0.043)	
BC/TE	–0.161	–0.0005*	0.712^{+}	–	–	0.221*	0.050	.058
		(0.0001)	(0.280)	–	–	(0.074)	(0.050)	

SOURCE: See text.

BC, TV/EV, and BC/EV for Republican candidates. (For definitions of these and other abbreviations, see the Appendix.) Conceptually these cases result from lower supply constraints, less concern with spanning diverse groups, or a greater proclivity to concentrate activities on a relatively homogenous population segment.

3. *Mobility.* As stated above, one hypothesis concerning immigration is that total expenditures and broadcast components of expenditures are positively correlated with mobility. It follows from two basic propositions. First, new immigrants into an area, especially from another state, are generally less committed to one particular candidate or party, subject to the caveat that generally "movers" are lower income and blue collar and tend to be relatively more "Democratic." Second, campaigners attempt to attract the attention of new migrants by means of broadcast appeals and additional expenditures. Thus one presumption is that total expenditures will be greater in those districts which have had a larger proportion of immigrants; in addition, the fraction of broadcast expenditures to the total will be larger.

Similar to the results derived for income inequality, regression coefficients tend to support the first part of this hypothesis. Estimated coefficients both for total expenditures and for broadcasting were significantly positive. The second portion is supported except in the case of Democrats and losing candidates: for these groups estimated coefficients are positive in the case of TV/TE but are not significantly different from zero at the 0.05 level of confidence.

4. *Age.* Hypotheses concerning the fraction of the district population between the ages of 18 and 21 and the measure of expenditures follow from several propositions. First, young eligible voters are presumed to be less committed to a particular party or candidate. This may lead to two alternatives concerning total expenditures. Younger voter contributions are probably minimal, restricting supply and limiting total expenditures. However, younger voters are fair game for campaign appeals, and candidates might be expected to spend more per eligible voter in districts which have a relatively young population. Also, prior work suggests that a preferred method of appeal to youth is through the media, especially broadcast expenditures. We should thus expect that TV/EV, TV/TE, TV/BC, BC/EV, and BC/TE would all increase with youth.

In large part these hypotheses are supported, with several exceptions. First, both total campaign expenditures and TE/EV are negatively correlated with the youth variable, suggesting a possible supply constraint. Lack of statistical significance of the estimated coefficients, however, limits definitive conclusions. Second, television and broadcast spending, in total and per eligible voter, are positively (but not significantly) correlated with age. Only coefficients for losing candidates were negative. Significantly positive correlation was, however, found in the relationship between youth and TV/BC, TV/TE, and BC/TE in the cases of winning candidates, Democrats, and both candidates. This result suggests a possibly successful appeal to youth.

5. *Race.* The impact of a district's racial composition, measured in terms of the fraction of the population which is white, on campaign expenditures followed a mixed pattern, consistent with our hypotheses. In most cases percent white is positively, but not significantly, correlated with increases in total spending, but negatively correlated with spending per eligible voter. Exceptions are total Democrat spending and TE/EV for Republicans. Further, in all breakdowns, except Democrats, the race variable and TV, BC, TV/EV, and BC/EV are positively correlated. More significant results are obtained for variables which measure allocation of spending: TV/BC, TV/TE, and BC/TE. All showed positive coefficients, but, again, Democrat spending patterns were relatively less correlated with race than other candidate groups; losers exhibited the greatest positive correlation.

6. *Incumbency.* Incumbent House candidates behaved somewhat differently than nonincumbents, depending on party. Incumbent Democrats had significantly less total spending, television, and broadcasting (per eligible voter and as a fraction of total expenses), while for Republican incumbents just the opposite occurred. Only in one case does incumbency have the same effect on Democrats and Republicans: a positive coefficient for the percentage of broadcast expenditures allocated to television.

The retrospective view of winners and losers in terms of incumbency is even more striking. Winning incumbents uniformly spent less on their campaigns and less on television and broadcasting than did losing incumbents. Possibly, incumbents who were unseated in the elections attempted to stave off defeat through expenditure allocations, or possibly they simply had greater "war chests" with which to conduct campaigns.

B. SENATE

Regressions for the 33 Senate races are given in Tables 10-14. In general, independent variables tended to explain a somewhat larger fraction of the variation in dependent variables due to the smaller number of observations; i.e., R^2's were a bit larger. However, there again remains unexplained variance that requires future research. Further, in many instances, estimated coefficients were not statistically different from zero at an acceptable level of confidence. Nonetheless, interesting patterns relating to our hypotheses may be identified.

For Senate contests we have not included regression equations for total expenditures; instead we limited work to the expenditure ratios and expenditures per eligible voter. Total expenditures are subject to substantial variation due to population sizes of individual states, a problem which is not present in the case of congressional districts (with the exception of several smaller one-district states).

1. *Income.* In Senate races the relationship between per capita state income and expenditure patterns does not conform exactly with results in House contests. In the first place, statistical significance of estimated regression coefficients is not great; for only a half-dozen equations is the coefficient significantly different from zero with a reasonable degree of confidence. Second, signs of derived results do not follow a consistent pattern across expenditure categories and groups of candidates. However, several of these results are quite interesting and suggest both behavioral patterns as hypothesized and areas for future work.

In contrast with House contests, income in Senate contests is not positively correlated with TE/EV; only in the case of losing candidates is the coefficient positive. Evidently Senate contests are either immune to income-determined supply constraints or require fixed levels of expenditure independent of state demographic characteristics. The ratios TV/EV and BC/EV follow identical patterns with respect to income. Coefficients are positive for eventual losers, Republicans, and total campaign spending, but they are negative for eventual winners and Democrats. Possibly the supply

Table 10. SENATE: TOTAL EXPENDITURES

Variable	*Constant*	*Income*	*GINI*	*Mobility*	*Age*	*Race*	R^2
TE/EV	–38.592	–0.0131	42.459	33.876	117.564	15.812	.294
		(0.0290)	(56.660)	(17.305)	(130.888)	(10.942)	
TV/EV	– 6.264	0.0007	10.315*	0.203	14.308	1.205	.431
		(0.0020)	(3.987)	(1.218)	(9.210)	(0.770)	
BC/EV	– 7.091	0.0004	11.678$^+$	3.416	16.214	1.273	.442
		(0.0029)	(5.637)	(1.722)	(13.022)	(1.089)	
TV/TE	– 0.835	0.0007	1.740	–0.625$^+$	1.233	0.051	.326
		(0.0005)	(0.896)	(0.274)	(2.069)	(0.173)	
BC/TE	– 0.659	0.0008	1.658$^+$	–0.535	0.595	–	.251
		(0.0005)	(0.752)	(0.287)	(1.999)	–	
TV/BC	– 1.796	0.0012	3.691$^+$	–1.715$^+$	6.124	0.262	.376
		(0.0011)	(2.093)	(0.639)	(4.836)	(0.404)	

SOURCE: See text.

Table 11. SENATE: DEMOCRAT EXPENDITURES

Variable	*Constant*	*Income*	*GINI*	*Mobility*	*Age*	*Race*	*Incumbency*	R^2
TE/EV	–20.443	–0.0078 (0.0185)	27.436 (35.136)	6.203 (10.617)	51.629 (80.804)	8.809 (6.754)	0.375 (1.013)	.151
TV/EV	– 2.038	–0.0015 (0.0012)	4.531 (2.358)	–0.109 (0.712)	3.598 (5.422)	0.662 (0.453)	0.025 (0.068)	.511
BC/EV	– 1.859	–0.0022 (0.0017)	5.109 (3.245)	1.024 (0.981)	2.035 (7.463)	0.636 (0.624)	0.062 (0.094)	.440
TV/TE	– 1.018	0.0003 (0.0010)	0.929 (1.824)	–1.098 (0.551)	5.596 (4.195)	0.266 (0.351)	–0.035 (0.053)	.202
BC/TE	– 0.648	0.0007 (0.0010)	0.981 (1.833)	–0.936 (0.554)	3.199 (4.215)	0.079 (0.352)	–0.022 (0.053)	.128
TV/BC	– 4.414	0.0009 (0.0014)	3.706 (2.716)	–3.316* (0.821)	23.954* (6.247)	1.150^+ (0.522)	–0.014 (0.078)	.569

SOURCE: See text.

Table 12. SENATE: REPUBLICAN EXPENDITURES

Variable	*Constant*	*Income*	*GINI*	*Mobility*	*Age*	*Race*	*Incumbency*	R^2
TE/EV	–19.571	–0.0014	15.259	27.222*	69.012	7.041	–0.396	.457
		(0.0160)	(30.185)	(9.137)	(69.072)	(5.809)	(0.896)	
TV/EV	– 4.390	0.0022	5.972+	0.298	10.998	0.573	0.010	.306
		(0.0015)	(2.909)	(0.881)	(6.657)	(0.560)	(0.086)	
BC/EV	– 5.558	0.0030	6.842	2.340	14.793	0.679	–0.015	.481
		(0.0020)	(3.826)	(1.158)	(8.756)	(0.736)	(0.114)	
TV/TE	– 1.239	0.0012+	2.996*	–0.468	–0.540	–	0.024	.357
		(0.0006)	(0.864)	(0.329)	(2.288)	–	(0.033)	
BC/TE	– 1.377	0.0017*	3.005*	–0.538	–	–	–0.008	.314
		(0.0005)	(0.917)	(0.298)	–	–	(0.036)	
TV/BC	– 3.987	0.0036+	9.401*	–1.049	1.171	–	0.058	.388
		(0.0016)	(2.455)	(0.935)	(6.502)	–	(0.093)	

SOURCE: See text.

Table 13. SENATE: WINNING CANDIDATE EXPENDITURES

Variable	*Constant*	*Income*	*GINI*	*Mobility*	*Age*	*Race*	*Incumbency*	R^2
TE/EV	−6.702	−0.0142	7.705	28.661^{+}	33.111	4.838	−0.493	.355
		(0.0178)	(35.054)	(10.601)	(81.261)	(6.847)	(0.928)	
TV/EV	−1.839	−0.0008	4.069	0.967	4.540	0.233	0.032	.476
		(0.0011)	(2.197)	(0.664)	(5.093)	(0.429)	(0.058)	
BC/EV	−1.617	−0.0013	3.920	3.385*	5.059	–	0.046	.561
		(0.0015)	(2.393)	(0.914)	(6.383)	–	(0.080)	
TV/TE	−0.597	0.0004	1.615	−0.415	–	0.037	0.016	.193
		(0.0005)	(1.138)	(0.284)	–	(0.200)	(0.030)	
BC/TE	−0.133	0.0002	1.038	−0.236	−0.560	−0.042	0.170	.104
		(0.0007)	(1.332)	(0.403)	(3.087)	(0.260)	(0.353)	
TV/BC	−1.872	0.0011	4.507	−1.324	3.133	0.377	0.012	.269
		(0.0013)	(2.617)	(0.791)	(6.067)	(0.511)	(0.069)	

SOURCE: See text.

Table 14. SENATE: LOSING CANDIDATE EXPENDITURES

Variable	*Constant*	*Income*	*GINI*	*Mobility*	*Age*	*Race*	*Incumbency*	R^2
TE/EV	−29.231	0.0014	32.146	5.202	77.433	10.231	–	.204
		(0.0139)	(27.160)	(8.295)	(62.742)	(5.245)	–	
TV/EV	− 4.723	0.0015	6.704	−0.780	10.137	1.025	0.057	.243
		(0.0016)	(3.178)	(0.956)	(7.229)	(0.604)	(0.112)	
BC/EV	− 5.926	0.0018	8.325	–	11.974	1.385	0.040	.229
		(0.0018)	(3.952)	–	(7.375)	(0.741)	(0.140)	
TV/TE	− 1.807	0.0013	2.300	−1.177	5.601	0.248	−0.025	.120
		(0.0010)	(1.919)	(0.577)	(4.365)	(0.365)	(0.067)	
BC/TE	− 2.091	0.0023*	2.986	−1.254$^+$	4.632	0.192	−0.055	.272
		(0.0009)	(1.841)	(0.554)	(4.188)	(0.350)	(0.065)	
TV/BC	− 6.694	0.0038	8.785$^+$	−3.095*	22.035$^+$	0.800	0.068	.425
		(0.0019)	(3.745)	(1.127)	(8.517)	(0.712)	(0.131)	

SOURCE: See text.

constraint is less binding for Republicans who feel obligated to utilize available funds for broadcast advertising. This result is more understandable for the losing candidates, most of whom are not incumbents; they presumably utilize broadcasting to enhance public recognition.

Distribution of total expenditures is more subject to income variations. The ratios TV/TE, BC/TE, and TV/BC are positively correlated with income per capita. However, as we might suspect, the coefficients are significantly different from zero only for Republican candidates and for the eventual losing candidates. These groups of candidates apparently do not have the manpower resources necessary for personal forms of campaigning (e.g., door-to-door canvassing); they do not incur expenses of organization and materials connected with such forms of campaigning and, as a substitute, spend relatively more on broadcasting.

2. *Income Inequality.* Values of estimated regression coefficients for Senate expenditures and the GINI measure of income inequality are similar to those obtained for the House. That is, in most cases states with higher inequality are also those for which expenditures per eligible voter and the importance of television and of broadcasting are significantly larger. Again, inequality appears to be associated with either a greater supply of campaign funds, with a greater perceived need for broad-based appeals for voter support, or both. This result is most significant in the case of Republican and losing candidates. In contrast, the GINI is positive but not significant for Democrats in all regressions and for winners in nontelevision expenditures.

3. *Mobility.* The effect of voter mobility—that is, a higher proportion of new voters—on expenditures is mixed. In general, candidates in states with the greatest influx of new voters spent more per eligible voter; estimated coefficients of mobility on TE/EV are all positive and, in two cases, significant. However, candidates in such states allocated significantly lower shares of total expenditures to broadcasting and specifically to television campaigning. Moreover, of the amount allocated to broadcasting, a significantly reduced share was allocated to television in states with increased numbers of new voters. Nevertheless, an increase of new voters has a significantly positive effect on broadcast expenditures per eligible voter for all

groups of candidates except losers. These results point out only minor differences between candidate pairs, centering around the relative importance of television and radio expenditures; Republicans and winners favored more television, while Democrats and losers spent relatively more on radio in response to voter mobility.

4. *Age.* Differences in the number of 18-21-year-old eligible voters between states had relatively little impact on differences in spending behavior; only 3 of the 30 coefficients are significantly different from zero. However, all but 2 of the estimated coefficients are positive, indicating that all candidates were probably cognizant of younger voters in spending decisions. This is particularly true in the case of TV/BC for losing candidates and Democrats.

5. *Race.* Similar to results obtained in the case of younger voters, the race variable follows no statistically significant pattern across states. Coefficients on the fraction of white population in a state are positively correlated with all variables with the sole exception of BC/TE in the case of winners. However, these coefficients are statistically different from zero only for losing candidate regressions on TE/EV and BC/EV and the Democrat regression on TV/BC. It does not, thus, appear that race had an impact on spending behavior of the Senate candidates.

6. *Incumbency.* Finally, whether a Senate candidate was an incumbent has at best a moderate role in explaining differences in spending patterns across states. However, the presence of an incumbent tended to increase total campaign spending and spending on broadcasting per eligible voter. Otherwise, standard errors are generally multiples of estimated coefficients, indicating essentially zero correlation. It might well be that spending by all senatorial candidates is subject to perceived minimum levels and form.

VII. SUMMARY

This survey has explored the extent to which congressional candidates are cognizant of, or constrained by, their environment in making campaign resource allocation decisions. We first outlined a model of rational campaign decision making and carved from that model several important components of campaign resources: total and broadcast (including television and radio) expenditures by candidates. We then formulated and empirically tested a series of hypotheses concerning the relationship between expenditures and five demographic characteristics of congressional districts and states.

Results of our analysis are promising; to a large extent empirical tests support the hypotheses. Three variables—per capita income, income inequality, and mobility—are particularly successful in "explaining" variations in expenditure behavior.

In both House and Senate contests, per capita income is positively correlated with total campaign expenditures and, with the exception of Republicans, negatively correlated with the relative importance of broadcasting. Party differences are particularly interesting here and merit future work.

Income inequality (GINI) and mobility (new voters from outside the state) are positively correlated with total expenditures and expenditures per eligible voter in both the House and Senate. Inequality is also positively correlated with broadcasting, especially television expenditures. However, mobility apparently reduces the importance of television in the Senate and increases it in the House. One interpretation is that Senate candidates indeed behave in a distinct manner. Another is that at the state level the impact of variables such as mobility is clouded by other factors—e.g., population size.

Two additional demographic variables were incorporated into the model with mixed success. In both House and Senate, age (fraction of eligible voters between 18 and 21) and race (fraction white) are not significantly correlated with total expenditures. Statistical significance is found for one or two candidate categories, but there is no uniform pattern. Similarly, the relative importance of radio and television in campaigns was not affected, with any regularity, by these variables.

Incumbency had mixed effects on resource allocation. In the House, incumbency is significantly positively correlated with Republican expenditures and with the relative importance of electronic media; for Democrats these correlations are all significantly negative. Senate results in part followed a similar pattern, but coefficients are not statistically significant.

We also found substantial differences between what proved to be winning and losing candidates, especially in the House. These results suggest that expenditure patterns may have an impact on electoral outcomes. Again, more work is necessary.

These empirical results are subject to an important caveat; we have found substantial correlation as hypothesized, but low R^2's in most regressions suggest the need to find additional determinants of campaign resource allocation.

APPENDIX

Variables

Information used in our report is found in four primary sources: the Common Cause (1973) survey of campaign expenditures (CC), a Federal Communications Commission (U.S. Senate, Committee on Commerce, 1973) survey of campaign broadcast expenditures (FCC), the Congressional District Data Book (CDB), and the Department of Commerce (1973) estimates of eligible voters published in the Federal Register (FR). The following is a list of all variables included in our survey and their sources:

Variable	*Definition and Source*
TE	Total Candidate Expenditures (CC): ($100s).
TV	Candidate Television Expenditures (FCC): ($100s).
RA	Candidate Radio Expenditures (FCC): ($100s).
BC	Candidate Broadcast Expenditures (FCC), consists of all radio and television expenditures: ($100s).
EV	Number of Eligible Voters (FR): (1,000 persons).
Income	Income per capita (CDB): (dollars).
GINI	GINI Coefficient (CDB).
Mobility	Fraction of individuals who moved into the state or congressional district from another state (CDB).
Youth	Fraction of eligible voters between 18 and 21 years of age (CDB).
Race	Fraction of population which is white (CDB).

Most variables are relatively self-explanatory. However, several conceptual problems and methods of estimation need to be explained.

First, the five categories of campaign expenditures come from two distinct sources: FCC and CC. The former derives from reports filed, with the commission, by individual broadcast stations. The information includes all station time (radio and television) purchased in the name of a candidate or party. CC results, on the other hand, come from reports filed by individual campaign organizations (candidates), according to a format specified by the Federal Election Office. According to this format, expenditures are disaggregated into two categories–media and nonmedia. Media include all broadcasting stations, newspapers, magazines, outdoor advertising, and direct telephone contact. Understandably, the two sources of expenditure information are not entirely compatible. Specifically, we found that, for a few candidates, broadcast expenditures from FCC exceeded media expenditures given by CC.

Per capita income is computed from two CDB series: income of families and of unrelated individuals, and the corresponding population series.

Several measures of income inequality were available for this survey; they include unemployment, the number of individuals below poverty income, and several measures of income dispersion. No single measure is entirely satisfactory. However, there is widespread acceptance of the GINI coefficient; it provides an adequate measure of inequality. Computation of GINI for each congressional district and state included one serious empirical problem. Data on family income distribution in CDB was expressed in terms of the number of families which had income in each of 15 categories: $0-$1,999; $2,000-$2,999; and so on up to $25,000-$49,999; $50,000+. To compute total income received by each class of families, we chose middle values of each income category. For the open-ended category, we followed a technique identified by the Census Office, U.S. Department of Commerce (1967); it involves estimation of the midpoint under the assumption of a log normal income distribution. Actual computation of the GINI coefficients followed the procedure set out by Bronfenbrenner (1971:41-75).

Mobility is an estimate of immigration into congressional district or state. Data is included in the CDB, and our measure is the fraction of the population which moved into the district from another state or country.

Age and race are, respectively, the fraction of all eligible voters in the district who are between 18 and 21 years of age and the fraction of all persons in the district who are white.

Contests and Candidates

The survey of campaign practices in Section V includes all 435 congressional districts and the 33 states which had Senate elections. However, for the analysis of Section VI, several congressional districts were excluded from the data set. This occurred because House elections pose a particular problem: in a number of contests one candidate ran uncontested in the general election. Because of biases that these elections would introduce, we included only those contests for which the winning candidate received less than 90 percent of the popular vote. This procedure excluded 52 districts.

A second problem results from contests in which there are more than two major contenders for a seat. No simple rule permits pairwise comparisons in multicandidate contests. As a consequence, we included information for only the winning candidate and the best losing candidate, defined by fractions of the vote received by each.

Party affiliations generally hold in our analysis. However, there are instances in which either both major parties did not field a candidate or the winning or best losing candidate was from a third party. For those few contests not excluded by the 90 percent rule we adopted the convention of classifying candidates as either Democrats or "Republicans," where the latter group included a few independents or third-party candidates. Further, candidates backed by both major parties were classified by their voting record; they were uniformly Democrats.

NOTES

1. Models of successful political resource allocation are made especially complex by possible variation in candidate and party outcome preferences. For candidates, three major alternatives have emerged from work on the theory of voting: (a) maximum number of votes, (b) maximum plurality, and (c) minimum vote necessary for election (Downs, 1957; Riker, 1962; Hinich and Ordeshook, 1970). These are the major preferred outcomes but do not exhaust the list of meaningful candidate campaign objectives. Elections are not necessarily zero sum contests in which what one candidate wins the other loses. The following are also reasonable candidate objectives: (d) increase the positive deviation from long-term or "normal" vote, (e) minimize, in conjunction with one's opponent, the third-party vote, (f) serve as a "sacrificial lamb" for one's party, and (g) erode the opposition's plurality in anticipation of future elections (Coleman, 1969; Davis et al., 1970; Ordeshook, 1971; Stigler, 1972; Wittman, 1973; Schlesinger, 1975).

Moreover, political parties have preferred campaign outcomes that may be at odds with candidate preferences. On this point, the literature suggests three major objectives for national party organizations: (a) maximum national vote, (b) maximum number of seats in the national legislative body, and (c) minimum number of votes for a working majority. Again, these zero sum alternatives do not exhaust the set of possible party objectives. Other objectives include (d) minimizing the expected cost per vote, (e) maximizing the national two-party vote (raising barriers to the entry of third parties), (f) maximizing the number of "safe" seats for long-term gains, (g) eroding pluralities in the "safe" districts of the opposition party, and (h) increasing the average positive deviation from the "normal" vote (Downs, 1957; Riker, 1962; Stokes, 1966; Buchanan, 1968; Coleman, 1969; Davis et al., 1970; Hinich and Ordeshook, 1970; Lindeen, 1970; Shubik, 1970; Tullock, 1970; Frey and Garbers, 1971; Ordeshook, 1971; Stigler, 1972; Wittman, 1973).

2. The 1972 congressional elections partially support this contention. Average fund raising, the difference between cash on hand at the beginning of the reporting period and total expenditures, for House and Senate candidates is as follows:

AVERAGE FUND RAISING ($1,000)

	Total	*Incumbents*	*Nonincumbents*	*Winners*	*Losers*
House:					
Democrats	40.1	41.3	38.5	35.2	45.2
Republicans	41.0	55.9	29.1	43.0	39.9
Total	40.5	47.8	33.3	38.4	42.2
Senate:					
Democrats	293.4	322.1	282.7	340.4	249.3
Republicans	394.7	417.5	373.2	530.4	250.5
Total	344.1	383.2	320.2	438.3	249.9

In Senate contests, Republicans are clearly superior fund raisers; Democrats were comparable to Republican candidates only in the case of losing candidates. House contests yield mixed results. Republicans raised more funds in the case of incumbent and winning candidates; Democratic efforts were more successful in the cases of nonincumbents and losing candidates. Overall, Republican candidates acquired 2.2 percent more than Democrats in the House and 34.5 percent more in the Senate.

An interesting subgroup in the House consists of nonincumbent winning candidates; the 26 Democrats and 44 Republicans in this category started their campaigns with only \$3,000 to \$5,000 and managed to raise over \$100,000 during the course of their campaigns, compared with an average of \$42,000 for all House candidates. Democrats were able to raise about 6.7 percent more funds than Republicans (\$113,000 compared with \$104,800).

3. For congressional districts the simple relationship between turnout and per capita income is:

$$\text{Turnout} = 0.268 + \underset{(0.00007)}{0.00079^*}\ \text{Income} \qquad R^2 = 0.208$$

The estimated coefficient on per capita income is significant at the 0.01 level of confidence. In alternative, and more complete, specifications of a model of voter turnout—which included income distribution, immigration, age, urban-rural differences, etc.—the coefficient on income remained positive and statistically significant, and values ranged from 0.0005 to 0.0008. Apparently this relationship does not hold at the state level (Zinser and Dawson, 1975).

4. The choice of five demographic variables for inclusion in our model follows from the review of available literature (Section III) and our own analysis of possible relationships. In addition to these five, several variables were investigated but then discarded due either to substantial collinearity with other variables or to a lack of statistical significance in estimated regression equations. Excluded variables include several measures of rural-urban district differences, district unemployment rates, and alternate measures of income inequality.

5. Much of the basic information in this brief description of the 1972 national elections is drawn from the Congressional Quarterly Almanac (1972:1010-1037).

6. For a more complete discussion of the law and an excellent analysis of its legislative history, see Berry and Goldman (1973). For a discussion of the 1974 amendments to this law, see Adamany and Agree (1975).

7. The Appendix includes an explanation of variables included in our analysis. "Republicans" includes several independent or third-party candidates.

REFERENCES

ADAMANY, D.W. (1969). Financing politics: Recent Wisconsin elections. Madison: University of Wisconsin Press.

——— (1972). Campaign finance in America. North Scituate, Mass.: Duxbury.

ADAMANY, D.W., and AGREE, G. (1975). "Election campaign financing: The 1974 reforms." Political Science Quarterly, (Summer):201-220.

ALEXANDER, H.E. (1966). "Broadcasting and politics." Pp. 81-104 in M.K. Jennings and L.H. Zeigler (eds.), The electoral process. Englewood Cliffs, N.J.: Prentice-Hall.

American Institute for Political Communication (1967). The new methodology: A study of political strategy and tactics. Washington, D.C.: Author.

ANDERSON, W. (1970). Campaigns: Cases in political conflict. Pacific Palisades, Calif.: Goodyear Publishing Company.

BERRY, J.M., and GOLDMAN, J. (1973). "Congress and public policy: A study of the Federal Election Campaign Act of 1971." Harvard Journal on Legislation, (February): 331-365.

BLACK, G.S. (1975). "A rational choice analysis of alternative party scenarios." Paper presented at the 1975 Annual Meeting of the American Political Science Association, San Francisco.

BLUMLER, J.G., and McQUAIL, D. (1969). Television in politics. Chicago: University of Chicago Press.

BONE, H.A. (1958). Party committees and national politics. Seattle: University of Washington Press.

BRONFENBRENNER, M. (1971). Income distribution theory. Chicago: Aldine-Atherton.

BUCHANAN, J.M. (1968). "Democracy and duopoly: A comparison of analytical models." American Economic Review, (May):322-331.

BULLITT, S. (1961). To be a politician. Garden City, N.Y.: Doubleday.

CLAPP, C.L. (1963). The Congressman: His work as he sees it. Washington, D.C.: Brookings Institution.

COLEMAN, J.S. (1969). "Beyond Pareto optimality." Pp. 415-439 in S. Morgenhesser, P. Suppes, and M. White (eds.), Philosophy, science and method. New York: St. Martin's.

Common Cause (1972). Congressional campaign finances. Washington, D.C.: Author.

Congressional Quarterly (1972). Almanac (92nd Congress, 2nd Session). Washington, D.C.: Author.

COTTER, C.P., and HENNESSY, B.C. (1964). Politics without power: The national party committees. New York: Atherton.

COTTIN, J; GORLASS, A.J.; and GREGORY, N. (1972). "Democratic National Committee." Pp. 225-259 in J.G. Smith (ed.), Political brokers: Money, organizations, power and people. New York: Liveright.

CROTTY, W.J. (1968). "The party organization and its activities." Pp. 247-306 (especially pp. 277-286) in W.J. Crotty (ed.), Approaches to the study of party organizations. Boston: Allyn and Bacon.

CUTRIGHT, P., and ROSSI, P. (1958). "Grass roots politicians and the vote." American Sociological Review, 23:171-179.

DAVIS, O.A.; HINICH, M.J.; and ORDESHOOK, P.C. (1970). "An expository development of a mathematical model of the electoral process." American Political Science Review, (June):426-448.

DAWSON, P.A., and ZINSER, J.E. (1971). "Broadcast expenditures and electoral outcomes in the 1970 congressional elections." Public Opinion Quarterly, (Fall):398-402.

DOWNS, A. (1957). An economic theory of democracy. New York: Harper.

ERIKSON, R.S. (1971a). "The advantage of incumbency in congressional elections." Policy, (Spring):395-405.

--- (1971b). "The electoral impact of congressional roll call voting." American Political Science Review, (December):1018-1032.

EULAU, H.; ZISK, B.H.; and PREWITT, K. (1966). "Latent partisanship in non-partisan elections." Pp. 208-237 in M.K. Jennings and L.H. Zeigler (eds.), The electoral process. Englewood Cliffs, N.J.: Prentice-Hall.

FISHEL, J. (1973). Party and opposition: Congressional challengers in American politics. New York: David McKay.

FRASER, J. (1972). "Why do high income people participate more in politics?–The wrong answers." Public Choice, (Fall):115-118.

FREY, B.S. (1971). "Why do high income people participate more in politics?" Public Choice, (Fall):101-105.

FREY, B., and GARBERS, H. (1971). "Politico-econometrics–On estimation in political economy." Political Studies, 19:316-320.

FROMAN, L.A. (1966). "A realistic approach to campaign strategies and tactics." Pp. 1-20 in M.K. Jennings and L.H. Zeigler (eds.), The electoral process. Englewood Cliffs, N.J.: Prentice-Hall.

GLASS, A.J. (1972). "National Republican congressional committee." Pp. 167-199 in J.G. Smith (ed.), Political brokers: Money, organizations, power and people. New York: Liveright.

HEARD, A. (1960). The costs of democracy. Chapel Hill: University of North Carolina Press.

HINCKLEY, B. (1970). "Incumbency and the presidential vote in Senate elections: Defining parameters of subpresidential voting." American Political Science Review, (December):836-842.

HINICH, M., and ORDESHOOK, P. (1970). "Plurality maximization versus vote maximization: A spatial analysis with variable participation." American Political Science Review, (September):772-791.

HUCKSHORN, R.J., and SPENCER, R.C. (1971). The politics of defeat. Amherst: University of Massachusetts Press.

HUTCHINSON, R. (ed., 1963). Finley Peter Dunne: Mr. Dooley on ivrything and ivrybody. New York: Dover.

JENNINGS, M.K., and ZEIGLER, L.H. (1966). "Electoral strategies and voting patterns in a Southern congressional district." Pp. 122-138 in M.K. Jennings and L.H. Zeigler (eds.), The electoral process. Englewood Cliffs, N.J.: Prentice-Hall.

JONES, C.O. (1962). "A suggested scheme for classifying congressional campaigns." Public Opinion Quarterly, (Spring):126-132.

--- (1966). "The role of the campaign in congressional politics." Pp. 21-41 in M.K. Jennings and L.H. Zeigler (eds.), The electoral process. Englewood Cliffs, N.J.: Prentice-Hall.

--- (1967). Every second year. Washington, D.C.: Brookings Institution.

KATZ, D., and ELDERSVELD, S.J. (1961). "The impact of local party activity upon the electorate." Public Opinion Quarterly, 25:1-24.

KATZ, R.S. (1973a). "The attribution of variance in electoral returns: An alternative measurement technique." American Political Science Review, (September):817-828.

--- (1973b). "Rejoinder to comment by Donald E. Stokes." American Political Science Review, (September):832-834.

KESSEL, J.H. (1966). "A game theory analysis of campaign strategy." Pp. 290-304 in M.K. Jennings and L.H. Zeigler (eds.), The electoral process. Englewood Cliffs, N.J.: Prentice-Hall.

KEY, V.O., Jr. (1964). Politics, parties and pressure groups. New York: Thomas Y. Crowell.

KINGDON, J.W. (1968). Candidates for office: Beliefs and strategies. New York: Random House.

KOSTROSKI, W.L. (1973). "Party and incumbency in postwar senate elections." American Political Science Review, (December):1213-1234.

KRAMER, G.H. (1970). "The effects of precinct-level canvassing on voter behavior." Public Opinion Quarterly, 34:560-572.

--- (1971). "Short-term fluctuations in United States voting behavior, 1896-1964." American Political Science Review, (March):131-143.

KRAMER, G.H., LEPPER, S.J. (1972). "Congressional elections." Chap. 5 (pp. 256-284) in W.O. Aydelotte et al. (eds.), The dimensions of quantitative research in history. Princeton, N.J.: Princeton University Press.

LEUTHOLD, D.A. (1968). Electioneering in a democracy: Campaigns for Congress. New York: John Wiley.

LINDEEN, J.W. (1968). "An oligopoly model of political market structures." Public Choice, (Fall):31-37.

MacNEIL, R. (1972). "Candidate exposure in uncontrolled media." Pp. 302-311 in R. Agranoff (ed.), The new style in election campaigns. Boston: Holbrook.

MAYHEW, D.R. (1974). The electoral connection. New Haven, Conn: Yale University Press.

McCALLUM, R.B. (1955). "The study of psephology." Parliamentary Affairs, 8:508-513.

McCRACKEN, P.W. (1973). "The practice of political economy." American Economic Review, (May):168-171.

OKUN, A.M. (1973). "Comments on Stigler's paper." American Economic Review, (May):172-177.

ORDESHOOK, P.C. (1971). "Pareto optimality in electoral competition." American Political Science Review, (December):1141-1144.

REES, A.; KAUFMAN, H.; ELDERSVELD, S.J.; and FREIDEL, F. (1962). "The effect of economic conditions on congressional elections, 1946-1958." Review of Economics and Statistics, (November):458-465.

RIKER, W.H. (1962). The theory of political coalitions. New Haven, Conn.: Yale University Press.

SALOMA, J.S., III, and SONTAG, F.H. (1973). Parties: The real opportunity for effective citizen politics. New York: Random House-Vintage.

SCHLESINGER, J.A. (1966). Ambition and politics: Political careers in the United States. Chicago: Rand McNally.

--- (1975). "The primary goals of political parties: A clarification of positive theory." American Political Science Review, (September):840-849.

SCHOENBERGER, R.A. (1969). "Campaign strategy and party loyalty: the electoral relevance of candidate decision-making in the 1964 congressional elections." American Political Science Review, 63:515-520.

SHARP, H. (1955). "Migration and voting behavior in a metropolitan community." Public Opinion Quarterly, (Summer):206-209.

SHEINKOPF, K.G., and O'KEEFE, M.T. (1973). "Political advertising and the 1972 campaign: A communication failure." Unpublished paper prepared for delivery to the Political Communication Session of the International Communication Association, Montreal, April 25-28.

SHUBIK, M. (1970). "Voting, or a price system in a competitive market structure." American Political Science Review, (March):179-181.

STERN, P.M. (1973). The rape of the taxpayer. New York: Random House.

STIGLER, G.J. (1972). "Economic competition and political competition." Public Choice, (Fall):91-106.

--- (1973). "General economic conditions and national elections." American Economic Review, (May):160-167.

STOKES, D.E. (1966). "Spatial models of party competition." In A. Campbell, P. Converse, W. Miller, and D. Stokes (eds.), Elections and the political order. New York: John Wiley.

--- (1967). "Parties and the nationalization of election forces." In W.N. Chambers and W.D. Burnham (eds.), The American party system. New York: Oxford University Press.

--- (1973). "Comment: On the measurement of electoral dynamics." American Political Science Review, (September):829-831.

TUFTE, E.R. (1975). "Determinants of the outcomes of midterm congressional elections." American Political Science Review, (September):812-826.

TULLOCK, G. (1970). "A simple algebraic logrolling model." American Economic Review, (June):419-426.

U.S. Department of Commerce, Bureau of the Census (1967). Trends in the income of families and of persons, 1947-1964 (Technical Paper No. 17). Washington, D.C.: U.S. Government Printing Office.

U.S. Department of Commerce, Office of the Secretary (1973). "Estimates of voting age population: July 1, 1972." Federal Register (July 11):18476-18477.

U.S. Senate, Committee on Commerce (1973). Federal Election Campaign Act of 1973, Appendix A: Political broadcasting and cablecasting by individual candidates. Washington, D.C.: U.S. Government Printing Office.

WASBY, S. (1968). "National party contributions to non-incumbent candidates: The Democrats in 1964." Social Science Quarterly, (March):573-585.

WITTMAN, D.A. (1973). "Parties as utility maximizers." American Political Science Review, (June):490-498.

WOLFINGER, R.E. (1963). "The influence of precinct work on voting behavior." Public Opinion Quarterly, 27:387-398.

WOLFINGER, R.E., and HEIFETZ, J. (1965). "Safe seats, seniority, and power in congress." American Political Science Review, (June):337-349.

ZINSER, J.E., and DAWSON, P.A. (1975). "Campaign behavior and voter turnout." Unpublished manuscript, Oberlin College.

Chapter 5

THE ITALIAN COMMUNIST PARTY AND ELECTIONS: THE NAME OF THE GAME IS "COMPROMISE"

ALASTAIR DAVIDSON

I. INTRODUCTION: THE RECENT SUCCESSES OF THE ITALIAN COMMUNISTS

In the administrative and regional elections of 1975, the Italian Communist party or Partito Comunista Italiano (PCI) again increased its share of the vote. (See Table 1.) Other left-wing parties, which have been allies of the Communists in the past or could become allies, also increased their share of the vote. On the other hand, the Christian Democratic party or Democrazia Cristiana (DC), which has ruled Italy since 1948, lost significantly in support. No longer does it seem impossible for the PCI to replace it as the party with the greatest support at elections. Whereas in the national elections of 1972 the PCI could only muster 28.3 percent of the votes against the DC's 38.4 percent, in the recent regional elections the former won 33.4 percent of the vote and the latter only 35.3 percent. Again, Communist projections of the probable nationwide support on the basis of both regional and administrative elections give 32.4 percent to themselves and 35.5 percent to the DC. While neither party could rule by themselves, even were their most sanguine hopes fulfilled,

AUTHOR'S NOTE: I wish to express special thanks to Joan Kirsop for her able research assistance.

Table 1

The Results in 15 Regions

	Regional 1970			*Political 1972*		*Regional 1975*		
	Votes	*%*	*Seats*	*Votes*	*%*	*Votes*	*%*	*Seats*
PCI	7,586,983	27.9	200	8,121,117	28.3	10,149,135	33.4	247
PSIUP	878,697	3.2	16	536,341	1.9	–	–	–
PDUP	–	–	–	192,389	0.7	411,725	1.4	8
PSI	2,837,451	10.4	67	2,798,781	9.8	3,636,647	12.0	82
PSDI	1,897,034	7.0	41	1,498,846	5.2	1,700,983	5.6	36
PRI	787,011	2.9	18	825,155	2.9	961,016	3.2	19
DC	10,303,236	37.9	287	11,017,525	38.4	10,707,682	35.3	277
PLI	1,290,715	4.7	27	1,131,047	3.9	749,749	2.5	11
PDIUM	195,373	0.7	2	2,316,757	8.1	–	–	–
MSI	1,425,807	5.2	32			1,951,011	6.4	40
Various	29,482	0.1	–	220,085	0.8	70,789	0.2	–
TOTAL	27,231,789	100.0	690	28,658,043	100.0	30,338,737	100.0	720

The Results in 86 Provinces

	Provincial 1970			*Political 1972*		*Provincial 1975*		
	Votes	*%*	*Seats*	*Votes*	*%*	*Votes*	*%*	*Seats*
PCI	7,400,418	26.7	701	7,975,941	27.2	10,101,761	32.7	860
PSIUP	958,296	3.5	73	595,128	2	–	–	–
PDUP	–	–	–	187,116	0.6	136,025	0.5	4
PC m/1	4,058	–	–	89,815	0.3	–	–	–
MP1	–	–	–	110,987	0.4	–	–	–
PSI	3,061,332	11.1	274	2,893,876	9.9	3,933,700	12.7	330
PSDI	2,019,366	7.3	177	1,522,738	5.2	1,800,127	5.8	142
PRI	823,869	3	60	816,054	2.8	1,048,868	3.4	73
DC	10,337,715	37.3	1,023	11,538,796	39.4	10,732,902	34.8	946
PLI	1,353,292	4.9	101	1,142,864	3.9	846,841	2.7	43
MSI	1,657,897	6	139	2,410,519	8.2	2,093,237	6.8	161
Various	98,682	0.4	7	29,628	0.1	177,216	0.7	6
TOTAL	27,714,925	100.0	2,555	29,313,462	100.0	30,878,687	100.0	2,565

PCI, Partito Comunista Italiano; PSIUP, Partito Socialista Italiano d'Unità Proletaria; PDUP, Partito Democratico Unità Proletaria; PC, Partito Comunista (Marxist-Leninist); MPL, Movimento Politico Lavoratori; PSI, Partito Socialista Italiano; PSDI, Partito Socialista Democratico Italiano; PRI, Partito Republicano Italiano; DC, Democrazia Cristiana; PLI, Partito Liberale Italiano; PDIUM, Partito Democratico di Unità Monarchica; MSI. Movimento Sociale Italiano (neofascists).

what is significant is the fact that the three main socialist parties—the PCI, the PSI (Partito Socialista Italiano), and the PDUP (Partito Democratico di Unità Proletaria)—together have won 47 percent of the vote in the 1975 elections. The goal of 51 percent is almost within the grasp of the Italian socialist parties.

What is more, the PCI and its potential partners on the left increased their vote throughout the country, while that of the DC fell in practically all regions. (See Figure 1.) This is particularly important for Italian politics, since until these elections there had been an apparent deadlock, with some areas unshakably in favor of the DC (Friuli-Venezia Giulia) and others unshakably in favor of the PCI (Emilia-Romagna). The pattern of Communist gains in 1975 suggests that the immobility of Italian electoral politics has at last been shaken and that its style could well change in the future as the Communists break out of their ghetto and finally win permanent footholds in the area which they, and many other Italians, have long considered crucially important in deciding who will rule Italy. In the Mezzogiorno, or Italy's South—to some her glory, to most her cross—the PCI had been faring badly since 1958. After doubling the party's share of the vote in the South from 10.2 percent in 1946 to 22.2 percent in 1958, the PCI stagnated in the early sixties, obtaining 24.1 percent of the Southern vote at both the 1963 and 1968 legislative elections, when its national average had reached 27 percent by 1968, and falling to 23.3 percent in the regional elections of 1970 at which the national average for the PCI was 27.9 percent (Tarrow, 1972:95-97). By 1972 the South not only seemed to be a bastion of conservatism but also threatened to become the "drill-square" of the fascist reaction, as Antonio Gramsci had feared nearly 50 years ago, when he elaborated the first PCI policies toward the South. The fascist MSI (Movimento Sociale Italiano) received considerable support in the area. This trend seems to have stopped in the 1975 regional election and been reversed in favor of the PCI and the other socialist parties. The "black vote" has fallen throughout Italy.

Similarly, the seemingly impregnable bastions of the DC in the Northeast appear to have finally been breached, even if it is still only a matter of the first step. This trend could already be seen at the September 1973 elections for three regions which function under special statute and which have long been considered DC preserves. In the elections the PCI made slight but indicative improvements, increasing the number of seats it held from 3 to 5 in Trentino-

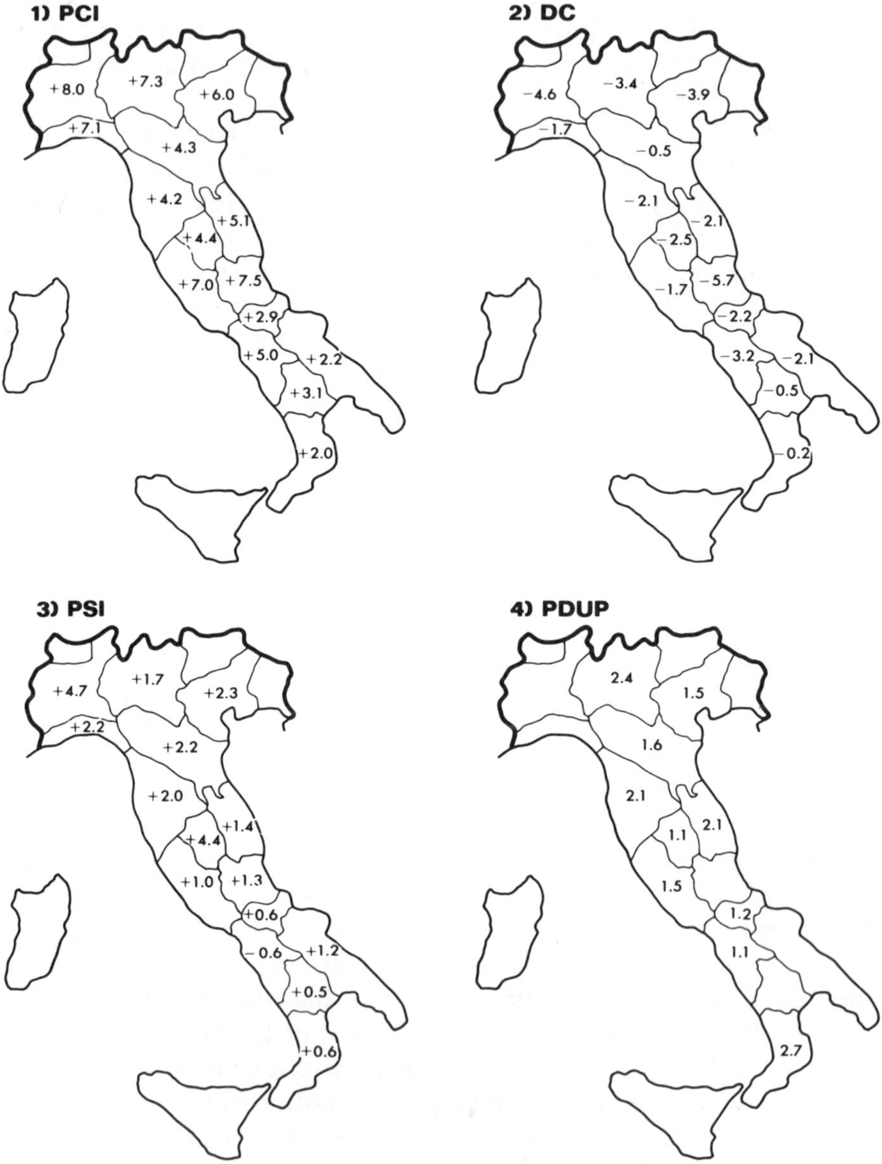

Figure 1: PERCENT INCREASE AND DECREASE IN VOTE BY REGIONS

Table 2. PCI SUPPORT AT NATIONWIDE LEGISLATIVE ELECTIONS

			Seats	
	Votes	*%*	*House of Deputies*	*Senate*
1948	8,136,637	31	183	72[1]
1953	6,120,709	22.7	143	51
1958	6,704,706	22.7	140	59
1963	7,767,601	25.3	159	85
1968	8,557,077	26.9	177	101[2]
1972	9,085,927	27.2	179	91[2]

1. In these elections the PCI and the PSI ran on a joint list as The Democratic People's Front for Freedom, Peace, and Work.
2. In these two elections the PCI ran on a "unitary" list with the PSIUP (Italian Socialist Party of Proletarian Unity) and the Independent Left.

Alto-Adige, from 12 to 13 in Friuli-Venezia Giulia, and holding its seats in Valle d'Aosta in the face of the national trend toward the right in 1972-1973 (Almanacco PCI, 1975:213, 218, 219).

In sum, the recent regional and administrative elections show that the gradual increase in popular support at elections for the PCI since 1946 is continuing, but that in 1975 it seems to have taken a qualitative leap in favor of the PCI after a long period in which the marginal gains in support did not really alter the political situation in Italy. (See Table 2.)

II. CAUSES OF ELECTORAL SUCCESS

What explains the continued increase in support for Italian communism, and, more importantly, how has it made the qualitative leap bringing it out of the ghetto and onto the national scene as a potential governing party? One reason is that Italy has been in economic, social, and political crisis since 1972. In 1976 life is "really difficult" for the average Italian. After a deficit in the balance of payments of 5,300 billion lire in 1974, Italy expected—despite its efforts to combat this deficit—a further deficit of 2,900 billion lire in 1975.[1] The consequent runaway inflation has forced consumer items up in cost: Italy has the dubious honor—in a list comprising Canada, the United States, Japan, France, West Germany, and England—of having had the greatest increase in prices since 1959, and especially since 1973. Between August 1973 and August 1974 the cost of consumer items for a family rose 21 percent. With people less able to spend, there have been cutbacks in production (14 percent between January and March 1975) and massive increases in unemployment.

In the cities the indices of crisis are obvious. Public transport frequently does not run; often there is no light or water (or the repairmen to fix them); mail is not delivered; money is so scarce that change is sometimes in the form of sweets. So bad has sanitation become and so dirty are the streets that cholera epidemics have occurred for the first time in decades. Hepatitis is rife. The police are increasingly unable to control the rampant, often parapolitical, criminal activities.

Italy's crisis is part of the larger worldwide crisis, but because of her dependence on importation of energy sources and her dependence on the rest of Europe as importers of her surplus labor, the crisis in Italy is much more extreme than elsewhere. However, her problems are also owed in considerable measure to the past misgovernment and present incompetence of the DC-led coalitions. The DC in its present form is greatly discredited. Gian Carlo Pajetta was not stating only the Communist position to the *New York Times* (March 13, 1975), when he wrote: "What is certain today is that it is becoming increasingly difficult for things to continue as they are—as they have been, molded by thirty years of a Christian Democratic monopoly of power.

"The economic crisis in Italy is aggravated by the survival of outdated social structures and the burden of vast parasitic and speculative interests. To these old ills, we must add the more recent, but by no means rational or modern, structures of a patronage-ridden state capitalism that is sinking (despite the efforts of its workers and technicians, which have produced many positive results) deeper and deeper into inefficiency, waste, and corruption because of the incompetence of a group of bosses placed in command, largely for their connection with Christian Democratic party. The victims are not just the workers, threatened with joblessness, or the farmers, living in a countryside devastated by the emigration of millions of its inhabitants in past years. Small and medium-sized businessmen are also paying the cost of the crisis, of the long-standing mismanagement of economic and social affairs and the inefficiency of the state machine."

Indeed, even big business has been pushed by the crisis to favor the PCI. In July 1974 a 36-page document emanating from a Fiat research office was leaked to the press. Its contents were so scandalous that Fiat had to deny responsibility. The document affirmed inter alia that "The PCI is the only Italian political force capable of assuming the responsibilities of government at a moment of grave crisis" (Padovani, 1974a:98).

The feeling of grievance in many sectors is compounded by the fact that the crisis came after the long and unprecedented period of well-being for wide sectors of the Italian community in 1960-1970. This "economic miracle" has clearly ended; many sections of the community have protested and are protesting in strikes and demonstrations and through the media. All the "antisystem" parties have benefited from this feeling. For example, in the first stage of the crisis the neofascists won considerable electoral support and have continued to encourage both confrontations with the left and acts of terrorism. More recently, support for their parties and organizations has dwindled as fascist terrorist outrages became a feature of life. As Table 1 and Figure 1 show, the PSI has also increased its support.

Without doubt the present crisis has facilitated and expedited Communist gains, but much more significant in explaining the PCI's present success in breaking out of its ghetto is its long-term and short-term political strategy. This strategy—or something very similar—is being followed by the other Italian socialist parties as well (*Rinascita,* March 14, 1975). The Communists have dubbed their version the "historical compromise." They trace its origins back 40 years but claim that it constitutes a new type of electoral politics. Given PCI success in 1975, an understanding of the nature of this new type of electoral politics is of utmost importance for political systems whose cornerstone is the belief that in conditions of affluence the majority of electors will not choose communism.[2]

III. THE EVOLUTION OF THE THEORY OF ITALIAN COMMUNISM

Under its first two leaders the PCI was intransigently committed to the need for violent revolutionary overthrow of the existing "bourgeois" state, together with the destruction of its institutions, and its replacement by a new form of socialist state: a soviet or conciliar system. Most of its members believed that the passage to a socialist society could be achieved in no other way and hesitated to regard as real allies those parties which disagreed, no matter how much they professed to be socialist. Even this sect of true believers was forced by the middle thirties to come to terms with the intractable world: to escape the persecution of fascism and to constitute a viable resistance to its tyranny, they were forced first into alliances with their erstwhile enemies, the Socialists, and then to work with men who were sometimes not even socialists. Accordingly, in 1934 the Communist leader, Palmiro Togliatti, gave up the intransigency of his predecessor and after 1935 deliberately encouraged his followers to play down the goal of "revolution" (Davidson, 1965:342-345). Ten years of conciliatory policies of working with Socialists, Christian Democrats, and Liberals facilitated the acceptance by the PCI of the "Salerno turn," which Togliatti proposed in 1944 and which constituted the formal origin of present PCI policy (Gruppi, 1975). Having returned to Allied-occupied Salerno from exile in the Soviet Union, Togliatti not only proposed that the PCI act as heir to the Risorgimento but also argued that only in democratic coalition with other progressive forces could the war be won and the basis laid for the postwar social and political order in Italy (Togliatti, 1958:98). The enforced policy of working with other parties had become a positive policy to be applied when wartime conditions no longer existed. The reasons were simple: there had been a massive increase in support for Italian communism in 1943-1944, and it did seem possible that the PCI might accede to power without a fight once the war was over. On the other hand, it would have been foolhardy to risk a violent revolution without majority support, given the presence of Allied troops in Italy who could easily have crushed any Communist government.

Even to the ever cautious Togliatti prospects must have seemed bright in 1945-1946. There was a massive increase in PCI membership to 1,776,013 in 1946. There was a widespread feeling in Italy that men of goodwill could work together to create a new, more just social order for Italy. In 1946 the PCI, because of this atmosphere and the electoral support it received in the elections for the Constituent Assembly, obtained five portfolios.[3] Communist and socialist influence was clear in the postwar Italian constitution, which could form the constitutional basis for a socialist state, although it has never been used in this sense. So in 1947 Togliatti extended the Salerno policy into a general strategy for making a socialist revolution in Italy: "International experience tells us that, given the present conditions of the class struggle in the world, the working class can find new roads toward socialism, namely to develop democracy to its extreme limit, which is precisely the same as socialism—roads different from those, for example, followed by the working class of the Soviet Union" (Galli, 1964:305).

The problem was whether he could convince the average Italian voter—especially the massive and timorous Italian middle class—that he really believed in and intended to make a socialist revolution only with majority support. By 1947 this was already becoming more and more difficult. Immediate fears of a Communist takeover had died down, but so had the euphoria of the "Resistance." The real power interests of the postwar world were already looming solidly through the mists of idealistic dreams of nations united in peace and harmony. The Cold War had started and Christian Democracy, backed by the United States, was beginning a determined anti-Communist bogey campaign in Italy. The main theme in this campaign was that the PCI was merely a tool of the U.S.S.R.'s international campaign of conquest and armed imposition of communism regardless of majority wishes. The DC argued that no one should be deceived by the sheep's clothing of commitment to democracy worn by the erstwhile members of the Communist International. It was a difficult charge for the PCI to rebut convincingly in 1947, and it became more difficult as each year went by. The PCI had been formally part of the Communist International between 1921 and 1943 and had been obliged to obey directions coming from Moscow. It had formally subscribed to the political theories of V.I. Lenin, which proposed that "a revolution could be made where the population already wanted one by a dedicated group of revolutionaries going out and propagandising marxist theory among the masses, who would, once the truth was told them, become revolutionaries knowing where the main blow should be landed; that it would have to involve a direct violent assault on the bourgeois State and its structures (which could not be utilised in the final analysis, for the advancement of socialism); and, finally, that the Communist party would have to work alone, independent of, and in hostility to, all other parties which professed the same goals as it did but which would not merge with it. So the Communist party would have to be an 'anti-system' party" (Davidson, 1969:5-6).[4] Many of its leaders, including Togliatti, had spent most of the thirties and the war in Russia. Worst of all, the PCI became one of the two Western parties (the other was the French Communist party) to join the Communist Information Bureau in 1947. Despite the Cominform's lip service to democratic ways to socialism, it was set up at Stalin's behest to coordinate all Communist activities in the interest of the U.S.S.R. In particular, member parties were called upon to subordinate all domestic policies to the needs of the Communist "peace-loving" bloc in the Cold War. After 1947 the Cominform coordinated or endorsed the seizure of power by Communists in Czechslovakia in 1948 and the crushing of all rebellions, popular or otherwise, throughout the Communist bloc. The years 1948-1952 were times of trumped-up treason trials, the Berlin blockade, the expulsion of Yugoslavia from the Communist camp, and the repression of revolt in Poland.

In the face of all these past and present associations, it was difficult for the PCI to achieve credibility. Moreover, it really was torn between its associations and its new democratic policies. Even Communists now admit that, while many of the rank and file were "aware that the defence of democratic liberties, that the use of democratic institutions was indispensable and just," they also "awaited a . . . sort of X hour, when they would suddenly pass to other objectives and other methods of struggle" (Gruppi, 1975:123). How quick and ready they were to resort to armed rising was made clear when there was a massive uprising of Communists after an assassination attempt on Togliatti on July 14, 1948. It took all their leaders' skill to defuse the situation. Moreover, many were loath to give up their support of the U.S.S.R. while there was at least half-truth in the Cominform's claim that every policy should be subordinate to that of fighting for peace. The Sixth Party Congress of 1948, which introduced the notion of "an Italian way to socialism," also affirmed that "the main enemy against whom we must direct our blows are the most reactionary forces of capitalism and reborn imperialism." The "Italian way" was thus reduced merely to taking into consideration "certain peculiarities" of Italy.

The results of the 1948 elections, which the DC fought on a platform of anticommunism, made clear that the PCI would not achieve credibility for its "Italian way" if it continued to hedge its bets as it had. It would have to prove that it had freed itself from the tutelage of the U.S.S.R. and no longer subscribed to Leninism. In this connection it is important to note that the PCI had been an undisciplined member of the Comintern for at least half its life, that it never undividedly adopted Leninism as defined above, that

Togliatti and other leaders were unusually independent even while in the U.S.S.R., and that, from its foundation, the Cominform had recognized these realities and had condemned the "opportunism" of PCI policies. Moreover, Luigi Longo had not replied to this condemnation in the craven fashion of the French Communist party delegate to the Cominform (Spriano, 1967-1970; Reale, 1970). It does not seem worthwhile to continue to deny the bona fides of Togliatti in his commitment to the "Italian way" even in 1948. At worst he tried to reconcile conflicting domestic and foreign policy issues in a delicate business of balancing institutional, organizational, and political pressures from all sides. Often he just, as was his wont, did nothing or, as was less characteristic, backtracked.

In 1948 the PCI/PSI vote had fallen to 31 percent from 39.7 percent in 1946. At the same time the DC vote rose from 35 percent to 48.8 percent. The PCI lost all its cabinet positions, and so did the PSI. Drawing its own conclusions, the PSI withdrew from the electoral coalition, and the PCI was confined to a ghetto. Although it increased its vote in 1953, what was important was that it still could not make the alliances that it considered all-important to its policy.[5]

Only in 1955-1956 did Togliatti begin the process of emancipating his party from the U.S.S.R. in a fashion which hostile observers were forced to acknowledge. Togliatti availed himself of the de-Stalinization campaign started by N.S. Khrushchev at the Twentieth CPSU Congress and declared a formal independence from the U.S.S.R. Where Khrushchev had blamed the failures of the U.S.S.R. on Stalin, Togliatti declared that "it seems to us that undoubtedly Stalin's errors were tied in with an excessive increase in the bureaucratic apparatus in Soviet economic and political life." He affirmed in indirect consequence: "the Soviet model cannot and must not any longer be obligatory. . . . The whole system becomes polycentric, and even in the Communist movement itself we cannot speak of a single guide but rather of a progress which is achieved by following paths which are often different" (*Nuovi Argomenti,* June 16, 1956). The skeptics had to wait some years for further evidence that the PCI was emancipating itself from the Soviet model. In 1960 the PCI took up positions against the Chinese in the Sino-Soviet dispute, although the Chinese were posing as defenders of Leninist orthodoxy. A year later, the PCI demanded complete autonomy from international regulation in deciding its own policy and organization. Moreover, in

1962 both Togliatti and Longo, his heir apparent as PCI secretary, said that Lenin's work no longer provided in any way a guide for party action. Indeed, Togliatti went further: he said in February 1962, "We have no experience whatever of how we can and should lead the struggle for socialism in a regime of advanced capitalism. . . . There do not even exist implicit indications in the classics of our doctrine" (Galli, 1962:127, 135; Bianco, 1967:117, 120).

Many critics of the PCI were not initially convinced, but such declarations of independent opinion by the PCI made it increasingly difficult to maintain that the party took orders from Moscow. Instead, the critics shifted the stress of their argument to the view that the institutions and the personnel of the PCI prevented its real commitment to a democratic road to socialism. To combat this, the PCI had to get rid of its Leninism both as an explicit guide to action and as the organizational system of traditional democratic centralism. It found this very difficult to do, and was only able to achieve these necessary objectives in the later 1960s.

Leninism had too long been *the* theory of the party's militants for it to be too hastily and explicitly discarded. Up until 1964 the PCI still explicitly remained a Leninist party. But who was prepared to risk joining the Communists in an alliance and to form a coalition government if the first thing a Leninist party proposed to do once in power was to install a dictatorship of the proletariat? Ignazio Silone, a former Communist, wrote:

> Since there has been no genuine ideological revision, I do not believe in the democratisation of Communism. Its alleged liberalisation is, in the first place, a matter of tactics or perhaps not even of that, but only a try-out tactic. [Schmid, 1966]

Only after its 10th Congress in 1962 did the PCI start adopting a new ideological system, that of Gramscian Marxism. Gramsci's *Prison Notebooks,* which supposedly contained his views of how a revolution could be made in conditions of advanced capitalism, had been published since the war by Einaudi after careful editing by the PCI. The Gramscian Marxism which the party first adopted thus filtered through to the party in garbled form via Togliatti in the fifties. Togliatti's real contribution was thus to make the first hole in the massive Leninist ideological dyke. By the early sixties Gramsci's work was widely read by party members, but it was the hybrid

"Leninist" Gramsci fostered by the PCI at the first conference of Gramscian studies in 1958, according to which Gramsci was the loyal developer of the little-studied Leninist theory of hegemony.

This conflation of Lenin's and Gramsci's theories had two effects. On the one hand, by securing the continuity from Lenin to Gramsci on a formal level, the party was able to placate its Leninists and maintain party unity to a considerable extent while in fact introducing a new non-Russian theory. It achieved this effect by successive redefinitions of Gramsci's theory to the point where he became "everybody's Gramsci" (*Giovane critica,* 1969, No. 21) and by a gradual discard of the equation of Lenin with Gramsci (White, 1971; Davidson, 1972). On the other hand, while the party continued to present Gramsci as the loyal continuer of Lenin's theory, critics of the PCI were still able to accuse the PCI of being committed to the Russian's theory and guilty of duplicity in its proposal to make a socialist revolution through existing institutions. So, while the 1966 constitution of the party stated that Gramsci's theory provided it with its guide to action, not until much later in the sixties did the critics really believe this.

Only in the seventies did the anti-Communist bogey used to such effect by the DC in the sixties finally fail to work. It became generally recognized by all but the diehards that the PCI had emancipated itself from Russian tutelage both in theory and in practice. The PCI could finally set out to make its socialist revolution by democratic means.

IV. GRAMSCIAN THEORY

The theoretical starting point for the party's activities was the Gramscian theory that it had developed by the second conference of Gramscian studies in 1967. At the core of the party's new theory was the belief that men make their own destinies and that there is no inevitability about history. A socialist revolution will not come, it will be made. Men would make the revolution once they accepted the ideology of revolution and not before. But in the PCI's interpretation Gramsci had argued that in hundreds of different ways the bourgeoisie of the West had secured an intellectual and moral hegemony over the people. It socialized and indoctrinated them with bourgeois values from the cradle to the grave. Thus the process of liberation involved first a vast reeducation to liberate the people from the bourgeois hegemony of values so that they could make a free choice about the sort of society they wanted; so that when presented with an alternative to capitalism, an alternative which Communists consider more rational and more likely to secure happiness for all, they will be able to perceive the real choice which is facing them. How, according to Gramsci, did a party go about breaking the bourgeois hegemony of values? First, it identified the inculcators of those values, and then it captured or converted or supplanted such inculcators. And the inculcators were the intellectuals—in modern parlance, the ideology makers. Then the institutional channels through which they worked to transmit their values were identified, captured, and restructured to work against the values of the system. This theory could obviously be interpreted in various ways, depending on the meaning attributed to "education." The PCI interpreted it primarily as meaning the establishment of Communist power in the mass media, the opinion-making organs, and the power structures of society generally. By a massive flow of countereducation the Communists could then gradually break the bourgeois hegemony, and, when faced with a true choice between going on under capitalism or changing to socialism, the populace would choose socialism because it was more rational.

Certain practical attitudes flowed from this view. First, it was preferable to have a plurality of ideas rather than a monopoly because the fewer the bourgeois ideas the tighter their control over minds. Thus democracy at all levels was of great value because it freed people from preconceptions by forcing them to cope with social problems. Second, any party which was progressive, that is, opposed to the established values, was an ally, as it was opposing further extension of the bourgeois hegemony even if it did so unwittingly. Third, since the process of conversion consisted of building up a counterconsensus among the people, the very transition to socialism could be consensual and not by conflict; and therefore no question would arise of a dictatorship of the proletariat against the bourgeoisie after the revolution. The change could come only after the vast majority of the populace had been converted to the more rational (socialist) system. The institutions traditional to the country would thus remain. Fourth, since Gramscian Marxism was concerned not with fundamental or metaphysical questions, but with making men conscious of their relationship with society and the best way of ordering society, it intended no totalitarian conformity to a single religion after the revolution had taken place. This was particularly important in Italy, where a modus vivendi had to be established with Roman Catholics, who usually believed that Marxism was atheism (Broadhead, 1972).

In sum, the PCI interpretation was one which put stress on providing education from above or capturing crucial institutions through top-level deals, alliances, and power games and, *without transforming the institutions,* using them to introduce the material and spiritual prerequisites for socialism. By 1966 Giorgio Amendola had become the major spokesman for this interpretation. So far did his belief in the possibility of deals at the top become that he was even prepared to advocate the dissolution of the PCI into a sort of progressive left front. Basically, the political goal associated with this line was that of establishing a left coalition government in Italy, and can be critically assessed as a "tendency towards reformism."

V. PCI STRATEGY PRIOR TO THE "HISTORICAL COMPROMISE"

Conditions were ripe for the acceptance of these "consensual" politics in the period when Gramsci was replacing Lenin as the party's somewhat bowdlerized Bible. Italy had experienced an "Economic Miracle," emerging from a poverty-stricken and rebellion-ridden history summed up in the two sayings—"Africa begins at Naples" and "Better to live one day like a bull than a lifetime like a steer"—into a condition of affluence characteristic of advanced capitalism. Whether the miracle was owed primarily to factors innate in the Italian economy or whether it was primarily a result of the stimulus of the European Common Market and more rational capitalist methods imported from overseas remains a matter for debate. However, it is certain that after the painstaking business of rebuilding the postwar Italy in the decade 1945-1955, Italy entered a period of economic boom and industrial expansion. Italy's expansion advanced posthaste until 1967, when the miracle started to end. The change in 1955-1967 was quite obvious. It started with the vast new factory complexes, which mushroomed everywhere, and the older ones, like Fiat, which expanded greatly. It was on the underpinning of a few of these vast industrial enterprises, sometimes state-owned, sometimes private (Agip, Olivetti, Fiat, and so on) that all the rest was erected. These companies were frequently international in their ramifications, and there was a vast amount of foreign capital invested in them. Consequently, to some extent their fortunes were bound up with the fortunes of international capital. On them, however, rested a host of smaller enterprises whose factories dotted Italy's landscape and penetrated farther and farther south each year. (The big companies did not at first waste much money on the South; investment there was more often by Southerners like Achille Lauro, who had controlling interests in Flotta Lauro.) The expansion of industry had two main effects. First, it resulted in a rapid urbanization of the former peasantry. This meant not only a mushroom growth in the cities and a consequent boom in the building industry but, to some extent, a solution to Italy's perennial problem of rural overpopulation. The drain of rural, and especially Southern rural, workers to the cities caused a constant migration pattern characterized by the yearly trip north to the industrial cities in the New Year and a return to the *paese* at Christmas. Not infrequently the women remained behind, but it is clear that more and more Southerners shifted to the North to seek factory work and settled permanently. Second, there was a rapid rise in the standard of living and a marked increase in wages. Italy became a place of the supermarket, the Alfa, and TV. All the chrome-plated monstrosities which constituted gadgetry and creature comfort sold very rapidly: washing-machines, refrigerators, even transistors.

Politically, the most significant development was the change in the DC from a party torn between service of God and Mammon, to the party of neocapitalism aspiring to regulate the consumer society so that it ran efficiently.

Overall, much of the old Italy remained even in 1968. The consumer well-being was not matched by a social and spiritual well-being. In one obvious sector, schooling, there was virtually no progress at all, and the universities of the sixties were still administered under a Fascist statute of extremely reactionary nature. The worst problem was still the *problema del Mezzogiorno.* Until late in the sixties the government's attitude was to let the North solve the problem of the South. We might characterize this as the "creeping well-being" theory, according to which the affluence and progress of the North could gradually spread south. The factories and development did creep south, it is true, but all in all there was a drastic lag in Southern development and much worse conditions south of Rome than north. The drain of Southerners to the North also depopulated the area and further complicated the problem of investment as the labor force varied in strength from period to period. The structure of landownership changed only gradually from its near-feudal and reactionary nature, partly because the DC allied itself with the notables who represented these reactionary interests and did little to combat them.

In the late sixties the Southerner still lived, if not in, then with many reminders of his millennial misery. This complicated the PCI's acceptance of Amendola's line, basically because the Southerner was much more ready to accept violent solutions than was the relatively affluent Northerner. Within the party, Gramscian Marxism was widely espoused, but since Gramsci went through at least two distinguishable stages in his theoretical development, at least two distinct brands of Gramsci emerged in the party. In opposition to the official brand of the sixties, which has been described above and is derived mainly from his *Prison Notebooks,* there is that espoused first by some Communists from the South, which stressed an earlier essay on the Southern question. What the Southerners for the most part maintained was that South was still at a feudal stage of its development and would have to have a bourgeois revolution first before there was a socialist one. So, unlike the party leaders, they maintained that in the South the use of democratic methods should be seen as contingent. With them were associated many of the intellectuals in the party, who were dissatisfied with the official brand both for theoretical reasons and for the reason that it was something dispensed from on high by Togliatti, who brooked no opposition to his interpretation. In the first half of the sixties the young Southerners who "had negative expectations for the future" showed some tendency to support Mao Tse-tung in defiance of the official party hostility toward China. Without doubt, the challenge of the party's "new left" was contained until 1968. Then came the first of two events which are crucial in explaining how the "historical compromise" differs from the policy of seeking electoral allies and coming to power which prevailed in the sixties. This was the May uprising in Paris.

Without doubt the party was completely surprised by the developments of 1967-1968 among the students of Italy and the world. The rising in Paris made clear that even in conditions of affluence a mass movement from below might still topple governments, especially if the Communist party was not caught napping as the PCF was. The party should develop a number of flexible formulas to cope with possibilities like this and reconsider its monolithism (*L'Unita,* October 19, 1968). The 12th Congress of the PCI of February 1969 marked a dividing line in PCI politics. The Amendolan line was under siege from several quarters. Amendola argued that the integration of the working class into Italian capitalism was impossible and therefore that "even the most elementary working-class demands were incompatible with the system, and therefore even reformist objectives took on a 'subversive form' " (Petracca, 1970:17). He proceeded to propose as the goal of PCI politics a new majority which would include not only the parties of the left as in the past but "socialist and democratic" forces in the DC. He thus emphasized his expectations that the PCI would enter the "governmental field" within a brief lapse of time. He denied forcefully that Italy was entering a period of "revolutionary crisis" and that policies should take that into account, and he continued past warnings that the party would have to struggle against left extremism. A third of the delegates at the congress heard this line rather bleakly, since they were from the "new left" in the party. Their leaders—Luigi Pintor, Rossana Rossanda, and Lucio Magri—countered Amendola *senza complimenti* with the assertion that Italy was in "revolutionary crisis" and that this should be crucial in determining policy. They demanded that the party open itself to the student movement; that it seek contact with dissenting Catholics; and that, developing on Gramsci's early writings on workers' councils, the PCI emphasize "new forms of assembly of direct democracy in the factory." Worst of all, they demanded more democratic practice in the party, treading on the secretary's toes (Iacono, 1971:111).

They argued—and continued to argue after the conference—that the "war of position" on which the Amendolan line was based was finished and that "we are in a moment when socialist revolution is the order of the day in Italy." Conditions were forcing a radicalization of the class conflict on a worldwide scale and especially in Italy, where the relative backwardness of the South made matters more critical overall. This meant that the movement should shift its attention from capturing democratic institutions and turn to "the real places of social power," the factories and the universities. Only through democratizing relationships in these important social activities could the representative institutions themselves remain viable for socialism.

The "new left" group, known as the *Manifesto* group from the name of the journal that it set up in June 1969, had considerable support, especially among the younger members of the party. Unlike other groups of rebels who had threatened the leadership in the past by setting up dissenting journals, they could not hastily be expelled–though they were later. Enrico Berlinguer, a Sardinian and a former head of the Communist Youth Federation, attempted a recovery to the left by attempting to wed the Amendolan and the "new left" lines. "The strategy of Berlinguer tended to the formation of a historical bloc, which, while privileging parliamentary mediation, did not exclude, indeed presupposed, the impetus *(spinte)* which came from society. Berlinguer in fact maintained that neocapitalism, although all-devouring and reinforced by international links, could not put into practice those of its promises ('reforms') which already bordered on socialism. It was precisely in this direction that the action of the PCI could succeed, and here Berlinguer's strategy sought to incorporate the groups and classes which the 'new left' represented" (Iacono, 1971:112). Berlinguer also came out against "the metaphysical cult of democratic centralism" and thus forestalled serious disciplinary sanctions against *Il Manifesto.*

After the 12th Congress Berlinguer's "third way" began to supplant that of Amendola, and about three years later he replaced Longo as party secretary. The "historical compromise" for which Berlinquer is also responsible started with this "third way."

VI. THE STRATEGY OF THE SEVENTIES: "THE HISTORICAL COMPROMISE"

The *Manifesto* group's criticism of the "reformism" of Amendola had considerable justification. Throughout the sixties the PCI had sought to build up alliances which would allow it to come to power, or at least to exert power. Practically all party attention had been devoted to winning such support no matter what the compromise. Yet all overtures had come to nought, even with the PSI, an erstwhile ally. The PCI therefore remained confined to its ghetto: in the 1963 elections it received 25.3 percent of the vote, and in 1968, 26.9 percent. At the same time its organized contact with the working class had been neglected, and its own membership had fallen greatly, from 1,792,968 in 1960 to 1,502,862 in 1968. So, while on the one hand the PSI preferred to experiment in "center-left" coalitions with the DC and ignore the PCI, the PCI was also losing its own base generally, and particularly in the working class (Magri and Maone, 1969).

This real failure of the Amendolan line did not even touch on the deeper problem: that Marxist theory and practice had always taught that it was impossible to use the existing machinery of the bourgeois state for socialism without transforming it.

The "third way" tried to cope with both these problems. Ingrao developed its ideas in this fashion: in regimes of advanced capitalism the movements of struggle in which parties had to develop their policies of political synthesis tended to become demands for "self-government" or participation in power. It was therefore impossible to think of effectively linking with these movements by monolithic methods or delegation of power. He therefore proposed a dialectical relation of "new left" and "old left," each reacting on the other so that any "restructuring" of the left would not merely be the addition of the Communists to the center-left or "slabs of Catholics and socialists to the opposition" but "the result of transformations and displacements taking place within the popular political forces engaged in common in the struggle for reforms." Thus the "elective assemblies would regain their capacity for renewal and reform."

Berlinguer made clear that this line meant both the rejection of any attempts at inclusion in the "center-left" coalition *and* rejection of the "council republic" in favor of an alternative "founded on the convergence and understanding of all left forces, lay and Catholic" (Petracca, 1970:21-22).

The Communists had a chance to test their new "third way" after 1970. The establishment of regional governments throughout Italy —some of which communists controlled even in 1970—facilitated the implementation of the new "third way" in practice. Even more importantly, the PCI started to test its new policy through more than two thousand town councils *(comuni)* which it controlled. The initial PCI move was to discard the residual "sectarianism" of the party representatives on these bodies. This encouraged even more unity among the different parties on the various *giunte* of the regions. In turn, this unity was strengthened by a campaign for more and more regional autonomy and more powers within this autonomy. Again, to win local support for the new line, the citizens had to be included as much as possible in the decision-making process. Here the party met its first stumbling blocks. The division of powers between the central government and the regions, especially in matters of finance, made it difficult for many locally laid plans to be more than pipe dreams. However, insofar as it was possible, the Red regions delegated as much power to local authorities as was possible in 1970-1971. In Emilia the communes decided how the available money of the region was to be distributed. Then, through a new organization set up by the regional assembly, the *circondario,* a mechanism was created for "popular participation in the running of decentralized regional functions." The circondario is composed of elected representatives of local assemblies. Again, in Tuscany, one of the first actions of the region was to remove the *comuni* and *provincie* from the administrative control of the prefect. Then, a whole series of laws delegating control of schooling, social services, markets, and other social activities were passed. The DC proclaimed that a "soviet" system was being introduced. Again, in Umbria a "law of participation" was passed. This made it mandatory "that any regional law or general administrative act undergo prior judgment by the regional society in its various articulations: communes and provinces in the first place; then union organizations, mass organizations, trade and professional associations *(di categoria),* etc. In this climate, and with these guarantees, approval of the overall plan for the region was reached" (Almanacco PCI, 1975:209-232). Even the PSDI (Partito Socialista Democratico Italiano), the DC, and the Liberals approved.

Even in early days, the object of this devolution of power and encouragement of mass participation in decision making was obvious. It directed popular attention to common interests and away from the ideological differences which had characterized interparty relations in the past. It coincided with the spontaneous demands from the base which had evolved since 1968, and it met with remarkable success. The first indications of how appealing the line was, was the increase in party membership after 1972. In 1971-1973 membership rose in this fashion: Turin, 31,188 to 35,950; Milan, 73,699 to 78,071; Venice, 14,948 to 17,080; Brescia, 20,515 to 24,998; Naples, 31,378 to 39,774; Taranto, 9,527 to 10,281. Emilia and Tuscany were obviously very important since 26 percent of the party resided in the former, and 14.9 percent in the latter. The greatest proportion of these new members were from the youth who in 1968 had given up the PCI as "reformist" and "bureaucratic." The problem in 1973 was to get all these new members active to further develop the cross-party unity which manifested itself (to the horror of DC officials) at the various regional and interregional conferences of 1972-1973 (Pecchioli, 1973).

A total of 283,069 members joined the PCI in the year from June 1972 to June 1973. In 1973 there was a determined attempt to ensure that they become active. This, it was argued, would rebuild the party's "mass" character and offset the trend in previous years when the membership/voter ratio changed in favor of a smaller party and a larger vote: for example, in 1958 there were 27 PCI members to every 100 Communist voters, and in 1968 there were 17 members to every 100 Communist voters. In 1973, the PCI therefore held 11,377 conferences of its basic units, the sections. "The object was to encourage the development of a type of section that, overcoming old schemes and habits, will be able to involve itself at the center of a mass political struggle for democratic reforms and renewal, basing its initiatives on the living needs of the population and on the capacity to interest social and political forces and representative institutions and to encourage new developments in the democratic organization of the masses, in their unity and autonomy." While the aim was therefore no longer to organize 100 percent of the members around a single party line, *in particular* the members were encouraged to direct their attention to winning women and younger members (Pecchioli, 1973) and were exhorted: "Not a single worker, not a single housewife, not a single employee, not a single pensioner must remain extraneous to the political attention of the section."

The section conferences were encouraged to adhere to the following guidelines in their work: (1) they should give up ideological battles and denunciations in favor of mass action on specific issues which "mature the conditions which allow organic reformist solutions"; (2) they should concentrate on raising their own cultural level so that they could supply information to the mass. In particular they were called upon to consider the democratic potential of the regional reform (*Note per la Convocazione dei Congressi ordinari delle sezioni,* November 1973-March 1974).

Facilitated by financial reforms in favor of the regions in 1972, the new activity did result in an enormous increase of popular participation in decision making and the burying of many political differences in common causes in 1973. The PCI was obviously pleased with its "third way."

Then came the news of the coup in Chile. Chile differs in many respects from Italy, but the Popular Unity government of Salvador Allende had been applying policies very similar to those proposed by the PCI; the Chilean socialists had been proceeding as if it were possible to introduce socialism through parliament and without destroying the traditional organs of power in the country. Their violent and bloody overthrow of the military, just as they began to win popular support of a significant sort, suggested the general validity of Lenin's lesson that the existing state machinery could not be utilized to introduce socialism, even in situations different from those of prerevolutionary Russia. ("Chile," 1972, is a useful introduction to the relationship between Chile and Italy.) The relevance of the coup to the PCI's "third way" was so obvious that the party had to consider what it meant for the future of its policy. Berlinguer argued in three successive articles in *Rinascita* that Chile showed that the main enemies of democracy in the "free world" were imperialism and the dominant bourgeois classes and that these forces could only be contained by a worldwide modification of forces in favor of the socialist camp. However, the further development in changing the present balance of power in favor of socialism depended on the struggle in each particular country, where the real relations of power should be coldly evaluated "as Togliatti taught us to do" and then overcome. Berlinguer then argued that, while there were analogies between Chile and Italy, in that Chilean socialists and Italian Communists both chose to follow a democratic road to socialism, there were also differences.[6]

What was the Italian policy? It was not merely the adoption of a parliamentary way to power, though the use of parliament was essential to it: "Parliament cannot be conceived of and used as it was in the time of Lenin and could be in other countries—namely, merely as a tribune for the denunciation of the evils of capitalism and bourgeois governments and for socialist propaganda." Rather, the more it became the "mirror of the country" the more it would work in a progressive fashion. This brought Berlinguer to the other, "more important" aspect of the democratic way, whose object was that all state institutions and the people who operated them be inspired by respect for the constitution and by intimate ties with the working population. From this it followed that what was most important and different about the PCI line was that it was directed at encouraging "measures and provisions of democratization in the organization and life of the judiciary, the armed forces, and all the apparatus of the state." This would avoid unilateral developments in which some sections of the community would not benefit.

The democratic path to socialism in Italy was thus a progressive transformation—one which could be realized through the constitution and one which would involve the entire economic, social, political, and ideological structure of the nation. This transformation called for both force and consensus, but the latter was more important, as no revolution could take place without it.

As far back as 1956 the PCI had recognized that there could be no change unless Italy's vast middle classes could be won, and they could only be won if their "economic activity" was guaranteed in a democratic society on the way to socialism. Naturally, the policy of alliances had its point of departure in the "convergence between the immediate and long-term interests of the working class and other social groups." But within a scheme in which the "other social groups" conserved their "role in society" it would be necessary to work for an evolution in their attitudes to a less individualistic and more social vision.

Thus the PCI was more sectionally than class-oriented and its goals were not only economic but also social. To establish a consensus called for a careful choice of priorities and timing in social transformations. Headlong clashes with other mass parties were to be avoided because they broke unity and threatened the democratic state. Rather, the PCI policy was to favor collaboration of all democratic forces.

The lesson that Berlinguer drew from Chile was therefore not that the PCI should make practical preparations for the violent, undemocratic methods of opponents when and if it came to power, but rather that it should rely on the mass movement's united strength. Rather than give up its belief in coalitions with other parties, the PCI should extend its democratic front to prevent a unity of the center and right. In view of the fact that, after Chile, it was no longer possible to believe that winning 51 percent of votes was any safeguard for a socialist government, even the democratic forces in the DC should be courted.

In sum, the PCI should seek a "historical compromise" between the forces gathered together and representing the great majority of the Italian people and should not revert to the time-honored views that the capitalist state can function only as an organ for the "oppression of the poor."

Overall, the policy of the "historical compromise" seemed to many observers no more than a reversion to the policies of the "Salerno turn." This was a justifiable confusion. For example, only a month after Berlinguer had advanced the notion of the "historical compromise" G. Chiarmonte explained it this way: "The sum total of our proposals tend to get the country out of its crisis. . . . This, then, is the political meaning of our proposal: in a society like that of Italy, in which corporative, particularist, and municipal tendencies toward disintegration are very strong—as a result of the current social structure and political economy—the historical and political task of the working class is to develop an action to recompose different social and political forces so that they can attain the objects of social and political transformation" (Chiaromonte, 1973). If we substitute economic crisis for war, this formulation does not seem greatly different from those of the forties. Again, Amendola, who naturally had been a little defensive about the defeat of his line at the 12th Congress, stated in an interview in February 1974: "this is not a new political line which our secretary general, Enrico Berlinguer, has launched. It is the line that we have always followed but which has simply become more relevant because of the economic and social crisis and fascist attacks and because of the 'iron arm,' as we put it, which exists between Christian Democracy and ourselves" (Padovani, 1974b).

However, as Berlinguer had made clear in his formulation of the "historical compromise," it was not the policy of winning parliamentary majorities which was crucial, nor the extent of the alliance; what was crucial was that both these goals, which were necessary for contingent reasons, were based on the development of popular participation in decision making at the base.

This distinction between his position and that of Amendola had become clear by the time preparations were being made for the 1975 14th Congress. In the extensive discussions held beforehand, many contributors emphasized that the "historical compromise" was not a short-term tactic for solving the crisis, but a strategy for the long-term. It accorded with the "democratic" policies of the past but differed in that it was not merely "receptive" but "propulsive." Put another way, the policy was intended to change the electorate as well as reflect it. This would mean a revolution which was not passive but active. Cesare Luporini made the effect clear when he wrote that the objective of all the democratic participation in decision making at all levels was to stir the DC up from within and isolate its conservatives, whose power had rested on the apathy of the mass of people who supported or constituted the party. We might say that if democratic politics had been based on apathy, the PCI intended to reverse the situation and galvanize the apathetic (*Rinascita,* March 14, 1975).

At the 14th Congress, held on March 18, 1975, under the banner of "Entente and struggle of all democratic and popular forces for the salvation and rebirth of Italy," Berlinguer made quite clear that the electoral politics of the PCI were not directed, as Amendola urged, at getting into government, though this would be a welcome by-product. His speech spelled out the full dimensions of the "historical compromise" in a fashion which left the Amendolas of the PCI dissentient. The firm rebuttal of Amendola at the Congress was very important because by 1975 "the Communist question" had become the key question in Italy. The presence of delegations from other parties, even from the DC, attested to the general realization that the PCI was no longer in its ghetto, but a clearer contender for power in Italy than it had ever been before.

Berlinguer's report started from a consideration of the world scene. He typified capitalism as being in growing and indefinite crisis, while in the socialist countries production was still improving. The old capitalist solutions to such a crisis were no longer viable because the area of imperialism was becoming more restricted and the work forces were becoming more militant. Capitalism was therefore turning toward the "right" and to warlike adventures. At the same time, socialist pressure was resulting in a relaxation of international tensions. Consequently, there were moves afoot to find some basis for cooperation to get out of the crisis. Of the many schemes, the only acceptable one was that which would include all global interests on the basis of real participation. It followed that, while on the one hand the dialogue between the U.S.S.R. and the U.S.A. should be strengthened, the autonomy of Europe should also be encouraged. At the same time, it had to be recognized that Europe was no longer the center of the world.

Berlinguer went on to say that in Italy the first immediate task was to prevent the crisis from becoming a collapse and that "the attainment of this goal calls for an exceptional effort for unity among all the forces of our people." This effort was needed because of the terrible outlook for 1975, which most of the populace did not realize, partly because the cliques ruling the DC had deliberately misrepresented the "historical compromise" to secure selfish personal advantages. However, 1974 had shown that the tendency was toward democratic rather than authoritarian solutions. The PCI should work to ensure the functioning of democratic institutions and a climate of civility through mass actions and direct pressure on the government. Berlinguer claimed that the support for the "historical compromise" after 18 months of rejection by the DC showed that the policy interpreted widespread and growing feelings in favor of political, social, and moral change and that its novelty vis-à-vis all other policies for 25 years was recognized.

It was logic chopping to argue that the search for so wide a majority as the PCI called for denied contradictions. All PCI activities were directed to stimulating unity. The fact was that since 1968 new popular democratic forms had emerged: workers' councils, cooperatives, consumer associations, womens' movements, and election of teachers. None had really been the single answer to what democracy was, but they had shown "how large masses of citizens, traditionally tied to center and even right-wing positions under the influence of prejudice, could move to more advanced positions in the democratic and reforming sense, insofar as they could become active, participate in a clash, be called upon 'in the first person' to live the democratic life. It is now necessary to engage to the end in contributing to make these new organizations live and work so that so much passion and popular participation are not frustrated and so that the elements of confusion which the first phase of this experience brought to light are overcome."

Berlinguer made clear that the emphasis he gave to what might be called base-level democracy did not mean that the PCI accepted abstruse theories about direct democracy being the only genuine form of democracy, as opposed to traditional channels of representative democracy. Rather, the organs of direct democracy strengthened the latter and enabled them to play their preeminent role more effectively and in a more timely fashion. In turning to political action, while not neglecting the battle of ideas, the PCI avoided the limitations of reformism and maximalism characteristic of the Second International.

In accordance with this stress on a molecular restructuring of society to complement the traditional political battle, Berlinguer suggested how the regional elections of 1975 should be fought. They would not be turned into some sort of a plebiscite or crusade as the DC wished. Instead, the battle would be between honest men who wished to solve the real problems of Italy and those who wished to continue the ideological dispute. The party would continue, as it had, to extend popular participation in regional and administrative decisions and, in opposition to the centralism of the DC, continue to argue in favor of self-management for the regions (*L'Unita,* March 18, 1975).

This last suggestion showed continuity with decisions taken late in 1973, when preparations for the 1975 elections had begun. Then, the PCI had also stressed the democratic possibilities of the regions and had declared that attempts by the DC to divert attention from the substantial achievements of the regional governments and to emphasize the ideological struggle should be repulsed. A conference held in association with the 14th Congress addressed itself directly to electoral policy, drawing on the experience of all party federations. This conference directed that all questions, lists, and programs be drawn up on the basis of concrete issues and decided by consultation below, rather than by direction from above. Pajetta recognized that this was not easy because "dialogue, exchange, capillary meetings house by house, public meetings organized on the basis of what the citizens want to know" required a massive labor. Much had been learned from the previous year's campaign on divorce, in which the PCI had been most prominent. The object was to force the opponent into debate where he could then be worsted. (*L'Unita,* March 21, 1975).

By mid-1975 the PCI certainly had much that it could point to by way of achievement. Bologna was a showcase of what "democratic control" meant. There, "groups discussed concrete matters about schools, health problems, the 'historical center,' traffic, public transport. There was not a beggar in a city of 500,000 inhabitants nor a single small or middle-sized industrialist who had a complaint about the mayor, who is a Communist, or about the president of the region, who is also a Communist. There was not a child who would not duly go to school. There was not a single decision about financial, political, or cultural matters in which the population was not involved.

"The 'historical center'? Well, it has been made as good as new. For whom? Precisely for those people who used to live there. It is the only example in Europe of urban renewal which was not funded by builders or accomplished by the classic process of sending the lower-class residents to the outer suburbs.

"Cooperation has improved in many ways: Since July 1973, Guido Fanti, president of the region, has proposed that the opposition (that is, the Christian Democrats) not only be consulted in every governmental decision but take constructive responsibility for it, just like the majority" (Padovani, 1974:98).

Indeed, with this record at the regional level, why not a Communist government at Rome? Despite a last-ditch anti-Communist campaign by the DC, which pointed indicatively to Portugal, this seemed to be the question which many citizens were asking themselves as they went to the polls for the regional elections and looked forward to 1977.

VII. THOUGHTS ON THE FUTURE OF THE PCI

There are problems with the "historical compromise." The first question is how far can it work. Tarrow (1972) pointed out that in southern Italy the PCI policy of working with the middle class in 1960-1970 resulted only in effects detrimental to the rural poor. The new policy continues this cross-class tradition as conditions become intolerable in the South, where the continuing readiness to resort to violent solutions was made evident in the fascist-inspired riots of 1970-1971. Party spokesmen seemed aware of the contradictions in their policy right from its inception. In October 1973 it was denied that there was need for "more opposition" in the South than on a national scale, even while taking into account the deeper cleavages of interest in the South than the North. Instead, the party somewhat ambiguously proclaimed that the policy of working on concrete issues would be accompanied by a concentration on the "worst off" in the community, without neglecting the interests of the middle class. Indeed, there was more than a hint of the desire to create more middle farmers to close massive gaps between the poor and their traditional enemies, the rural middle class.

This policy seems designed to encourage those objective conditions in northern and central Italy which allowed the PCI to win or influence regions. In the South the PCI cannot test its line in practice because it is completely outside the regional governments. None of the participatory activity of the North is possible, and earlier loyalties and political styles are not broken. The regional conferences at Cagliari and Naples in 1973 and 1975 were characterized by the usual Southern political style—"vetoes, threatening phone calls, orders not to . . . appear" (*Rinascita,* March 14, 1975). The overall result is a growing gap between PCI power in the South and PCI power in the North, with no exceptional policy for the South. The recent gains in members and votes may again be frittered away unless more is achieved. Yet, an exceptional policy seems unlikely: the trend of the PCI since the conference of European Communist parties in Brussels in January 1974 has been to regard Italian developments more and more as subordinate to overall European developments.

It has also been pointed out by recent observers that even the participatory politics of the North tend to result only in quantitative changes rather than qualitative changes in economic, social, and political life in general. As the opening pages of this essay suggested, the PCI is posing as the latest efficiency expert carrying out popular wishes—no matter what they may be—while attempting to change popular attitudes from "individualism" to something approaching "social vision." In a recent article about the Red belt of Emilia-Romagna (Stern, 1974), it was suggested that in the 1960s Communist party officials had climbed socially and had frequently gone into private enterprise themselves. At the same time, there was a lack of active popular participation in PCI organization. Too long supping with the erstwhile bourgeois devil had created "family circles." The contemporary problem is not that this will prevent the policy of the "historical compromise" from taking root, but that it may slow it down and result in maximizing local as against national interests of the party. The new line risks a revival of the old *campanilismo* and *anarchismo* characteristic of Italian socialism before 1921.

Finally, the student of revolution feels a certain unease about how responsible socialists will be affected by this apparently "responsible" policy. It may appear to be, as has been argued, close to the Gramscian conciliar theory, and therefore a laudable return to Marxism from the travesty which that doctrine became under the Communist International. It may even be beyond Gramsci's theory, as has also been argued, in its realization of the importance of the objective strength of imperialism. On both counts, it heralds a much needed return to the propositions in Marx's sixth thesis on

Feuerbach. To some degree the PCI's renewed appeal to the young may be attributable to this new militancy.

But, unlike Gramsci's theory, the new policy does not see base-level democracy as an alternative to parliament, and it contains no thought-out theory of the organic relationship between the activity in the former and the activity in the latter. Gramsci's theory was that of building a new consciousness prior to overthrowing the bourgeois state, precisely because there are irreducible contradictory class conflicts which cannot be reconciled. In this connection the most telling speech at the 14th Congress was that of Carlos Altamirano of the decimated Chilean Popular Unity. He appealed in touching terms that the lesson of Chile be learned. For him this lesson added up to the idea that socialism cannot be introduced through parliament alone. Those who try this, without building up a dual system of power which challenges the interests of capitalism by force, risk failure. "We should have defended our conquests, according to Lenin's teaching, using every form of struggle" (*Corriere della Sera,* March 21, 1975).

NOTES

1. Figures are in U.S. billions.
2. The policy of the PCI has been adopted by the French Communist party as well and by minor Communist parties like the Communist party of Australia.
3. In the first De Gasperi government the PCI had the ministries of Justice, Finance, and Agriculture and Forests. In the second De Gasperi government the PCI had the ministries of Justice, Finance, Agriculture and Forests, Transport, and Postwar Assistance. In the third De Gasperi government, which lasted until May 1947, the PCI had the ministries of Justice, Public Works, and Transport.
4. Of course, this is an "ideal type" Leninism, and in practice the Russians frequently diverged from these precepts. See the article cited.
5. The PCI received 22.6 percent of the vote for the House of Deputies and 20.2 percent for the Senate.
6. Allende in fact encouraged the development of base-level democratic organizations in the later part of his presidency. However, it appears that the Chilean Communists believed that socialist measures could be voted through parliament and that no further organs were needed to ensure their implementation or defense.

REFERENCES

Almanacco PCI (1975). Rome: Sezione centrale di stampa e propaganda.
BIANCO, G. (1967). "Culture, dogma and the PCI." Survey, (January):114-122.

BROADHEAD, S. (1972). "Togliatti and the Church, 1921-48." Australian Journal of Politics and History, 18:76-91.

CHIAROMONTE, G. (1973). La lotta per le riforme sociali e la democrazia nell'attuale situozione interna e internazionale. Relazione al CC. October 18, Rome.

"Chile, France and Italy: A discussion" (1972). Government and Opposition, 7:389-408.

DAVIDSON, A. (1965). "Tendencies towards 'reformism' in the Italian Communist party." Australian Journal of Politics and History, (December):335-349.

——— (1969). "The dissenters: Italian Communism." Unpublished paper delivered to Dante Alighieri Society Conference, Brisbane.

——— (1972). "The varying seasons of Gramscian studies." Political Studies, (December): 448-461.

GALLI, G. (1962). "Italy." In L. Labedz and W. Laqueur (eds.), Polycentrism. New York: Praeger.

——— (1964). "Italian Communism." In W. Griffith (ed.), Communism in Europe (Vol. 1). Cambridge: Massachusetts Institute of Technology Press.

GRUPPI, L. (1975). Togliatti e la via italiana al socialismo. Rome: Editori Rinuniti.

IACONO, F. (1971). "Il PCI fra centralismo e apostasia." Nord e Sud, (September):94-113.

MAGRI, L., and MAONE, F. (1969). "L'organizzazione comunista Strutture e metodi di direzione." Il Manifesto, (September):28-40.

PADOVANI, M. (1974a). "Le scenario rouge." Le Nouvel Observateur, (September):16-22.

——— (1974b). "Le sens d'un compromis." Le Nouvel Observateur, (February):11-17.

PECCHIOLI, U. (1973). "Politica e organizzazione nel PCI." Critica marxista, May-August.

PETRACCA, O. (1970). "I 'contrastanti' futuri del PCI." Tempi Moderni, (Winter):17-22.

REALE, E. (1970). "The founding of the Cominform." In M. Drachovitch and B. Lazitch (eds.), The Comintern: Historical highlights. New York: Praeger.

SCHMID, P. (1966). "The perplexities of Italian Communism." Dissent, September-October.

SPRIANO, P. (1967-1970). Storia del partito comunista italiano (3 vols.). Turin: Einaudi.

STERN, A. (1974). "The Italian CP at the grass roots." Problems of Communism, (March-April):42-55.

TARROW, S. (1972). "The political economy of stagnation in Communism in southern Italy." Journal of Politics, 34:93-123.

TOGLIATTI, P. (1958). "Il partito comunista italiano." Milan: Nuova Accademi.

WHITE, S. (1971). "Gramsci and the Italian Communist party." Government and Opposition, 2:186-205.

Chapter 6

INFORMATION ON FRENCH POLITICS

ALFRED GROSSER

Traditional classifications of political systems emphasize the relationships among governmental powers, the number of political parties, the degree of individual freedom. However, in each case the oft-neglected question of how political information is disseminated should be taken into account. Interest groups could not gather opinions and influence government, political parties could not act as a link between the citizen and his government, the choice of representatives in elections could not be interpreted as referenda on the policies of those in power (*consultations* as they are often called in France), if a sufficient amount of political information were not spread throughout the polity.

This diffusion of political information has at least two interrelated but distinct aspects. On the one hand, each actor in a political system—citizens, interest groups, political parties, members of parliament, the government in power—must make its ideas and aspirations known to the others. On the other hand, each of these

AUTHOR'S NOTE: The author and the editor would each like to thank Dace Weiss, who translated this chapter from the French original. This is a slightly altered version of a chapter which appeared as Chapter 6 of *La Politique en France* by Alfred Grosser and François Goguel. We would like to thank Armand Colin for permission to publish this translation.

must have access to a wide range of information, economic and social as well as political, international as well as national; for it is these factors which shape the future of any country. "Freedom of information" in a truly democratic country should be understood as a twofold right to information: the right to communicate information and the right to be informed, the right to make known and the right to know.

One often makes the distinction between news and propaganda—that is, the diffusion of unbiased, honest, objective facts as opposed to the diffusion of the biased, dishonest, and subjective. In fact, any news item, solely by virtue of the facts that it was chosen over another and that it was presented in one form rather than another, is biased. "The right to make known," then, might well be controlled or limited because inherent in that right is the right to influence. Individuals and groups constantly seek to influence others by the information they exchange. This is a perfectly legitimate desire, whether on the part of trade unions or the part of governments. But there is inevitably an inequality among individuals' and groups' capacities to exercise this right. This inequality could be diminished if channels of communication were as accessible to those out of power as they are to those in. Obviously this solution is somewhat utopian, since privileged access is most often both an expression of and a source of the power of those in control.

Those in power are inevitably tempted to reduce the news communicated to that which is useful for their purposes and to limit and tamper with the news that is disseminated. We have already noted that total objectivity in the selection of news is impossible, because all news results from a selection based on subjective criteria. No message is ever detached from the subjective views of the transmitter and the intermediary. Therefore, democracy cannot be defined in terms of the objectivity of news coverage. However, when both the sources of political information and especially those who relay news to the public strive for objectivity, then a democratic model is approached. The goal for a democracy should be a set of institutionalized procedures which permit reporters to be independent interpreters of the news, not merely instruments in the hands of politicians seeking solely to enhance their own positions.

I. POLITICAL INFORMATION FROM AND TO THE GOVERNMENT: PUBLIC OPINION POLLS

When a government wishes to make its policies known to the public, when it has an important news item to communicate, how does it proceed? The parliamentary tradition offered a clear response: the government made a declaration before the assembly or answered questions put forth by opposition members. The information was then circulated through two channels, the press attending the parliamentary session and commenting on it and the members of parliament returning to their constituencies to explain their judgments of the government's policies to local leaders.

This description does not represent an accurate assessment of the situation in any one country today. In the first place, the existence of highly organized parties often leads the government to channel information through the organization of the majority party. More important, the development of the mass media has increasingly diminished the role of parliament as either a representative of public opinion or as a link between the government and the public. Radio and television allow for direct contact between those who govern and the governed, raising questions about the very nature of representative democracy. During the fast-moving political period surrounding his accession to power, Pierre Mendès-France, imitating Franklin D. Roosevelt's "fireside chats," addressed the French people regularly on radio. Starting in 1958, General de Gaulle extended this policy widely. In France today the use of televised speeches, press conferences, and interviews has nearly eliminated parliament as a channel for transmitting information to the citizens.

The reverse process—the government gaining information about public opinion—is slightly different. In this process the members of parliament have two rivals in their roles as relayers of information, the press and the polls. At the same time, however, if there is a majority and not a proportional electoral system, members of parliament can safeguard their representative function because they are able to sense the psychological feeling of the public, a feeling which the bureaucrats, the other source of information for the government, often miss.

It is most important that the government in power make its decisions based on as much information as possible. But can this be so? Certainly less than one would expect. In economic matters, for example, the necessary condition for developing a sound policy —namely, rigorous statistical information—is only beginning to be filled in France. Looking back, it is still unclear whether the economic policy of the Popular Front in 1936 was good or bad. It is better to emphasize that it was based on uncertainties, because knowledge of the relevant parameters was still highly embryonic at that time and because there are still many gaps in available economic data. In foreign affairs the intentions of others and often even the elementary facts of a situation are not precisely known. What, one may ask, actually did happen at a given place in the world at a given time? The minister often knows no more about it than does the reader of the major newspapers.

The natural tendency of citizens to overestimate the amount of information possessed by the government has two unfortunate consequences. It brings about both abdication and intransigence. In not realizing that serious reading of a responsible newspaper puts him in as good a position to judge a political situation as a minister, the citizen is resigned to passive acceptance rather than active will. In believing that the minister has made a decision with all the relevant information at hand, the citizen is prepared to condemn him severely in case of failure. However, the statesman cannot wait to know everything: he must act even if he is caught at fault by later historians who have more information available. Thus, in any situation requiring a political decision, an element of chance is present; this ought to cause the governed to be slightly more indulgent toward their governors.

Those who make political decisions must seek as much information as possible. This is often not the case. A close tie often exists between the refusal to properly inform the public and to make it aware of existing problems and the acceptance of not being very well informed and failing to recognize this situation. It is easier to reassure the public if one does not have to be concerned with reassuring oneself first.

In general, however, those who rule do at least want to understand public opinion. Napoleon found a good way to reconcile his need to provide information with his denial of freedom of information; he arranged to have a free newspaper published by a well-informed and intelligent journalist—in one single copy.

The press, elections, parliament, group demonstrations, all of these are the traditional sources of information on the state of public opinion. For some years now we have had to add to this list the public opinion polls. Without even emphasizing the possible risk of manipulation of results, we must be aware that polls involve two serious dangers, manifest in the countries where they are most used (the United States and Germany) and already visible in France, where their implementation is more recent. Governments and parties attach too much significance to their results; they tend to bend their policies (or require that those in power bend theirs) according to the latest results. The government thus deprives itself of an important prerogative, that of taking an unpopular measure and of being judged over the long run on the results of that action. Thus while appearing to be democratic, the polls constitute a sort of invitation to demagoguery. They also detract from the active and informed citizen by seeking out the "man in the street," who is only drawn out of his passivity by the question of the pollster. This said, if polls are conducted seriously, as are those of the IFCP and the SOFRES, the major French polling organizations, they incontestably acquaint one with the movements of public opinion, with orientations and even aspirations of different social groups, and with consequences –positive and negative–of possible policies or of policies already in effect.

The debate over the use of polls was particularly sharp at the time of the 1974 presidential campaign. First, this was because of the excessive duplication, with poll findings, statistics, and commentaries often occupying more space on the front pages than the actual debates of the parties. Second, and more important, the debate was aroused by accusations that the pollsters were falsifying their results. In fact, the polls exercised a definite, but a limited, influence. They noted, but they did not create, the sudden break between Giscard d'Estaing and Chaban-Delmas. The arguments of these men on television played a much more important role. However, solely by affirming the break, they did modify the strategies of the antagonists and undoubtedly brought Giscard d'Estaing extra votes because the polls made his victory over Mitterrand seem as plausible as that of his adversary in the majority camp. The phenomenon was reversed for Royer: the polls showed his following weak from the beginning and caused him to lose the additional votes of those who thought him already out of the running. It is also evident that the closeness of the election, as predicted by the polls, was a major influence in mobilizing the electorate and bringing about the record turnouts, although it remains difficult to judge in whose favor this mobilization acted.

Should polls be outlawed? Would the destruction of all thermometers be useful as medicine? Of course, neither of these is even conceivable. Well-conducted polls have proven themselves too valuable to be given up. The real temptation is to reserve the temperature reading to those who call themselves doctors—the large company promoting its sales or the head of a government or party making its policies more acceptable or catering to the public. Just as with news reports or television programs, polls can be done poorly or presented dishonestly. These are the inevitable risks when information is freely circulated, mistaken information as well as accurate. It is not impossible to minimize these risks. This can be done mainly through education, by teaching the public from grade school onward just how a newspaper is put together, just how a poll is conducted.

Polls are but one of the means through which government gains information. The government also has both a right and a duty to provide information. The tendency of the French is to label as propaganda and to discredit any government effort to inform. However, silence from the government is surely less democratic than the willingness to explain, to justify, to convince. Moreover, the exercise of power implies a certain pedagogy, the will to have the governed see political problems in the same terms as those who govern.

But pedagogy does not mean authoritarianism or monopoly. The government's efforts at explanation and persuasion must be countered, in a regime which prides itself on pluralism, with an equivalent effort on the part of those who aspire to rule in its place. This condition, partly achieved in the press, has never been met in France with regard to news coverage on the radio and television.

II. RADIO AND TELEVISION

In a rather paradoxical fashion, the political discussion about the monopoly of governmental powers over radio and television has become more intense as new statutes in 1959, 1964, and 1972 have in theory assured more autonomy for radio and television. This intensified debate is easily explained, however, if four factors are taken into account.

The first fact is the changed role of television. When the Fifth Republic came into existence in 1958, there were roughly one million television sets in France. There were more than five million in 1964. In 1967, for the first time, owners of televisions outnumbered those who owned only radios. In 1969, Frenchmen owned more than 10 million television sets. During the 1974 elections, this number reached approximately 14 million.

The second fact is that the power of the government has been very stable since 1958, whereas under the Fourth Republic the influence of the government and of political parties over radio and television was obscured by the instability of the government and the intense infighting within the parties.

The third fact is that General de Gaulle quickly acquired the habit of addressing the French people directly over television. This again reinforced the belief–rather prevalent in the early sixties–that television exercised a decisive influence on the political behavior of citizens. Today this belief is more widespread among politicians than it is among scholars, who prefer to speak of lasting influences on attitudes rather than of factors with short-term impact.

In fact, the essential factor has remained the same under the Fifth Republic as it was under the Fourth: the confusion between the concept of a national collectivity and the concept of a government. In the United States, the breadth of the area covered by television news programming is guaranteed by commercial competition between private networks and by the way in which journalists view their profession. The journalists' task is to offer more than his competitor does. The American journalist views his profession as a sort of news "hunt," in which he must bring back more game than his competitor; this led to the astonishingly wide coverage of the Vietnam War and the riots in the black ghettos. In Great Britain and in Germany there is public ownership of radio and television without governmental regulation. In France, to the contrary, broadcasting is the monopoly of the state. Private networks cannot broadcast on French territory, even if, as is the case of Radio Luxembourg and Europe 1, they are permitted to locate their main offices in Paris. This monopoly was established, as were other nationalized industries, under the terms of a concept expressed in the preamble to the Constitution of 1946, the validity of which was echoed in the Constitution of 1958: "Any property or enterprise whose exploitation has or does acquire the character of a national public service . . . must become public property."

The importance of radio and television in the realm of news coverage is such that this concept of public ownership can easily be applied to them, the principle being to avoid the influence of money, particularly through advertising. But the doctrine of all French governments, from 1946 through 1976, has been that "public ownership" and "government" are synonymous. Elsewhere, mainly in Great Britain and in Germany, the "government" is seen to be the political majority in parliament at any given moment, and the "public" comprises all existing currents of opinion. Thus the BBC in London and the various German networks in Cologne, Hamburg, or Munich have statuatory independence both with regard to money and with regard to government interference. German federalism sets up a supplementary guarantee against government intervention, while in Great Britain the custom of noninterference forbids the government from intervening even if it does possibly have the jurisdiction to do so. The German doctrine was formulated very precisely by the Federal Constitutional Court on February 28, 1961, when it decreed that the government had no right to control a television network because such control would constitute an attack on the freedom of expression as it was set down in the Constitution. The Court stated in particular:

> Radio and television are much more than simple conveyor belts in the formation of public opinion. They play an eminently creative role. Their participation in the formation of opinion is not limited to news programs, political commentary, or special series devoted to the politics of the present, past, or future. Dramatic and musical programs, variety shows, these also influence opinion. Each broadcast or televised program will have a certain leaning due particularly to those decisions on what must not be broadcast or on what is not considered of interest to the listener or viewer. The result is that institutional freedom is no less important for radio or television than it is for the press.

The French situation has been radically different. In 1945, after broadcasting licenses awarded to private companies before the war were withdrawn, and after the state monopoly was established, the French broadcasting system, which eventually became the Radiodiffusion-Télévision Française (RTF), was created as a special administrative unit under the Minister of Information. A first important step was taken at the start of the Fifth Republic with the ordinance of February 4, 1959, which converted the RTF into a public institution of an industrial or commercial nature. It thus acquired its own administrative existence but continued to depend directly on governmental authority. The obvious consequence of this was that the real director of the RTF was not the man who held the title but in fact the Minister of Information. Whether he wished to do so or not, even the most liberal of ministers was obliged to weigh the news coverage on the RTF as well as its cultural and artistic programs. Since he had the power to select or prohibit any single item, every program was considered to be aired with his approval. The law of June 27, 1964, transforming the RTF into the ORTF (Office de Radiodiffusion-Télévision Française) was supposed to put an end to this situation. From then on, the power of the minister was limited in principle to that of administrative supervision and financial control; the law created a powerful board of directors whose chairman was to supervise the affairs of the organization.

The June 27, 1964, statute granted specific and important responsibilities to the board of directors. That board members were appointed by the government did not necessarily mean that they would be dependent on it, since the council of the BBC was in the same situation. However, the age of most of the members appointed in 1964 and the fact that a good number of them had no expertise in the field of radio and television limited the activities of the board severely. Moreover, the board itself and its chairman had little power over the director general, who was appointed by the government and subject to recall in conformity with French tradition, the head administrator of the Comédie Française standing as the only exception to that tradition.

The director general could have secured independence from the government for himself and his subordinates if he had leaned heavily on the precise text of the law, which was clear in its intent, and if he had appealed to public opinion in the case of conflict. In reality, however, the 1964 statute brought little change in customs, at least not until the crisis of 1968.

Sparked by a ban on the broadcasting of a series of programs on the troubles in the Latin Quarter, the ORTF strike became one of the longest strikes in the spring of 1968. It consisted of various episodes, ranging from dignified demonstrations of solidarity with the strikers to rather ridiculous spectacles in the occupied Sorbonne. The strikers were criticized for revolting against something they had accepted for such a long time; they responded that that was the nature of all revolutions. Negotiations conducted during the strike produced no results. Management and government made commitments which they did not keep. In the end an appreciable number of the journalists were dismissed, supposedly as an economy measure, but in fact as a sanction for striking and other related activities.

Paradoxically, the strikers eventually won. During the 1969 presidential campaign, liberalization of the ORTF was an important issue; right from the time that Pompidou was installed in the Elysée and Chaban-Delmas in the Hotel Matignon, the government's willingness to withdraw from its position of direct control over the ORTF became evident. A study was undertaken to reform the statute governing the ORTF. It addressed itself particularly to the way in which the statute had been applied, admitting as fact some of the principles which had inspired the 1968 strike. In November 1969 the board of directors finally issued precise directives to the new information services set up by the two networks—services which were established, incidentally, by government decision when they should have come under the internal jurisdiction of the ORTF.

The statute of 1964 was rather abruptly changed in 1972, Parliament quickly passing a bill initiated by the President of the Republic and his advisors. Under the new system, the board of directors lost even more of its influence, as it no longer had any control over the director general, who was now concurrently chairman of the board and was still directly appointed by the government. An important new feature did appear: the director general was appointed for a fixed period, three years. However, despite the fact that he was a faithful supporter of the President of the Republic, the first appointee did not last even half this fixed term. Wishing to protect his prerogatives, the director general found himself in conflict with the Minister of Information and was dismissed by the government in October 1973. The government justified this dismissal by manipulating the law in a fashion which was probably illegal: the statute stipulated that the director general had to be a member of the board, and, since appointments to the board were revocable, the government ended Arthur Conte's tenure as director general by dismissing him from the board and consequently making him ineligible for his position as director general. Conte had been a political appointee; his successor was an upper-level bureaucrat. The new director immediately informed the press that he viewed his job as he would view any other responsibilities conferred upon him by the government.

The second statute governing the ORTF had an even shorter life than the first. Since his accession to the presidency, Giscard d'Estaing had decided not to reorganize the ORTF but rather to do away with it. Drafted and adopted in great haste, the new law of August 7, 1974, retained the idea of monopoly and reiterated the declarations of purpose expressed in the two previous statutes, but it left many important questions unanswered and at the discretion of governmental decrees:

> Article I. The French national radio broadcasting and television public service, within the limits of its capabilities, assumes the responsibility of meeting the needs and aspirations of the public in all that concerns news coverage, communications, culture, education, entertainment, and all other values of civilization. Its foremost objective is the promotion of the general interests of the people in these areas.
>
> It guarantees equal access for the expression of the main currents of opinion and the principal lines of thought. All of them will regularly have the opportunity to air their views.
>
> It participates in spreading French culture throughout the world.
>
> These responsibilities carry with them the obligation of maintaining and supervising the quality of the French language.

However, the new law eliminates any central unifying organization and creates six national agencies: the public broadcasting agency, the production agency, and four programming agencies, one "in charge of the conception and programming of radio shows," the three others "in charge of the conception and programming of television." All four are run according to the same principle:

> Article II. The Board of Directors of each agency is composed of six members: two representatives of the state, one parliamentarian, one journalist, one representative of the agency's personnel, and one person drawn from the world of culture.
>
> For the agency mentioned in Article X, the member will be drawn from the cinema (the former third network).
>
> The members of the Board of Directors will have a tenure of three years.
>
> The personnel representative is to be appointed from a list drawn up by the unions representing the personnel.
>
> The Chairman, chosen from among the members of the Board, will be named for three years by decree of the Council of Ministers. He is to organize the management of the agency and appoint the administrators.

It is highly improbable that these new structures will cause any basic modification in existing procedures, nor will they reduce significantly the possibilities for influence exercised by those in power. Not that the ORTF journalists are all "lackies of the government" or subject to permanent censorship, but the fact remains that there is a considerable amount of self-censorship, typified by the statement, "It is a fantastically tricky subject; you really have to watch your step!" Journalists do not want to displease or provoke those in charge; in short, they seek to avoid problems.

Exactly who should not be displeased? The government, of course; but to end there is to simplify reality. One does not wish to displease either the mass of television viewers or the social groups which make them up. Hence, countless fears. Fears expressed in contemporary history, where only established truths (on the war period, the Fourth Republic, etc.) occupy the screen. Fears about discussing political or social problems; as soon as an inquiry begins to get at the heart of a matter, the chances that it will be seen on television are sharply reduced. Doctors, teachers, peasants, veterans, administrators all make certain that they are not criticized excessively.

Thus one finds a fundamental phenomenon which is shared by the monopolistic press, which also must address itself to the broadest of all possible audiences: a hesitancy, a sense of moderation, even a prudishness, which is imposed by no one directly but which nonetheless dictates that one write nothing which could possibly shock anyone. Without doubt this represents something more important than government control of news coverage. This is even more true in an election period, when a rather remarkable balance is established—in a very transitory fashion—between the various candidates who, according to the law (and a special regulatory commission), must be treated equally.

In April-May 1974, this equal-time provision became rather absurd, in part because the serious candidates could not address the public one minute longer than the frivolous ones, but more so because no flexibility was possible. This prevented the serious candidates from confronting one another during the first round. The outlying transmitting stations were able to profit tremendously from this state of affairs.

The broadcasting monopoly has in fact been somewhat altered since the early postwar years because of transmitting stations located just outside of French territory, run by companies whose offices and studios are still centered in Paris. There is Radio Monte Carlo, a corporation of the principality of Monaco, which is in fact controlled by an agency belonging to the French state. Radio Monte Carlo also has television broadcasting.

More importantly, there are the two large competitors, who vie with each other as well as with the national radio and television corporations: Europe 1, whose transmitter is in Felsberg in the Saar (in the Federal Republic of Germany), and Radio Luxembourg, whose transmitter is in Beidweiler in Luxembourg. Europe 1 is controlled by Sylvain Floirat, a powerful self-made man who is now 75 years old, and by Sofiräd, each controlling more or less one-third of the shares. During 1974 Radio Luxembourg was the scene of a bitter and subtly complex conflict between Belgian and French financiers (including Hachette and the advertising agency Havas, which belonged to the French state); the conflict centered on the future successor of Jean Prouvost, another powerful old man, who wields tremendous de facto power while controlling only a minority of the stocks.

Europe 1 and Radio Luxembourg enjoy much greater freedom than does the ORTF, Radio France. Although they are limited by certain taboos, as is the ORTF, especially since they depend entirely on advertising, their reporters nevertheless can do much more, from commentaries put together by prestigious journalists (the ORTF never tolerates personalized news commentary) to improvised confrontations, to reporting events where anything may happen that could possibly interest the public. Nearly anything which will draw an audience for their advertisers is possible.

III. THE PRESS AND ITS INFLUENCE

The starting point in the history of the press after the war is peculiar to France, but the main lines of evolution are not. At the Liberation, in 1944, a revolutionary decision was taken. The newspapers which had appeared under the German occupation saw their operations ended and the organs of the Resistance installed in their place. Only the Catholic daily *La Croix* and the conservative daily *Le Figaro,* which had ceased publication in Lyons shortly after the Germans crossed into the unoccupied zone in November 1942, were not subject to this interdiction. The purpose of this action was to create a press which was independent of political and financial control.

For a great number of reasons, financial independence was quickly revealed to be illusory. The new newspapers, gradually and under a variety of circumstances, soon became "normal" commercial enterprises. The break in 1944, however, caused important modifications in the image of the press. One of these modifications resulted from the division of France in 1940: if before the war the Paris press had many readers in the provinces, since 1945 the provincial press (much more prosperous than the Paris press) has become master of its own house. A small portion of the regional economic, intellectual, and political elite reads *Le Monde, Le Figaro,* or *La Croix. France-Soir* also has a limited circulation outside the Paris area; but it is certainly the local press which forms the basic reading of the vast majority of the non-Parisian population.

There are three caveats attending this statement, however: first, the urban area in question represents approximately one-fifth of the French population; second, the news in the provincial dailies is largely taken from the previous afternoon's edition of *Le Monde;* and, third and above all, the weekly press remains almost exclusively Parisian. It nevertheless remains true that it is wrong to judge the French press and its role on the basis of the Paris press alone.

The two most important developments in the postwar period are the same in France as in the other Western European countries: the erosion of party control over the press and the concentration of the press. In the mid-1940s, the main political parties owned or directly controlled certain important dailies. Today party newspapers are, as they have been for a long time, in a period of crisis.

As of 1945, the Radical party had lost, in addition to its electoral power, control of its two pillars of the press, *Le Progres* of Lyons and *La Dépèche* of Toulouse; the latter, however, still tended to be radical when it became *La Dépèche du Midi,* continuing in its broad zone of influence in the Southwest to play an important role in opposing Gaullism. Of the three main parties of the Liberation, one, the MRP, saw its daily, *L'Aube,* disappear in 1951; the second, the Socialist party, managed to retain *Le Populaire* as a daily until 1966; while the third, the Communist party, still succeeds in maintaining its national daily, *L'Humanité,* although it has a daily printing of only 190,000 and a circulation of 150,000 for more than 5,000,000 Communist voters. *La Nation,* the organ of the remaining large party of the Fifth Republic, with its four short pages and its circulation of a scant 12,000, would have been considered nothing more than a mere internal news sheet had its editorials not been quoted by the newspapers and by radio and television. *La Nation* survived only because of governmental subsidies. These subsidies were withdrawn in August 1974, when *La Nation* sharply criticized the new president, Valery Giscard d'Estaing; it disappeared shortly thereafter.

The figures in Table 1 show the concentration process dramatically. A few further explanations are necessary. In the first place, there has been a global decline in the production of dailies, particularly since the number of copies published, already dropping in absolute terms, is declining even more if one takes into account constantly rising population figures. In 1946 there were 25 million French voters; in 1974 there were 30 million; in addition, the 18-to-21-year-olds, not yet voters but certainly readers of the newspapers, are much more numerous now than they were three decades ago. The Frenchman is not a large consumer of newspapers —and what he reads in his usual daily paper is not necessarily party news. Second, the concentration of the Paris press, even if discernible between the prewar period and 1946, still remains weak in comparison with the world's other large cities. The Parisian situation is better than that in London and certainly better than that in New York.

On the other hand—and this is a most important point—the concentration of the provincial press is actually much more pronounced than one would be led to imagine from Table 1. A large number of the titles counted are those of newspapers which are members of chains, with only the local news actually written by the papers' editors. Even between large newspapers, situations of

Table 1. CONCENTRATION OF FRENCH NEWSPAPERS

	Paris		*Provinces*		*Total*
Year	*No. of Titles*	*No. of Copies Printed**	*No. of Titles*	*No. of Copies Printed**	*No. of Copies Printed**
1914	60	5	242	4	9
1939	31	6	175	6	12
1946	28	6	153	9.2	15.1
1956	14	4.4	111	7	11.5
1966	14	4.4	91	7.8	12.2
1972	11	3.9	78	7.5	11.4

*Average number of copies printed per day in millions.

interdependency can exist. The two most significant examples are, first, in the Rhone-Alps region, where the two large dailies, *Le Progrès* and *Le Dauphine Libéré,* have divided the area and established a common newsgathering source, the Aigles agency, and, second, in Marseilles, where *Le Provençal,* edited by the socialist leader Gaston Deferre, bought out its chief rival, *Le Méridional,* in order to control the entire political arena. In the latter case, *Le Méridional* is allowed some editorial latitude and is to the right of *Le Provençal.*

Concentration has created real monopoly situations in large areas of France. Typical are the case of *Sud-Ouest,* which is published in Bordeaux, and above all that of *Ouest-France,* which is published in Rennes and which, with a daily circulation of close to 700,000, is largely without competition in many départements. The problems caused by this state of affairs have been decried throughout the Western world and will be analyzed from a French point of view later. However, such concentration also has certain advantages. When the same newspaper is read by all varieties of people, social communication between groups becomes much easier than it is when each group reads only the newspaper which suits it. (It is not at all certain that cable television would end up giving better news coverage; it could establish "ghettos" of purely internal communication.) In any case, the monopolistic newspaper should at least transmit a wide variety of news, and this is only done to a limited degree. However, during the 1974 presidential campaign, the attitude of *Ouest-France,* for example, was found to be remarkably balanced, serious, and impartial, providing its readers with accurate information about the candidates and their platforms.

The problem of power within any newspaper's organization and the way that this is tied to the independence or dependence of the editorial board is the same in France as in similar countries, with certain unique characteristics. Different newspaper chains have different sets of relationships. A few examples can illustrate this point. Robert Hersant, "centrist" member of parliament from the Oise, publishes eight regional dailies (of which one, *Centre-Presse,* was the product of takeovers and mergers of 11 others) and controls a series of weeklies and monthlies, ranging from *L'Auto Journal* to *La Bonne Cuisine.* Jean Prouvost, the great wool manufacturer who launched two unprecedented successes, *Paris-Soir* and *Match* before the war, keeps up his incredibly energetic pace despite the fact that he is nearing 90. Not only does he still control the weekly *Paris-Match,* which he started in 1949 (and which has long been declining) and not only does he still share with Hachette control of the largest radio and television weekly, *Télé 7 Jours* (with a weekly circulation of between 2.5 and 3 million), but also from 1950 to 1975 he was in charge of *Le Figaro,* which he acquired in 1972 after having been co-owner since 1950; in 1975, though, he sold his shares to Robert Hersant, who is now the new master of the old paper and dictates a conservative orientation.

Prouvost's power, in terms of financial resources and the variety of publications controlled, is more limited than that of the Hachette group, but he undoubtedly has more direct influence on editorial boards than does anyone in Hachette. La Librairie Hachette, founded in 1826, deals not only with newspapers. Its bookstore and publications section–with its division that publishes textbooks, its divisions that publish series of editions (including the largest French company producing pocketbooks), and its publishing houses (Hachette, Fayard, Grasset, Stock)–allow it to control approximately one-fifth of all French publishing. By holding 49 percent of the stock–as against that held by five newspaper cooperatives–in the NMPP (Nouvelles Messageries de la Presse Parisienne), Hachette also occupies a central position in the distribution of newspapers and magazines in France. In advertising, in record distribution, in television film production, in the use of videotape and cassettes, and in printing, Hachette is omnipresent. Hachette has total or partial control of all sorts of weekly and monthly newspapers; but it controls only one daily, *France-Soir,* and that has been steadily on the decline as its sensationalist headlines and pictures are displaced by television news coverage. The most political weekly controlled by Hachette is *Le Point,* which was started in 1972 by a team of journalists who had left *L'Express.*

If Hachette has no real counterpart in other countries, much the same can be said of Bayard-Presse, the largest Catholic publisher in the world. Its 18 different publications, each addressing its own audience, stand as models of openness. This spirit is seen in *La Croix,* in various publications for young people of all ages, in the monthly *Notre Temps,* which is addressed to senior citizens, and in *Presse Actualité,* the French publication which best deals with the problems of journalism.

When one speaks of an individual or group controlling a

newspaper, does one mean that editorial freedom does not exist? There is no clear answer to this question. In September 1971, Simon Nora, a high-level advisor to Premier Chabon-Delmas, became managing director of Hachette. Immediately the questions arose: To what extent does political power influence a private enterprise? To what extent can this group gain more from those in power? How much can an individual's loyalty and perceptions change, just because he has changed jobs? Other questions followed: When *Le Point* was launched in 1970, it showed no hostility to Chaban-Delmas. Does one attribute all subsequent political stances taken by *Le Point* to Simon Nora, despite the fact that the editorial board enjoys wide autonomy and, during the presidential election, along with support for the Gaullist candidate, a number of editors also were sympathetic to Mitterrand?

On the other hand, *France-Soir* took a very clear position–in both the presentation of its news and its commentary–in favor of the mayor of Bordeaux. This seems to confirm the notion that this paper's orientation could have been predicted. Shortly before Pompidou's death, the editor of *France-Soir,* who had been associated with the President, was replaced by Henri Amouroux, an excellent journalist who until that time had been the editor of *Sud-Ouest,* Bordeaux's major daily. (Amouroux, though, was fired a few months after the electoral defeat of Chaban-Delmas.) At the same time, Prouvost was installing the author Jean d'Ormesson, a faithful follower of Valéry Giscard d'Estaing, as the new editor of *Le Figaro.* Certainly it is evident that Jean Prouvost is much more concerned with controlling the content of the newspapers he controls financially than is, for example, Marcel Boussac, the industrialist who has financial control of *L'Aurore,* or F. Beghin, the sugar manufacturer who used to be co-owner of *Le Figaro.*

In order to protect their freedom and to fight against the power of owners who sell their journalistic enterprises (and their journalists) just as they do their industrial enterprises, editors have tried –probably at an earlier date and more frequently than in other countries–to obtain certain guarantees. In 1969, the editors of *Le Figaro* were protected by a hierarchical administrative set up. The editors of *Paris-Normandie* (Rouen) and of the largest political weekly, *L'Express,* also gained certain protections which were theoretically quite important. However, this movement was slowed down and its momentum has been reversed. No association of editors has achieved decisive results; *Le Monde* remains an isolated example.

Le Monde, founded on December 11, 1944, is the only enterprise of its kind. Its capital is divided into 1,000 shares, grouped into three categories. The A shares, 400 of them, belong to individuals such as Hubert Beuve-Mery, the editor from 1944 to 1969, who with his sons owns 155 shares. The B shares belong to personnel associations –400 to the Association of Editors, 50 to the association representing other officials, 40 to the association of the employees. Lastly, the C shares belong to the existing editors, 70 to Jacques Fauvet, the editor-in-chief, and 40 to the business manager. *Le Monde* has continuously increased its circulation and its advertising revenue, and, because it is a profitable venture, the question of assigning fresh assets does not arise. This assures the Association of Editors a privileged position from which to exercise a certain amount of control, if not actual direction, over the newspaper, a situation which also has some drawbacks.

To what extent does the need for advertisers limit a newspaper's freedom? Again, the answer is not simple. The limitation is not strictly political, but the list of economic and social problems with which advertisers might be concerned would be long–although this does not necessarily mean that large newspapers, considered as good vehicles by advertising agencies, will necessarily bow to the interests of the advertisers. However, especially when compared to papers in other countries, French newspapers must gain a high proportion of their revenue (up to 80 percent) from advertising, largely because few Frenchmen take out subscriptions. (Distribution to newsstands is so costly that lack of subscriptions effectively cancels out receipts from readers.) In 1972, *Le Monde,* with a circulation of 360,000, had only 77,000 subscribers; *Le Figaro,* with a circulation of 724,000, had only 6,000 subscribers. Only *La Croix* is sold mainly to subscribers (114,000, for a circulation of 131,000); this has permitted it to survive despite very low advertising revenues, as its readers are not considered to be as "consumer oriented" by advertisers as are those of other publications. This touches upon a fundamental aspect of the leverage exerted by money: the more readers a newspaper has and the more money its readers have, then the more advertising the newspaper will acquire, thus allowing it to expand further and thereby attract even more advertising, thus allowing it to expand still further, and so on and on.

In principle, the "revolution" which affected the press in 1945 was to have led to state protection of the newspapers from the control of moneyed interests. While this protection is largely illusory, the state does actually subsidize the press. The state subsidizes newspapers by permitting the French press to buy paper below international rates, by giving it privileged postal rates, and by providing tax exemptions. However, this subsidy has two serious drawbacks. First, it favors the well-off. Since the larger newspapers use more paper and send heavier packages through the mails, they receive proportionately more assistance than do the smaller ones. In 1973 a small supplementary subsidy was given to those papers with the smallest advertising revenue. However, even this did not compensate for the "supersubsidy" which the large papers receive through their advertising—advertising which on top of everything else enjoys more tax exemption than does anything else in the paper. More important, the government wields a formidable instrument of pressure against the newspapers, for it can always threaten to revoke the subsidy inherent in lower paper prices and postal rates.

IV. WHAT INFLUENCE?

Let us assume that the essential function of a newspaper is to inform the public. What type of information is most easily transmitted? In the provinces it is easy to answer this question. Newspapers permit people to keep in touch with what is happening locally. When a strike kept *Sud-Ouest* from appearing in February 1972, the nature of the "news" in its local editions became abundantly clear. Suddenly there were fewer people at funerals and at weddings; country people stopped frequenting local movie theaters; no one was certain when any of the local clubs were to meet. These were not momentous political events, but they were important to the paper's readers.

Newspapers also carry a good deal of "information," whether true or false, which helps the readers to escape from the dullness of their daily lives. (When Queen Elizabeth visited France, the *Sunday Times* of London published an amusing "roundup" of "news" about the Queen which had already appeared in a certain segment of the French press in the preceding year. In all, so the reports went, she had been pregnant 92 times, had had 149 accidents and 9 miscarriages, had been on the point of abdication 63 times, and had been close to separation from Prince Philip 73 times!)

Daily information such as the weather report and entertainment notices publicizing such events as a local brass band concert also contribute to the depoliticization of the news. This phenomenon is accentuated by the numerous weekly and monthly "popular romance" publications, replete with their endless, illustrated serials of romantic fiction. The office girl who spends her time reading about the "true romance" of another office girl who ends up marrying the boss or the boss' son is evading reality and can hardly be thinking of improving her fate through trade union action.

In France as in other countries, however, newspapers and television do have good reasons for not dwelling on in-depth analyses of delicate and complex social, economic, and political questions: the reader and the television viewer do not want these. If the audience does not demand these programs and articles, it is because they are not accustomed to regarding the media critically. They are not taught to question in grade school, in high school, even in the university. The French school system (and this fault is common among other systems as well) does not prepare future citizens for practical criticism of the media. It does not even provide the tools so that the citizenry can draw proper conclusions from bits and pieces of information.

It is difficult to measure the effect of newspapers on the public—whether this effect is positive or negative. At best one can find a few clues. One such clue points to the limits of direct political influence. Just as the Republicans would always win in the United States if editorial writers determined the vote—since a vast majority of the American newspapers are controlled by Republicans—in the same way the residents of the "red" outskirts of Paris would long ago have ceased voting Communist, if they had followed the non-Communist *La Parisien Libéré* and *France-Soir,* which they read, rather than the Communist *L'Humanité,* which they scarcely read. *La Parisien Libéré* does not even attempt to hide its right-wing Gaullist orientation, while *France-Soir* shows evidence of a more insidious progovernment stance as well as a more open "Chaban-ism." It is possible to see, however, how *Le Parisien Libéré* caters to the petty bourgeois tendencies of the working class, particularly working class people confronted with immigrant laborers, how it relies on sensationalist headlines and the appeal to facile indignation against all that disrupts the proper order.

Traditionally the editorial writer and the reporter, each in his own way, has attempted to express the thoughts and the feelings of the readers and of the public as a whole. Their articles have contributed greatly to popular views of public opinion. Today public opinion is translated (and partially created) by the polls, just as newspapers create in part the currents they claim to reflect.

The large newspapers have thus lost, to a great extent, their role as representatives or spokespersons of the voting public vis-à-vis the politicians and ruling groups. This phenomenon has coincided with another which further diminishes the influence of newspapers on the public. Under the Third and Fourth Republics, leading newspaper editors and journalists were in constant communication with political figures who felt they needed the journalists as sources of information in times of rapidly fluctuating political and governmental situations. This type of direct contact has perceptively diminished since 1958, though it does remain stronger than one might guess.

The section of the press which is influential in political matters is relatively easy to delimit. Within this section we have neither a widely read newspaper such as *Le Parisien Libéré,* which everyone knows is hardly representative of its readers, nor a quality paper such as *La Croix,* because its sphere of influence remains unknown to politicians. We certainly do find *Le Figaro,* the three weekly journals *L'Express, Le Point,* and *Le Nouvel Observateur,* and, above all, *Le Monde,* which, in addition to their news and editorial commentaries, often publish positions taken by political leaders and are, even for those most critical of them, a sort of debating ground for the political milieu—a milieu which is highly difficult to define because its borders are so flexible and its composition so varied.

Other social groups are perhaps easier to define but not easier to analyze in terms of the long-lasting influence that the press holds over them. First, the most relevant segment of the press is probably that which has not been discussed at all, specialized weeklies and monthlies which are aimed at definite professional groups and which are being read more and more. One example suffices: it is highly probable that *Agri-Sept* contributes more to forming the opinions of farmers than do the regional dailies which they also read. Second, available statistics are not necessarily relevant. For example, the far-left weekly *Politique-Hebdo* did a study of its own readers which revealed that its audience was not necessarily working class; the readership was comprised 30 percent of university and high school students, 22 percent of teachers, and 5 percent of factory and farm workers. However, a good many of its readers are militant, and their ideological influence is not negligible.

In any case, influence is always reciprocal. One must not exaggerate the distinction between those who inform and those who are informed, nor between the dispensers of propaganda and the subjects of propaganda. Just as directors, ministers, or parliamentarians, heads of companies or union leaders, newspaper editors and journalists act, so they are acted upon; just as they form the views of others, so their views are shaped as well. It is this interaction which makes the problem of information one of the most complex, one of the most important, and one of the most deceptive in politics.

Chapter 7

A MATURING TELOCRACY: OBSERVATIONS ON THE TELEVISION COVERAGE OF THE BRITISH GENERAL ELECTIONS OF 1974

ANTHONY SMITH

A General Election Campaign ought to provide the ideal testing ground for theories of media influence: an election is a political set piece with skilled performers, an organized audience ready to take concerted and measurable actions at a given moment. The evidence for the "who," the "what," and the "to whom" is virtually public from the start. But elections in practice have been notoriously difficult areas for media study: the lessons from one electoral situation are difficult to transfer to another; the periods between elections are normally long enough for the theories, conceptions, and methodologies to shift significantly and the researchers to move on to other fields; the great techniques of propaganda itself are, many of them, inapplicable to the short period of time in which electoral battles reach their peak. "A campaign is the simplest, most imperfect form of modern propaganda," wrote Jacques Ellul, "the objective is insufficient, the methods are incomplete, the duration is brief, pre-propaganda is absent, and the campaign propagandist never has all the media at his disposal. . . . the one case in which the measurement of effects is comparatively easy . . . is also by far the least significant" (1973:261). The difficulty has perhaps been that researchers have tended to separate the content of propaganda from the events and the audience concerned; we examine constraints upon the media themselves as if these were separate phenomena from the effects of the media upon the public; an examination of the forms and methods of electoral television, as it is developing in Britain, would suggest that the constraints (of impartiality, say, or the exclusion of particular groups or parties or issues from coverage) are also constraints upon the ability of the audience to perceive an event in a particular way. The *expectation* of impartiality as a prescribed constraint within broadcast content might itself affect the audience's willingness to vote or to participate in the electoral process. An audience cannot be influenced by a medium which is visibly constrained; it can be entertained and informed, but it is less likely to be persuaded if it is constantly reminded that the forms in which the communication occurs are somehow prearranged precisely to prevent the audience feeling the full impact. British general elections have been haunted by the constant specter of information withheld. "We are not being given the facts," say many voters to pollsters, although information is pouring at them through print and electronic media in unprecedented quantity. It could be that the program formats have created or reinforced a kind of cognitive reticence, which defies measurement.

It seems necessary to this observer to adjust our mental pictures of political communication to take into account the dominant nature of the genres within which political programs are beamed at the audience, genres which are supposed to act as simualted models of "real" political activity. The phone-in show, for example, gives the impression of direct inquiry or inquisition by a doubtful voter of a political candidate; but it is simultaneously one segment of a prepared pattern of programs in which a broadcasting authority, operating under license and in the light of precedent and policy, is attempting to provide no advantage to any party other than that which news events (i.e., political "history") necessitate. The discussion program or debate, which is presumed to present a balanced presentation of arguments, carries with it an aura of having been transported from the real scene of political battle into the studio. It is a *version* of the political debate carried on spontaneously elsewhere.

Television has acquired the additional function of being the register of which historic events are significant, and the process of event→news coverage→critical assessment→point scored→voter influence begins to feed upon itself. The original "event," which may be a speech or the announcement of a statistic will be monitored and timed in its announcement to feed into the pattern of other events, to prevent risk of an accusation of bias; the events are selected partly to fit into the needs of the genres within which coverage is to be slotted. Of course, great pains are taken to separate news bulletins from the strict application of the rubric of impartiality; comment is deliberately balanced while news is supposed to follow its own nonbalanced set of "values," but the total machinery of broadcasting has now become so important to electoral activity that that distinction tends to be obliterated under the sheer weight of the overall necessity to balance. An "unbalanced" item in a news bulletin takes on the feeling of a major piece of editorializing during the tense weeks of an electoral campaign, even though it is formally permitted within the broadcasting rules.

In the relatively small quantity of literature which the two British general election campaigns of 1974 have hitherto generated, two views emerge, views, in fact, which reemphasize the trends of what has been said in studies of previous elections ever since the mid-1960s. The first asserts that television dominated the election to the point at which it has become impossible to say that any election existed at all outside its televisual manifestation. "The General Election Campaign as the creation of organised parties is made to exist by them in ways dictated by the presence of the mass media in general and television in particular" (Pateman, 1975:2). Senior party leaders organize their walkabouts to get the best coverage in the early evening bulletins on all three channels. The content of the big set-piece speeches at public halls in the evenings is designed partly to catch headlines the following morning, but mainly to get live coverage in the midevening news bulletins and the later discussion programs on television. The morning press conferences given by all three parties are designed to get pithy statements into the early afternoon radio news programs and the afternoon papers. The audience, therefore, experiences its election largely through the mediation of television, and the flow of debate and argument is made to fit the contours of program scheduling.

The second discussion to emerge is whether the collectivity of constraints which affect broadcasters' activity "sanitizes" the content of the programs and angles the whole election to the needs of those groups already dominating political life. "Rather than employing the medium to cast a journalistic eye over the political questions of the election, studios and facilities were effectively given over to the propagation of the ideas and feelings of the three main parties" (Tracey, 1975:490). The constraints in this argument are twofold: there are those which emanate from the organizational hierarchy, the broadcasting authorities, the party leaders, and to some extent the electoral law itself, and there are others which arise from the professionalized assumption that the audience finds politics boring and that their needs and interests can be satisfied only through the sacrifice of adequate reflection of political issues.

An older line of research, into the effect upon voting of the mass media coverage of a campaign, is gradually gaining less attention than the modern and more subtle issues of social control through constraints upon content. Most modern discussion about propaganda has emphasized that campaigning is itself the least effective because it is the shortest-term means of influencing opinion. Opposing arguments neutralize each other: the population is indifferent to the material offered; none of the really powerful techniques of modern mass propaganda can be effective in a few short weeks (Ellul, 1973:19). The first full-scale study of television's influence on a British general election reached the conclusion, consistent with that of similar studies in American elections, the previously held presumptions of the persuasiveness of television were gross exaggerations (Trenaman and McQuail, 1961). Throughout the sixties the view prevailed that election campaigning on television was helping to improve the level of general political education in the country but not to influence attitudes. "Television may inform or reinforce attitudes, but it rarely converts," was the view of one of the Nuffield College electoral studies (Harrison, 1965:156). Later and more elaborate studies of television effects in elections have tended to explode even more of the common assumptions which have been held: for instance, examination of the 1966 election indicated that television is far less of a personalizing medium than has been thought. "Impressions of politicians are no more susceptible to media influence than are attitudes towards the parties" (Blumler and McQuail, 1968:262). The findings of the same study tended toward the abolition of other prevailing notions too: television did not tend to force the election more toward national at the expense of local issues than would have been the case anyway, nor does it tend itself to "moderate the tone of political argument," that process has been the result of the growth of a more affluent voter learning to appreciate practical rather than ideological argument. Nor even was there convincing evidence that television had helped to raise voting turnout, although there did appear to be in broadcast coverage a positive aid to the rise of third parties in a traditional two-party situation (Blumer and McQuail, 1968:261-281). (Certainly, in the context of the partial fragmentation of the party system in the general elections of 1974, the allocation of broadcasting time to the new spectrum of small parties was felt to be of crucial importance.)

What has happened, broadly speaking, in the study of media influence on elections since the first "television election" of 1959 is that a series of wide-ranging assumptions of media power have been refined into a series of supposed special tendencies latent within broadcast coverage; these, in turn, have been dethroned as the political circumstances of one election after the other have exploded one theory after another. We are left with all the old hypodermic theses in ruins, and in place of them what we have acquired is a view that television professionals merely reinforce the prevailing set of political relationships and, in the interests of viewer appeal, emphasize conflict among policies and politicians. The media, it is argued, have come to define the campaign more than the contending parties themselves. One observation of the whole trend of mass media coverage of elections in the postwar period argues that the media "struck the balance between issues and personalities, seeking continually to impose a differentiation on the parties, in the interests, presumably, of clarifying the choices open to the electorate. They sought also, doubtless for the same reasons, to avoid a 'quiet' campaign" (Seymour-Ure, 1974:233). Some observers have tried to argue a much more vigorous case, alleging the complete trivialization of politics by the media; television has been responsible for the vitrual elmination of cognitive activity by the voter. "We have already indicated that the classical Jeffersonian image of the voter—the voter who is capable of making purely rational judgments based upon the (factual) political information he seeks out and receives—is simply a quaint hyperbole in light of present social-science evidence. . . . Politics on television affords voters a sense of participation in the dramatic political events of their time without the work that is involved in understanding the serious abstractions involved" (Mendelsohn and Crespi, 1970:294-295). Television, so goes this argument, has changed the patterns of political campaign activity, the habits of the thoughtful voter, trivializing the political process at every level.

What we are seeing is a unitary concept of television being applied as a necessary and sufficient cause of whatever changes have in practice occurred in the conduct of electoral and other political activity. The very nature of the tendencies within the political scientists' arguments between the sixties and the seventies indicates a consistent willingness to label television as the cause of a series of everchanging circumstances. The development of political television since 1959 has enabled more and more elements in the campaign in the "real" world to be reflected on the screen; that, in itself, reflects the increasing willingness of the various actors within the arena of politics to permit the access of television. It also reflects the increasing versatility of television in developing formats and professionalism which exploit the increasing opportunities. As more of the activity is tailored to the needs of broadcasting, it is inevitable that more of the actual changes in the conduct of politics will be ascribed causatively to the medium through which they are reflected. In one sense this process of argument is quite logical; in another it becomes increasingly tautological. In an era of prosperity, an election will inevitably appear to involve the auctioning of material goods more than the debating of serious historical questions. In periods of major economic and social tension, third and fourth parties will tend to emerge, or fragmentations will occur within existing parties; all these processes will be increasingly apparent from watching television. Whether, in any real sense, the medium can be properly seen as the historic "cause" is doubtful.

That is not to say that television is a crystal mirror passively reflecting the circumstances of history. Television encompasses a series of institutions operating a series of technologies which transmit heavily processed and predetermined images within a series of genres, which range from advertizing to news bulletins. Broadcasting will tend to portray different images of political activity—from occasion to occasion—within different dominant genres. Since television, as we shall see, has acquired the taste of *mobilizing* the society to vote as well as that of presenting the electoral options, then it has to turn ceaselessly from genre to genre in order to keep the material interesting and therefore politically effective. The broadcasters exercise a sufficient range of professional options to be blamed for the effects of political activity as portrayed on the screen, but within politically prescribed constraints so tight as to make their medium a secondary one. The initiatives within the world of political communication have to come from elsewhere—from newspaper journalists, from politicians, from community leaders. Yet the broadcasters must devise formulas which unite two contrary impulses, of independent thought and of independent arbitrage of an objective struggle. As one major figure in British television, Sydney Bernstein, said in a *Times* article in 1961: "The two streams of British journalism—the journalism of protest and the journalism of authority—meet uneasily in television today. It is one thing for a newspaper to canvas a variety of opinions in its features and editorials over the year. It is another thing to impose upon an editor the responsibility of producing every feature and every editorial in such a way that exactly balances the conflicting opinions of every situation" (Granada Television, 1974c).

In many respects the British electoral system has slipped painlessly into the era of television. We are now a case of advanced telocracy. Electoral contests in Britain are relatively brief three-week affairs preceded by a period of speculation as to the date likely to be chosen by the reigning Prime Minister. Television, restlessly searching for novelty and for the dramatic, builds up the audience's interest in the forthcoming spectacle and then throws enormous resources into the coverage of the brief campaign. In British politics the basic cast of characters is quite small; a brace of party leaders, already known but perhaps not fully tested in advance of the big match, pitch into the fray, one or more of them knowing that his political life as well as his party's chances of office may well be at stake in the struggle. Although our constitutional life is not what has come to be labelled presidential in style, our electoral life does necessitate the projection of a few people to the mass electorate.

In the actual conduct of national electoral warfare, day-by-day television has entrenched as much as changed many of the traditional practices. It has enabled senior politicians to go on the stump and yet be seen night after night by the whole electorate as well as those in a particular region of the country. Senior party men and women, always with their eye on the clock, must organize their key statements around the anticipated requirements of newspaper editions, long-distance trains, and the engineering of front-page layouts, and they find it sometimes easier to cope with the needs of television politics. They emphasize, of course, the difficulties when asked to comment on the impact of television on their professional lives as politicians, but at least they know that once their skills are acquired, the timings of television are predictable, precise, and zealously fair between sides. Communicating with a mass electorate entirely through the press and the platform involves pitting one's wits against a wall of doctrinal hostility on the part of at least some of the newspapers. With television (and radio) at least the politician enjoys *rights* as well as undergoes risks. There is, among the various added frustrations, the appalling problem, in live performances, that one political gaff or one piece of unfairness on the part of the broadcasters can bring terrible penalties, when the whole of the rest of the media can seize upon it and exploit it for days. But in the rapidly flowing three-week campaign the skilled politician also has the opportunity to exploit the instantaneity of television for himself.

I emphasize the convenience of the television campaign to the politician in the British context not merely because this is sometimes overlooked but because we are beginning to see certain changes in the public acceptance of political (and especially electoral) activity on the screen. The two general elections of 1974 might well, when looked back on with the hindsight of a decade, prove to be some kind of turning point. The first of these elections took place on a day in late February—a time of year when television viewing is usually fairly high and the long winter evenings conducive to long hours of continuous passive reception. In any case, the sheer volume of political broadcasting was greater than in any previous election. Between the dissolution of Parliament and the day of polling, the two BBC television channels projected 11½ hours of coverage of actual politicians, excluding the 14 programs which are transmitted on all three channels simultaneously and are under the editorial control of the parties themselves rather than the broadcasters (Windlesham, 1975:146-147). (In Britain, where no political paid advertizing is allowed by law, the broadcasting authorities by agreement between themselves and those parties contesting a modicum of seats, allocate various periods of time between the parties in which they can transmit their own programs of propaganda. At these times no other competitive broadcasting is allowed on any channel, leaving the politicians, for a brief period, with a wholly captive audience.) Each evening on BBC-1 there was a one-hour block of news and politics between 9 and 10 p.m. On BBC-2 a 40-minute discussion program was presented at 11 p.m. Five other major current affairs programs, which normally deal with the whole range of public matters, presented special editions dealing with the election during that brief campaign period. Three editions of the weekly "Panorama" (50 minutes in length) were devoted to the British economy, and two editions of "The Money Programme" looked at the problems of food and other prices and at questions of industry. There were also three editions of a program entitled "Election Forum," long periods of program time in which the three party leaders, each in a program of his own, answered questions submitted by viewers. (On radio nearly one hour every morning was bring dedicated to an innovation in British election broadcasting –direct telephoned questions from listeners.) Some of the party election broadcasts, in addition to other election programs, were transmitted regionally rather than nationally, to give opportunities for local issues to be dealt with by politicians contesting seats in those regions; these gave an opportunity for Welsh and Scottish nationalist parties, for instance, as well as the right-wing extremist National Front party, to have their own broadcasting time, although the Communist party, which had fielded the necessary 50 candidates to qualify for television time in the 1970 general election, failed, in February 1974, to put up the necessary modicum of candidates. Altogether, in February 1974, the total amount of BBC television time devoted to the election was a third higher than in the previous general election (Harrison, 1974:146-169).

On the Independent (commercial) channel a similar pattern of increased attention to politics was apparent. During the campaign period, there were 3½ hours of party election broadcasts, plus 16 hours of national news coverage by ITN (the special national news unit which operates within the basically regional structure of the British Independent system), plus 8½ hours of nationally disseminated programs dealing with discussion and comment on political topics. In addition to all of this there were 52 hours of regional material broadcast by the regional companies which compose the Independent system. It was clear that British broadcasting was not playing down the "snap" election called by Prime Minister Edward Heath in the complex political circumstances of winter 1974.

There had been tense circumstances which had given rise to the election and to the one which followed it in the autumn of the same year. In February 1974 Britain passed through the most serious and the most tiresome of its many financial-industrial crises in the postwar period. A long-drawn-out national miners' strike was depriving the country of coal supplies necessary to maintain industrial activity; the international crisis in energy was simultaneously beginning to bite deep. The government under Edward Heath refused to concede the pay claim of the miners and the entire country was put on a sort of war footing; television closed down at 10 p.m.; the whole of the working population was put on a three-day week; an atmosphere of appalling gloom was made suddenly to envelop a population which still, despite all the trappings of national emergency, was failing to take its economic disasters seriously. Television ran a governmental "Switch Off Something" campaign, and we all dutifully looked for some convenient appliance to turn down. We shivered patriotically while waiting for the posturing to cease. The climax was an announcement that Edward Heath was to call a general election as the result of which he hoped to achieve a reaffirmation of his leadership from the people so clear that the miners would capitulate and accept a lower pay increase and the government's policy of sternly controlled wage rises would be saved.

What happened at the end of a very brief and intense electoral campaign was that Edward Heath lost office and Harold Wilson, former Prime Minister and opposition leader, returned to office, but without an overall plurality of votes in Parliament behind him, which betokened an inevitable repeat election within a brief period. In October 1974 that election was held, and the country gave Wilson a tiny overall majority in Parliament, sufficient to govern, but insufficient to claim any total mandate. One quarter of the electorate had voted for parties other than Labour or Conservative, a proportion unprecedented in modern postwar politics. Parliament henceforth was to contain a cluster of small parties, nationalists of various half-submerged Celtic nations, the odd independent, a minibusful of Liberals.

The tenseness of the general political atmosphere during the miners' strike had encouraged most commentators to predict an explosive election campaign. Class conflict of the kind experienced in the prewar period was thought to be about to return. Violence was even expected by many. In the event, the first election campaign of 1974 was fought in gentlemanly fashion, the claims and counter-claims of the politicians being far less shrill than political circumstances had led the public to expect. Only Enoch Powell, the maverick Conservative right-winger, became a major source of interparty tension when he recommended the public to vote Labour, on the ground that the election had been called on a false basis and that a Labour victory would ensure the departure of Edward Heath and the establishment of a government more likely to take Britain out of the Common Market. The only television program to cause an important rumpus during the campaign was one (an edition of "Panorama") dealing with the Common Market in which Mr. Powell was intended to play an important part; even in this case the row blew over when the BBC agreed to use, not a live appearance by Mr. Powell, but a recorded extract of a speech previously made by him on the Common Market issue (BBC, 1974a:19). Both Labour and Liberal parties made protests during the campaign at various aspects of the coverage but not of a very strident nature. It was a quiet campaign which seemed all the quieter for the atmosphere of extreme drama in which it had been precipitated. Perhaps it was not surprising that the BBC began to receive complaints that television was overdoing its coverage (Dunkley, 1974). Night after night the audience looked in to prolonged periods of political discussion and reporting, waiting in vain for the gladiatorial combat between Heath and Wilson, between class and class, between unions and public interest, which various influential "experts" had promised.

The BBC conducted an Audience Research Inquiry shortly after the election which showed that a large proportion of the electorate thought that television had concentrated too much on the campaign. Even among that category of the sample who were "enthusiastic" in their political interest, one-third thought television coverage excessive. Among those who described themselves as "apathetic" toward politics, nearly 90 percent held this view (BBC, 1974a:22-23; Harrison, 1975). It was inevitable that in the next election, imminent because of the indecisive nature of the February one, the broadcasting authorities would reduce the total coverage for fear that, by boring the audience, the broadcasters might inadvertently be doing a disservice to the democratic system (BBC, 1974b). In the event, the total coverage was reduced by about a quarter, and much of the time that was devoted to political material was no longer concentrated in peak hours; in particular the one-hour band of news and comment between 9 and 10 was abandoned by the BBC and divided into separate parts, as had been the pattern in many of the general elections of the previous decade.

One Conservative politician, who is himself a writer on media questions and a broadcaster, analyzed in a speech delivered in the summer of 1974 some of the implications of excessive coverage of an election. Lord Windlesham invited his audience to consider whether this might induce "cynicism" in the audience, whether the tone of political debate as presented to the public in hour after hour of political discussion in television studios might not bring discredit on the practice of politics. "Is it necessary," he asked, "that the conventions of political broadcasting should result in transposing to the media the confrontation style of politics which marks the proceedings on the floor of the House of Commons?" (Windlesham, 1975:148). It is worth paying a great deal of attention to the question of "overkill," of inducing boredom or cynicism, because it is through this fear that one can observe the role played by broadcasting in doing more than report, as if it were a whole series of newspapers, a quantity of political activities. In taking deliberate measure of its own excessive attention to political activity, the broadcasters, in a sense, are acknowledging a power different from that traditionally ascribed to the press. It is the power to shape a society and a power inescapably molded by mass communications; it is the acceptance of a manipulative function in society, a realization that the broadcasting environment of a society is an element in the political environment and has responsibilities to it, not merely to reflect it but to sustain it (Curran, 1973). In the early months of 1975, as another event unique in British constitutional history drew near—a referendum on whether the country would retain its membership of the European Common Market—the broadcasters took a further deliberate decision not to overplay their coverage. The rules of impartiality, of strict minute-for-minute balance between major parties with due acknowledgement of the minor parties, was no longer a sufficient doctrine for broadcasting coverage of political campaigns; henceforth an additional consideration would become crucial—that of whether the total range of material offered to the public might be likely to deter them from playing their part as citizens, whether by implication it might even have the effect of making them turn aside from the electoral process toward other forms of political expression. Among the various social phenomena for which television is henceforth liable to be blamed is any clear disillusionment within society at the overall political process. The broadcasting authorities in their commitment to impartiality in all its forms are coming to accept a more far-reaching responsibility, harder to guarantee: that of keeping a society wedded to its political structure. The coverage of major political events, therefore, such as general elections or a referendum, is by implication expected to do more than maintain unbiased news values but in fact to act as cosmetic artist to the political system. "If I read the signs aright," said the chairman of the BBC in a speech at Leeds University in which he summarized the BBC's experience of the two elections, "I believe the greatest risk we all face is that the public cries a plague on both your houses and proceeds to abstain from voting" (Swann, 1975). Looking forward to the referendum campaign of 1975 he saw that television, by presenting "too much wrangling," could produce dangers. "We in the BBC–and our colleagues in the IBA–have a major responsibility here. I am in no doubt that we overdid things a bit in the February election. . . . We took note of the fact, and in October I believe we got the emphasis more nearly right. But now we look like having a third major election-type campaign within eighteen months, and a campaign moreover restricted to the one topic. The risk of overdoing things is a very serious one, and we shall, I expect, set, or endeavour to set a slower tempo and a lower key than we have done for ordinary elections" (Swann, 1975). Almost unnoticed, the BBC was accepting the job of official guardian of democracy, a role which other senior broadcasters had been proclaiming in various degrees of enthusiasm since the attempt began, in the 1970s, to recover from the alleged breakdown of consensus in the previous decade (Dearlove, 1974).

Electoral broadcasting is caught in a double bind: in fulfilling a journalistic role it has to confront those in public life with the views of the broad mass of the governed–to put the questions, as all interviewers incessantly repeat, "which the average man would like to ask if he had the opportunity." However, as a medium which is obliged to operate within rules of impartiality of an extreme nature (especially during election campaigns), it finds itself reflecting the great center block of national opinion at the expense of the fringe views and therefore finds itself responsible for a bias against certain forms of political initiative. Since a broadcasting organization must orchestrate its overall approach to a major political event, it finds itself creating a simulated model of the political process which it is supposed to be displaying. The forms of programs which it divises and the genres within which it conducts its political communication are produced both by the rules of balance and the desire to present the election to the public. The election is presumed to have some independent historic existence; it is a contest conducted within its own traditional rules and customs, and these are transferred to television through television's own acquired responsibilities and norms. The two have on the whole fitted well together, but, as television has tended to obliterate the original form of the hustings and the practices of the platform and the press, it has had to accept this new responsibility, that of providing the *basic* structure by which politicians communicate with people. Today, if the fears of the broadcasters in the aftermath of the February election are to be taken as evidence, it has to guarantec the satisfactory mobilization of the public, it has to guarantee the *effects* of its forms upon political life, even though these have grown up primarily in the attempt merely to mirror traditional electoral genres.

A great deal can be learned about the political content of a society by examining the structures and forms of progams in which political material is transmitted. British television, like English literature, is particularly rich in forms or kinds, and the audience is felt to be highly sensitive to changes in structure. The basic fact about the relationship between the audience and the medium of broadcasting is that the former in a sense chooses the genre but not the content. The purchaser of a newspaper has at least the opportunity, in certain cases, of looking at the banner headline before he buys the paper. The reader of novels can read the reviews. The television audience is made to associate certain times of the week with certain strands of programming and he learns to choose the series, the slot, or the generic title. In the case of political television, every genre represents or encompasses a sector of the overall political process; it provides an image of what politics is, while allowing the political debate to move on one stage.

We have already referred to the role of the party election broadcast, which is presented to the viewer as a propaganda form, like the pamphlet or squib of the past. It is not a program which itself contains controversy, but it is intended to be received as a shaft of polemic; the parties adopt different forms for these programs from election to election, ranging from the strip-cartoon approach, adopted by the Labour party in 1959, to the extremely serious and carefully argued 10- or 15-minute speech by the party leader which many such programs have consisted of in recent years. The objective, in the latter type of programs, is to make the party leader as weighty as possible, to make him appear a real leader, serious, worthy of attention, treating his audience as adults. The audience is informed before and after every one of these broadcasts that the program is a party broadcast and therefore outside the editorial control of the broadcasters themselves.

In complete contrast is the case of the constituency report. In these, which are normally sections of news bulletins or of one of the major regular weekly current affairs programs, a reporter tours a given constituency and interviews all the candidates and emphasizes the special issues of controversy or political circumstances which might influence the result of the campaign in that particular place. The rules about appearances in such programs are extremely complicated and are controlled by the provisions of the Representation of the People Act (1969) and the Independent Broadcasting Authority Act (1973). A candidate is considered to be taking part in a program if he "actively and consciously participates." If he is seen in a piece of film as a result of a deliberate arrangement, then all the rules of balance have to apply: he may only take part if all the other candidates take part or if they agree that one of their number may appear without them. If one candidate refuses to appear, the others may do so, and the views of the absent candidate will be presented in some other way (over a still picture or in a reported statement by himself or his agent); however, in such a case, no debate is allowed between the other candidates actually taking part. A candidate in a particular constituency may, of course, take part in any other type of program, including a party election broadcast, but he may in no circumstances refer to the name of his constituency without infringing the rules of balance (ITCA, 1974). The reporter acts as interviewer and attempts to describe impartially the circumstances of the constituency concerned; he may sum up but obviously must do so in such a way as to enable the viewer to reach his own conclusions. Reporters who have strong personal styles take good care to keep them firmly under control at election times when politicians are seldom shy of crying foul. Harrison describes some of these reports in the October election as "unhelpfully inhibited." "Campaign Special," the BBC's nightly television program which provided large amounts of election news (in both elections), was the main vehicle for such constituency reports. The reporters are allowed to exercise their usual imagination and their verbal ability but within the very firm structures which the rules of appearances of candidates have created. The constituency report is like a sonnet, a form with extremely rigid rules of form and shape which exudes always a highly predictable sentiment: the voters of X-land or Y-land must make up their minds between three, four, or five candidates, some of whom are politically and intellectually marginal but are taking part in a solemn political ritual. The image of the "real" election provided by the constituency report, as a form, is quite false; the viewer knows it is false, but, like the audience of the Elizabethan sonnet, he becomes a connoisseur of the form, knowing that the content is utterly predictable and, as if it were, irrelevant.

The creation of program formulas is influenced more by inhibition toward politics than creativeness, and several of the most familiar formats can be traced back through the years to various ordinances or negative declarations by the politicians. For instance, ever since a program called "The Last Debate" in the 1959 election, politicians at election times have refused to face live audiences; neither side has been willing to run the risk of facing an audience the composition of which might be fixed by a competing party or its supporters. The subject has been one of recurrent contention. In most general elections an attempt has been made by the boardcasters to coax the politicians from this collective coyness, but so far in vain. Only if the audience members are handpicked by the party organizations and tickets given out in carefully worked out proportions, will the party leaders participate. When that formula is employed, the results are not only dull but occasionally offensive: each party group in the audience feels it has to support its side and shout down or laugh down the efforts of the other to deal with questions. The spectacle of the democracy provided is a caricature of free discussion—a slanging match—and is apt to confirm the uncommitted viewer in his distrust of the political process.

In the 1964 election the BBC managed to take one important step toward confrontation between politician and public. A series of programs called "Election Forum" were started in which the leader of each party was invited in turn to spend 40 minutes or more answering questions sent in by viewers: the first time that this format was employed, over 30,000 postcards arrived and a small team of (professional) interviewers made a selection and put a series of often highly testing and provocative questions to the three main party leaders. Although this formula would seem hardly different from a press conference situation in which a panel questions a single individual, in practice the flavor of viewers' questions turns out to be quite different from that normally provided by professional interviewers even though the viewers' questions are actually chosen and put by a group of professionals; the viewer is sometimes more direct, not afraid to put the naive question, nor to put it again and even again. "Election Forum" became a central format in the elections of 1966 and 1970, but in the February election of 1974 the brief space of time available between the announcement of the election and the transmission of the program meant that the questions had to be put in the studio by a panel.

In 1974, however, further important steps were taken toward bringing voters and politicians together before the cameras: one of these was the introduction of the election phone-in, which was used in a long one-hour program every morning on radio but also in several television programs. Sometimes the viewer putting the question was invited to a studio in some other part of the country; sometimes an ordinary telephone handset was used in the studio. It was not difficult to notice an increased freshness in the questioning and in the answering. British television interviewing has been dominated for over a decade by a small group of extremely skilled professionals, and the composition of this band has changed only slowly throughout that time. Nor indeed have the politicians changed so greatly; the result is the sense of an increasingly skilled group of insiders all involved in playing the same game. The introduction of the telephone has created several new genres in political broadcasting and has helped to break down the deep-rooted inhibitions of the politicians toward meeting live voters.

Nonetheless, the attempt to persuade the politicians to give up their objections to live audiences has continued. The BBC advisory council report of the February election explained that "the main parties would only agree to allow their spokesmen to appear when the public were chosen on a fixed ratio of party political allegiance. The same consideration applied to interviews outside the studio. The difficulty of deciding in each case which particular political interest was represented by each individual had an inhibiting effect on prospective items of this type" (BBC, 1974a:21). In the course of "Campaign Special" in the October election, an ingenious and partly successful effort was made to evade this problem. A series of short films was made about a single constituency in the north of England, Keighley, which has always chosen its Member of Parliament on a knife-edge of votes, an evenly divided community which has won the election over the whole nation. The Keighley programs were made by a team who spent the whole election in the town and singled out a group of undecided voters, returning to them frequently during the campaign to see which way their minds were turning and to analyze the influences which ultimately persuaded them to decide their vote. In the last of this series of programs all the candidates for the Keighley constituency were persuaded to face a selection of the voters, an unusual event.

In the Independent system the broadcasters had taken a slightly tougher attitude toward the politicians on the question of crowds. The IBA itself decided to inform the Committee on Political Broadcasting (the semiofficial group of politicians and broadcasting officials who plan the allocation of party air time and arrange other matters of joint importance affecting broadcasting and politics) that it would, in the February election, allow programs in which politicians faced voters and their questions. The Independent system consists of a group of regional companies (14 of them) each of which operates with a very large degree of commercial and creative independence under the supervision of the IBA. Several of the companies, working under the general protection of the IBA's statement, did manage to create successful program formats involving live audiences. Scottish Television presented two one-hour debates, involving representatives of five parties speaking to audiences of several hundred voters. Thames TV (one of the London companies) managed to get one such program on the air, but was then faced with an embargo by the politicians on any further experiments with live voters. Yorkshire Television planned a series of nine such programs but found that it had to use retired politicians because the actual candidates in the election refused to face live questioning from voters. Thames TV then managed to get five more programs on the air with live and participating audiences, although these were of the specially selected variety rather than the spontaneous (the panel did eventually contain a modicum of uncommitted as well as loyal party-chosen voters). An embargo by politicians can thus prevent the evolution of program formats according to the predelictions of the broadcasters; in fact, the image of the overall electoral activity presented by television can be and frequently is profoundly affected by the constraints imposed by the political establishment itself. The whole problem of the politicians and the crowds is merely one of a long series of now traditional inhibitions which in one sense hamper, and in another actually encourage, the development of political genres in broadcasting.

In the Independent system, there is one company, Granada TV, which has, since its founding in the 1950s, attempted to act in the forefront of the evolution of television politics. It was the first company to cover an election at all (in February 1958), when in the famous Rochdale by-election it managed to force the candidates to take part in a television discussion based on questions put by a panel of journalists (Granada, 1974a). In the 1959 general election it broke new ground by giving television time to every single candidate of every party fighting an election in every constituency in its region (Granada, 1974b). In the February 1974 election it mounted a series of seven television programs, each on a different subject (prices, energy crisis, housing, government, Common Market, poverty, and the election itself), in which large audiences of electors took part and put questions to a panel of experts. The chairman of the programs ruled out of order all questions of a partisan nature, in an effort to move the discussion to the plane of factual analysis and keep it there. The project was called the "Granada 500" because the audiences were drawn from a large sample of voters from one town, Preston in Lancashire, which has an age distribution roughly similar to that of Britain as a whole. The voting intentions of the sample were checked at the beginning of the campaign, and the idea of the producers was to feed the sample with large quantities of clear, factual political information and then check the actual effect on their voting by following up the sample after voting day. Another sample, taken from the same town of Preston, but not allowed to participate in the television project, would serve as a control group. The operation proved to be extremely complicated to organize; the sample had to be kept fed with printed factual information throughout the campaign and had to be transported from place to place as the series of programs progressed. The project naturally became a major subject of conversation and comment within that part of northern England in which Granada's programs are seen.

In the last stages of the campaign the producers tried to get the candidates in the area to attend one of the "Granada 500" live sessions to answer questions and debate. All but one candidate agreed, but the dissenting candidate refused to waive his rights or representation and thereby allow the public debate to take place under the 1969 Representation of the People Act. Granada was forced to concede defeat, while promising to keep the struggle for live-audience questioning going until the next election (Granada, 1974d).

In examining the influence of any forms of mass entertainment, one must accept the centrality of the genre. It is the genre which links the two ends of the communication process by means of a series of strands and influences which pass through the society as a whole. To guarantee an audience, the communicator must offer an overt or implied promise, and, since the material may be unfamiliar to the audience, the vessel in which it is served must be recognizable. The creation of genres, however, involves the whole cultural tradition of a society; it has to be founded on elements which are known in advance not to be "boring." Television, more than any other medium, is obsessively concerned with the problem of confronting the impending boredom of the audience; and, in dealing with politics, it is trying to grapple with the transmission to a mass audience of a part of the culture which, without television, would probably not be part of mass culture at all. The concept of boredom therefore is the dominant element in a political broadcaster's view of his audience. His genres are the product of the dual desire to avoid boring the audience while carrying the burden of the preservation of the political culture. The audience is therefore loaded with information which is difficult to separate from comment, although the canons of traditional journalism command that this be done; and at the same time the audience is presented with image after image of the electoral process, in terms of argument or confrontation or the questioning of experts or as a mass decision-making process by the multitude. All of these images are in a sense wrong, or partial. Each new genre in political broadcasting attempts to capture one of those images and force it home, thereby sustaining the validity of the political system while trying out a simulation of one of the supposed central processes of democracy.

REFERENCES

BLUMLER, J.G. (1969). "Producers' attitudes towards television coverage of an election campaign: A case study." In P. Halmos (ed.), The Sociological Review (Monograph 13). University of Keele.

BLUMLER, J.G., and McQUAIL, D. (1968). Television in politics: Its uses and influence. London: Faber and Faber.
British Broadcasting Corporation, General Advisory Council (1974a). The BBC and the February 1974 general election. London: Author.
——— (1974b). BBC coverage of the general election September/October 1974: Summary of public reactions. London: Author.
CURRAN, C. (1973). A maturing democracy. London: British Broadcasting Corporation.
DEARLOVE, J. (1974). The BBC and the politicians. London: Writers and Scholars International.
DUNKLEY, C. (1974). "Overkill on television." Financial Times, February 28, 1974.
ELLUL, J. (1973). Propaganda: The formation of men's attitudes. New York: Vintage.
Granada Television (1974a). Granada goes to Rochdale: The first series of television programmes on a by-election. Manchester: Author.
——— (1974b). A first report on constituency television in a general election: The Granada election marathon. Manchester: Author.
——— (1974c). Prelude to Westminster? Manchester: Author.
——— (1974d). The Granada 500: An experiment in collective discussion of election issues. Manchester: Author.
HARRISON, M. (1965). "Television and radio." In D. Butler and A. King, The British general election of 1964. London: Macmillan.
——— (1974). "Television and radio." In D. Butler and D. Kavanagh, The British general election of February 1974. London: Macmillan.
——— (1975). "Television and radio." In D. Butler and D. Kavanagh, The British general election of October 1974. London: Macmillan.
Independent Television Companies Association (1974). ITV's guide to television for parliamentary candidates. London: Author.
MENDELSOHN, H., and CRESPI, I. (1970). Polls, television, and the new politics. Scranton, Pa.: Chandler.
PATEMAN, T. (1975). Television and the February 1974 general election (Television Monograph 3). London: British Film Institute.
SEYMOUR-URE, C. (1974). The political impact of mass media. London: Constable.
SWANN, M. (1975). Problems in broadcasting (Annual address at the University of Leeds Television Seminar). London: British Broadcasting Corporation.
TRACEY, M. (1975). "The production of political television in Great Britain." Unpublished doctoral thesis, Leicester University.
TRENAMAN, J., and McQUAIL, D. (1961). Television and the political image: The study of the impact of television on the 1959 general election. London: Methuen.
WINDLESHAM, Lord (1975). Politics in practice. London: Jonathan Cape.

Chapter 8

THE RENAISSANCE OF THE SCOTTISH NATIONAL PARTY: FROM ECCENTRIC TO CAMPAIGNING CRUSADER

VICTOR J. HANBY

The spectre of the Scottish National party (hereafter the SNP) rising Phoenix-like from the ashes of the Labour and Conservative parties continues to haunt the imaginations of the leaders of the latter parties, even after the stalemated and somewhat ambiguous results that the October 1974 election produced. Yet it is probably precisely because the October election did little actually to clarify the balance of elective political power in Britain or indeed to definitively detail the precise position of the SNP in the minds of Scottish voters and in the overall firmament of British politics that the SNP continues to cause unease to the managers of the two major parties. Undoubtedly such concern coalesces around two related points. Did the October 1974 level of SNP support represent a commitment to the party to the lasting detriment of the Labour and Conservative parties? Is the SNP a sufficiently well-organized body to capitalize on any such commitment, or it is merely a loose aggregation of individuals tied together by "a collective assertion of Scottishness" (Kellas, 1971: 452) around a series of emotive "gut" issues paraded before the public by way of a hard-hitting publicity machine and slick media techniques? Such considerations form the basis of the present paper.

I. RECENT ELECTORAL HISTORY OF THE SNP

It is of little account for our purposes to detail the history of the SNP since its inception in 1928 (see MacCormick, 1955; Hanham, 1969; Wolfe, 1973), but, for this study, its experiences since 1960 are of sufficient consequence to merit some consideration. While an SNP member had sat in Parliament in 1945, albeit only for a short while,[1] it was a series of Scottish by-elections in the early 1960s which caused the first ripples of concern to the established parties at Westminster.

> The Bridgeton (1961) and West Lothian (1962) elections had the twofold effect of increasing the opportunity for the S.N.P. to appear as a credible political alternative, in a way it had not been since the war and of recruiting a core of party workers some of them returning from voluntary exile in England. [McLean, 1970:361]

Such creditable performances as Bridgeton and West Lothian, however, were not immediately repeated and the SNP reverted to low polls in by-elections over the next two years. SNP support was next to experience an upturn in the period 1967-1969 when the party won one by-election (Hamilton, 1967) and achieved creditable showings in two others.[2] However, the Hamilton success was overturned at the 1970 general election, and it indeed appears that SNP support was in decline throughout 1969-1970 from its high point in 1968,[3] as reflected in the party's declining share of local election votes and contemporary opinion polls. Indeed, the parlous and mutable nature of the party's relationship with Scottish voters in the period 1960-1970 is well exemplified by the fact that the 1970 election saw it win its largest share of the Scottish vote ever (11 percent) and win one seat it had never held but, as indicated, lose another (Hamilton) upon which it had invested so much effort and prestige. The 1970 general election indicated therefore that while the SNP had a numerically respectable electoral base, this base itself was somewhat insecure and amorphous and constantly in a state of flux from by-election to by-election, from local to general elections. While the existence of such fluctuations is common to all British parties, it is the degree of change which is most relevant to the fortunes of the SNP, particularly when seen against the light of the arcane workings of the British electoral system.[4] In 1970, therefore, the party was still regarded nationally as little more than an eccentric political joke which had on occasions shown some flashes of political acumen, in particular the ability to stir those deep-seated emotions that most commentators assumed had taken second place to the everyday problems of existing in a fundamentally class-ridden society.[5]

SNP support next showed a significant retrenchment to pre-1970 levels in two by-elections held a few months prior to the February 1974 general election. In Dundee East it ran a close second to Labour and in Glasgow Govan actually won the seat. In addition, opinion polls published prior to the February election showed quite clearly that SNP support was on the increase throughout the period leading up to the election, rising from the 11.5 percent *actual* vote in 1970 to an expressed, *intended* 18 percent vote on the eve of the election ("S.N.P. campaign," 1974: 1). In effect, such polls slightly underestimated the level of support that the SNP was to receive. Final figures indicated a percentage rise in popular support over the 1970 figure to just under 30 percent of the Scottish vote. More importantly, this percentage translated into victory in 7 constituencies and second place in 17, compared with the 1970 figures of 1 win and 9 second placings. At first sight such figures were quite dramatic and clearly represented a body blow to traditional two-party politics in Scotland and, to a lesser extent quantitatively, in Britain. For most objective commentators,[6] therefore, the question became one of deciding whether such a body blow was of the fatal or of the merely ego-bruising variety, particularly in view of the volatile nature of the SNP's past electoral record.

To those individuals who subscribed to the "flash in the pan" thesis,[7] the subsequent October 1974 election could have provided little consolation. Neither, it is clear, was the Nationalist millennium around the corner. With 30 percent of the Scottish vote, 11 seats in Parliament, and several constituencies in which they placed a close second, the SNP clearly constituted an important force in Scottish politics and, by force of circumstances, in British politics generally. But October 1974 certainly was not the "breakthrough" presaged in the months prior to the election. If anything, it was a tribute to Labour's ability to consolidate its electoral position as the dominant party in Scotland, in the face of what seemed hitherto an SNP flood.

While this particular election could be construed therefore as a setback to the SNP's dream of Scottish political supremacy, it cannot, on the other hand, be seen as any kind of electoral defeat.

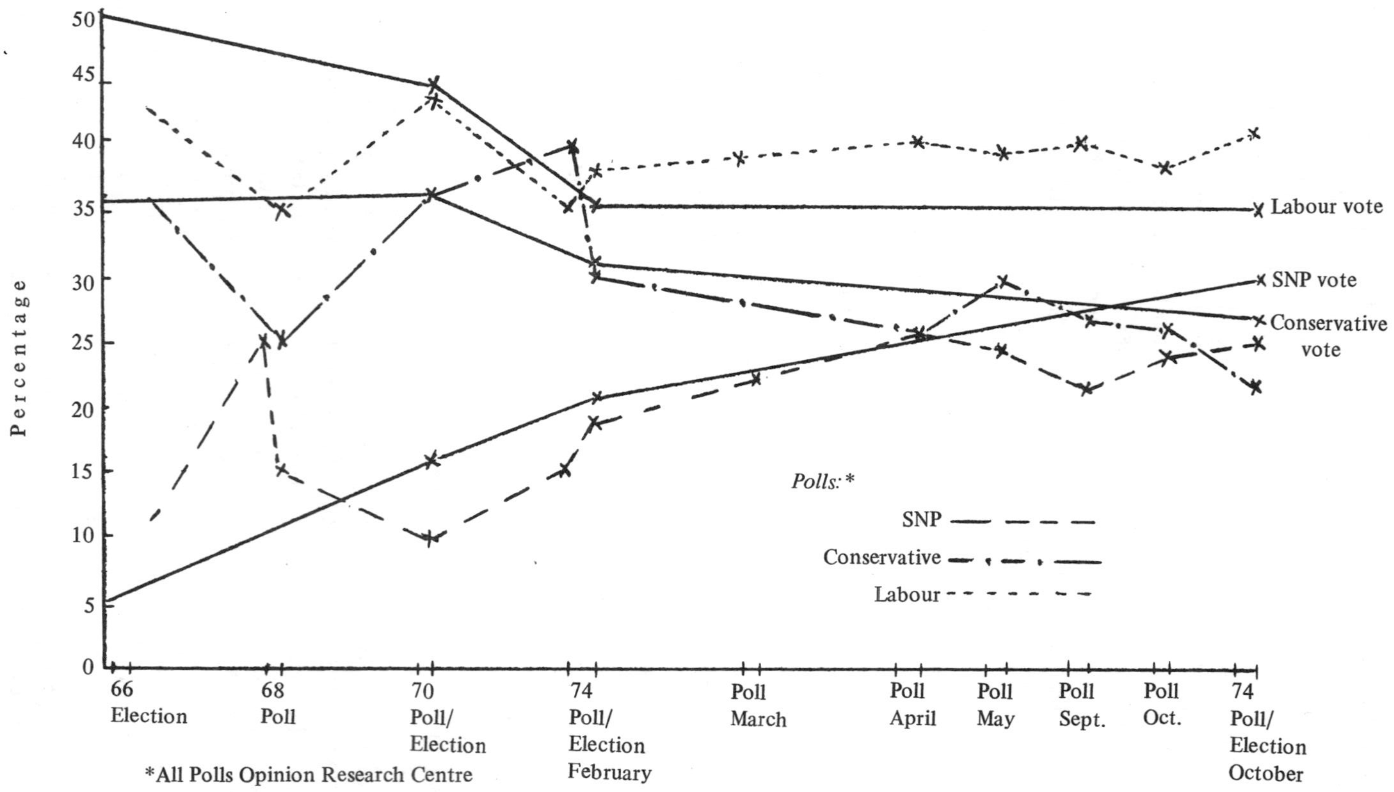

Figure 1: PARTY POPULAR SUPPORT IN SCOTLAND 1966-1974

On virtually every political index, the SNP October figures were highpoints in its electoral record. But questions that remained unresolved after February continued to demand answers after the October election. In particular, how significant a threat was the SNP to the traditional Labour-Conservative hegemony of British and Scottish politics, and was there something more to the SNP's appeal than attractively wrapped, emotive, public issues?

II. SNP ORGANIZATIONAL DEVELOPMENT AND POLICES IN 1974

Bochel and Denver's convincing critique (1972) of an early application of some aspects of these considerations to the fluctuating fortunes of the party in 1961-1970 (see McLean, 1970) concludes:

> One might ask in passing whether the lower morale of the S.N.P. in the second half of 1968 and in 1969 was symptomatic of the rather tenuous and frivolous nature of S.N.P. support generally. We suspect that S.N.P. activists knew better than commentators the source of their support and the poor foundation upon which it was built.... We believe that this assessment has been confirmed by events. People were prepared to vote for the S.N.P. in their disenchantment with the Labour government but their psychological commitment, their party identification, remained with their old party. [p. 315]

There seems little doubt, in fact, that such an analysis pinpoints quite accurately the dimensions of electoral volatility that underpinned the SNP's aspirations and disappointments in this earlier period. But is it stretching credibility to argue that similar reasons account for the successes of the mid-1970s? Particularly when the 1974 results seem considerably different in degree to those of 1968. Alternatively, Bochel and Denver's analysis (1972) might provide one of several elements accounting for the SNP's most recent rise. At its most extreme, such an interpretation argues that the SNP Is less a vehicle to win votes than one to receive them as a result of the political "mistakes" of other parties.[8] Any "nationalist revival," therefore, is really more a question of semantics than of substance. On the other hand, it could be argued that while their assessment was pertinent to the 1968-1970 situation, the tenor of British politics changed drastically in the period 1970-1974, making such simplistic interpretations indexically refutable. The SNP'S latter-day successes could therefore be considered necessary milestones on the road to political maturity of an organization which received its baptism in the late 1960s and early 1970s and subsequently assimilated lessons learned then into its later practices. The February and October elections, according to this viewpoint, reflect significant party realignments in the electorate, such that the SNP constitutes a stasis point in the fundamental equilibrium of the traditional British two-party system. It is to such considerations that we now turn.

In the past the SNP suffered from an organizational image that was clearly an embarrassment to a party working to create a major electoral base. Leadership wrangles fractured its nationalist appeal in the 1950s (see McLean, 1970). Its temporary and limited resurgence in the sixties, as indicated, suffered strongly from connotations of political eccentricity and the continuing, disparaging gibes of "tartan Tories"[9] did little to help project an independently identifiable and credible image. In addition, at the height of its 1968 renaissance the party was considerably embarrassed by revelations concerning its membership figures. The by-election and local government victories of 1967 and 1968 had been accompanied by strident claims about the fast-increasing party membership, and a membership roll of 120,000 was actually claimed in the latter year. However, such claims were subsequently followed by revelations that many so-called members were in fact schoolchildren under voting age. The party reaction was to refuse at all later dates to publish any membership figures so that most membership counts for the contemporary period are informed guesses and not official party statistics. However, it is possible to gain some insight into the number of committed supporters[10] through an analysis of the organization's infrastructure.

In the August 1974 *National Organiser,* John McAteer claimed that since the preceding February election, following an intense constituencies campaign, the party had enrolled 145 new branches throughout Scotland (Faux, 1975:4). Quite a remarkable achievement when one considers that at the beginning of the past decade they numbered only about 25 in toto! What is even more significant is the fact that this growth rate seems to have continued to the present. By October 1975 the party was claiming over 475 branches (Faux, 1975:4) with an average of roughly 150 individuals per branch, giving it a base of committed supporters of roughly 70,000. Financially as well, the SNP has moved from being a shoestring operation to an organization with sufficient resources to mount comprehensive national and local campaigns (Faux, 1975; but see also Butler and Kavanagh, 1975:241).

While the SNP therefore seems to have adopted some of the trappings of conventional parties, in one fundamental respect its structure differs quite considerably from the structure of its main opponents. Unlike them, the primary organizational emphasis is one of decentralization and branch autonomy, a fact which seems to have clear implications for the tone and type of campaign that the SNP mounts at any given election and may contain a germ of an explanation detailing the reasons for their meteoric success in particular constituencies in 1974. Branch initiative provides the dynamism that the national leadership must channel into electoral productivity. Branches dominate the major policy-making organ, the National Conference, and have full representation on the National Council, after the Conference the most important executive structure. The net result is a party organization with immense flexibility both in its day-to-day political practices and on specific occasions such as general election campaigns.

> The branches give a community identity to the party. It is entirely up to them to raise the money and project the party on the doorstep. There are three full-time senior staff members operating from headquarters in Edinburgh: the national organiser, the senior research consultant and the information officer. [Faux, 1975:4]

While it is true that such decentralization is important first in terms of merely increasing constituency feedback to headquarters, it is not immediately clear why it should seem such an important factor in the February 1974 election but not in 1970 when the results for the SNP were so minimal. After all, the dominant themes of 1974—"Scottish independence and Scottish oil"—were being articulated in 1970. However, the political background against which such articulation was taking place had fundamentally changed from 1970 to 1974, as reflected partly in the fluctuating SNP fortunes mentioned earlier.

First, the growing world oil crisis reinforced the importance of British marine deposits, and hence as the size of the energy problem grew, so proportionately did the political importance of Britain's potential economic savior. It is not inconceivable that many Scots became concerned about the apparent and obvious lack of Scottish voice in Conservative government plans for the development of a British oil industry. Parallel with such concerns, the appeal for "independence" had been well served by the publication of the Kilbrandon Commission's recommendation in November 1973 for a Scottish Assembly. Public events had therefore presented the SNP with some external evidence for the validity of their electoral claims. A move for independence would be well served by the establishment of an assembly, even the somewhat emasculated structure that was then under consideration, and Scottish oil provided the ready-made economic resource upon which independence could be founded. In addition, a somewhat fortuitous decision by the SNP to declare February 1974 a National Oil Month, in advance of the election announcement, was clearly supportive of this public momentum. The net result of the combination of both such sponsored and unsponsored Scottish emphases was to produce a campaign blitz by the SNP that was both strikingly effective and unrepentently ostentatious in particular constituencies.

In terms of the headquarter's participation the tone of the SNP's February campaign was clearly in line with the basic party tenet of decentralization and local initiative. The contribution of the national headquarters was limited to the provision of abundant supplies of posters and window stickers proclaiming the twin themes of the campaign, and a handful of party position papers on a selection of topical issues. Even the position papers were little more than priming material for local candidates and bore little resemblance to the more orchestrated campaigns of the two major parties. Labour adopted a particularly slavish approach to its constituency activities.

> The General Secretary's letter to candidates on February 16 urged candidates to fight "A synchronised campaign with the accent on Labour's *positive* proposals–taken straight from our Manifesto." [Butler and Kavanagh, 1975:232]

The SNP national TV broadcast[11] was a hardhitting program, structured around the nationalist appeals of independence and the promise of new prosperity from oil, with such emotive appeals being linked with a parallel attack on the duplicity and opportunism of the major parties. While the national headquarter's involvement in the campaign was therefore limited to little more than setting directions, it was clear that for the majority of constituency campaigns there was no shortage of initiative and dynamism. In those particular constituencies where they felt they had their strongest chances of success, the campaign took on an intensity hitherto considered alien to traditional British election practices. The ground rules were quite simple and varied little from constituency to constituency: saturate the area with party bill-posters, drive home with meetings and rallies the campaign themes, obtain maximum public exposure for the candidate, convince the electorate through maximum canvassing that the SNP's and Scotland's time had come. With the exception of the last, it might seem that such emphases would not have differed significantly from those of the major parties. However, as electoral organizations, both major parties over the years had atrophied in Scotland. Grown overconfident in some constituencies, rent with factionalism in others, neither party was really suited to fight an intense campaign in February 1974 (see also Butler and Kavanagh, 1975:217), nor, more specifically, were they prepared except in a few constituencies to meet a campaign effort of the intensity mounted by the SNP. The enthusiasm of the SNP and its party workers carried their campaign and its emphases forward with a momentum that the other parties could not seriously match in many vital constituencies.

III. THE SNP CAMPAIGNS OF FEBRUARY 1974

Populist appeal and hyperelectioneering fused, in their most extreme form, in the personality and antics of George Reid in the small but politically vital constituency of Clackmannan and East Stirling in central Scotland.[12] While Reid's background was not typical of the new generation of SNP candidates, the infectious enthusiasm for the task at hand and the easily communicated belief in the justice of the cause were common bonds between himself and his fellow candidates elsewhere. Within the constituency, Reid, though politically relatively inexperienced, had two advantages that even the Labour incumbent could not match. First, he was known publicly as a political commentator through his work on the Scottish Independent Television Service; his personal appearances in the constituency had the dual appeal of professionalism and TV celebrity. Second, he was born and raised in a small town within the constituency and through his media expsoure had clearly achieved the status of local-boy-made-good. With Reid's background, it is no surprise that the campaign that he so successfully engineered was based on a complex package of personality, SNP primary themes, intense and vigorous electioneering, and unadulterated showmanship. With a series of election practices that are best described as American, Reid blitzed the opposition with such determination that it drew comments of "circus practices" from one Labour agent and a clear implication from a Conservative worker that Reid had somehow cheated by adopting the techniques that he did.[13] The usual practices were present here as elsewhere, such as poster saturation, vigorous door-to-door canvassing, and well-organized and well-attended public meetings with the candidate; but two additional refinements seemed to have been particularly successful in projecting Reid and the SNP's image and appeal—the motorcade and the walkabout.

The standard approach of a single loudspeaker-laden vehicle touring the constituency publicly proclaiming the candidate and the party paled into insignificance against the motorcade tactics of the SNP. Some days, motorcades of up to 70 vehicles, each covered with party posters detailing policy on various issues, accompanied by loudspeakers blaring assortments of Scottish tunes, simply roamed from one end of the constituency to the other. On other days, their arrival presaged the appearance of the candidate; it is no wonder that on such occasions Reid was assured of sizable audiences, while the opposition in their spontaneous appearances often had to be satisfied with a mere handful of passersby.

While the walkabout had been a feature of Harold Wilson's behavior in the 1970 election and was in fact similarly adopted by Edward Heath in February 1974, it had hitherto not been traditionally associated with candidate behavior in individual constituency campaigns.[14] Indeed, the Labour candidate's approach in Clackmannan and East Stirling was very much in the traditional mold. Mingling with the population in any area, he emphasized essentially personal questions about family occupations and day-to-day money problems—the standard kiss-for-the-baby approach of British constituency electioneering—and responded to complaints with a short litany covering party policy. In contrast to this style, Reid's walkabout techniques were considerably more purposive, with the unmistaken intention of projecting the candidate and creating as much candidate-voter contact as was possible in the available time. Each walkabout was stage-managed in one of two ways. On some occasions a party worker introduced the candidate as he moved through the locality. On other occasions, two of Reid's ever-present assistants performed this function, marshaling and organizing the public as the candidate moved from individual to individual, from group to group, ensuring that he never stayed overlong with anyone, ever mindful that each individual was worth only one vote. Whichever form of walkabout was operative, the net result was the same; each contact was brief and candidate-voter coverage was extensive.

While Reid's electioneering tactics were more extreme than those of the remainder of his party colleagues, variations of his motorcade and walkabout tactics and techniques were employed in the other constituencies where SNP chances for success were considered strong. In two northern Scottish constituencies, East Aberdeen and Moray and Nairn, the by now standard "a sticker on every tree" effort[15]—buttressed by the usual vigorous campaign drive, concentrating on well-organized meetings and extensive public appearances by the candidates—was combined with limited motor cavalcades and candidate walks through the constituency. On occasions in East Aberdeen the candidate's walkabouts were accompanied by groups of young people chanting SNP slogans. Though such a tactic drew a charge of "Nazi tactics" ("S.N.P. campaign," 1974:5) from one of the losing parties, it is not at all clear that such a feature was a deliberate part of the SNP campaign, because on occasions the noise proved clearly dysfunctional to the candidate's public appeal. In addition, in Dundee East, the SNP's hard and vigorous campaigning enabled the candidate to build successfully on his by-election vote. In the Western Isles a combination of personal vote (Butler and Kavanagh, 1975:260) and saturation electioneering projected the SNP appeal and vote to the point of a massive majority for the one 1970 SNP parliamentarian. While the SNP energies and tactics were successful in helping win all the above constituencies, similar promotional tactics helped project their cause close to victory on many other occasions.

In Glasgow Govan, fighting to hold the constituency gained at the by-election in November 1973, the party found that even its easygoing populism was unable to defeat the class-based appeal of a revitalized Labour party, campaigning for its traditional support in a traditionally Labour area. Though the Govan campaign lacked the flamboyant techniques of Clackmannan and East Stirling, there was little doubt that the party was "fighting hard for the seat this time and [that its] campaigning style has none of the blandness which afflicts many election battles" (Mackie, 1974:6). While motorcade tactics would have been badly out of place in the decaying industrial area of Govan and while even walkabouts in George Reid style would probably have produced hostility and skepticism rather than support, the party candidate was able to produce a brand of electioneering which came close to helping retain the seat, in fact losing by only about 500 votes. The tactic in Govan was the usual massive poster campaign and intense canvassing, but this time it was supported by a "schedule of daily improvised street corner meetings, factory gate meetings" (Mackie, 1974:6), plus a major effort to visit every part of the constituency to establish the personal contact that the SNP considers vital to its election effort. No doubt too, the SNP campaign in Govan benefitted partly from the fact that the candidate, Margo MacDonald, played a prominent part in the party national television broadcast and that the program itself recalled the Govan by-election victory. Generally speaking, though the Govan campaign was unsuccessful, it did represent an interesting amalgam of traditional and unorthodox campaign techniques. In Stirling, Falkirk, and Grangemouth constituency, the impact of its political neighbor Clackmannan and East Stirlingshire was felt. Though the advanced age of its candidate[16] precluded as flamboyant a campaign, nevertheless the party did mount an impressive onslaught on the traditional Labour dominance with the usual saturation techniques being supplemented by a limited motorcade and public appearance tactic.

As a political proving ground there can be no doubt that organizationally and electorally, the SNP must have been considerably satisfied with its February 1974 effort. The vitality of its appeal and its ability to produce a vehicle for such an appeal could no longer be in doubt. Clearly, as demonstrated, it had received immeasurable help from the particular development of the national political agenda, but it had made a particularly individualistic response to such opportunities and had worked in an innovative and unorthodox fashion to create tactics that could best sustain them. While it was possible to conclude that Labour had been the major electoral victim of the SNP's rise, it did not seem possible to assess as accurately the SNP's probability of survival at 1974 levels. Certainly, both major parties adopted name-calling and insult-exchanging as expedient tactics to diminish the electoral impact of the SNP,[17] and thus is seems clear though circumstantial evidence that the SNP was not alone in its belief that it had damaged the traditional Conservative and Labour hegemony in Scotland. However, the efficacy of its new campaign techniques might be open to question. Though there was more than superficial evidence to suggest that its well-organized campaigns had played a large part in the successful articulation of its policies and themes and were a strong ingredient in its success in places, it is also true that in many areas the opposing organizations were weak and inefficient and would likely be revitalized for future operations. In a sense, therefore, the SNP was in rather a dilemma after February 1974. If its electoral support was largely transient and likely to return to its original home in future elections, then an efficient electoral organization had to be kept in order to minimize such losses. If, on the other hand, a large part of the electoral support, transient or otherwise, was due to electioneering efficiency, then the party likewise had to ensure the continual readiness of the electoral machine. If, however, it was clear that in spite of an efficient party machine, present gains were still transient, then what use would such a machine be in the future in preventing voter slippage? Regardless of the resolution to such a dilemma, SNP efforts in the months after the February election were devoted to the continued strengthening of the party machine at all levels, activity which, as it turned out, seemed to be rather a fortuitous choice from the viewpoint of October 1974.

IV. THE SNP CAMPAIGN OF OCTOBER 1974

At first sight, the pre-October political scenario seemed to have strong resemblances to pre-February features. Political circumstances kept the issue of North Sea oil and questions of Scottish independence alive in the media. The respective Scottish conferences of the major parties devoted much time and energy, not always positively, to discussions on the allocation of oil revenues and various forms of devolved assemblies.[18] The SNP Elgin conference in May expended a great part of its deliberations spelling out the specifics of policies resultant on the new revenue. Such debates culminated in

September 1974 in the publication of a white paper detailing inter alia the government's commitment to some form of governmental devolution for Scotland and Wales. While such devolution is considered by the SNP only a halfway house to its aim of independence, the document ensured the continuance of public debate on the matter, a fact that the party attempted to turn to its advantage by claiming that such concessions were the result of its political impact and agitation.

In addition, throughout the period, as mentioned before, the party had been steadily establishing its membership base. In June, in association with such activities, it had launched an intensive publicity campaign on oil, aimed at projecting the SNP theme into every house in Scotland. This saturation leaflet campaign was followed later in the summer by an extensive poster campaign. Such was the intensity of SNP activity over the summer of 1974 that on the day that the October election was announced, the *National Organiser* was able to state, "It has been non-stop action since the February election. We assumed there would be a quick election again this year and we mounted a campaign throughout the constituencies to make sure we were not caught out" (Kerr, 1974:8). While the preamble to the second of the 1974 elections therefore looks remarkably like the preamble to the first, such resemblances in some of the most important features are only superficial and mask considerable qualitative differentiation between the two periods.

Most importantly, the Conservative government's ambiguity over certain issues of the February 1974 campaign had been removed by the succeeding Labour government. The devolution white paper, though far from being any form of definitive statement on a new Scottish Assembly, was a welcome and considerable advance for those nationalists who were antipathetic to claims for total independence but who wanted an end to Scotland's "second best" relationship with the Westminister government. Second, the detailed and clearly projected Labour plans for oil development–an immense improvement over those of its Conservative predecessors–had been well publicized in the months prior to the election. The bulk of the Labour and, to a lesser extent, the Conservative constituency organizations had undergone considerable revamping in attempts to reconstitute electoral machinery that had clearly been unprepared for the vigorous campaigning of the SNP.

Though the bases upon which the election was fought were

therefore different in degree to those of February, the SNP campaign was mounted with a vigor which demonstrated the preparation by their organization throughout the intervening period. With the additional aspect of detailing with some precision the specific benefits that oil revenue would achieve in Scottish society, the SNP campaign in October primarily followed the blueprint of February. Constituency saturation techniques were well in evidence as were the now almost traditional panoply of motorcades and walkabouts in those constituencies where the SNP felt it had its strongest chances. Indeed, though George Reid claimed to have "cooled" his campaign, the available evidence is that his tactics not only were increased in his own constituency but actually spilled over into neighboring districts. On many occasions the traveling motorcades moved from constituency to constituency, effectively ignoring boundaries as neighboring party branches organized joint motorcades and campaign events. There is little doubt that those constituencies bordering Reid's anticipated a degee of electoral spillover. In Kinross and West Perthshire such tactics came near to being spectacularly successful, as a Conservative majority of several thousand was reduced to one of a few dozen votes.

While the decentralized nature of the campaign did not deviate overmuch from the model of February, in one important respect there was greater central organization. The October election saw the party MPs play a much larger and more directing role in the overall functioning of the campaign. Clearly this was partly a function of available numbers, but to some extent too it was a realization that the party could obtain maximum impact for its cause by greater utilization of a resource that already had demonstrable public recognition. Individual constituency MPs therefore performed a more general, peripatetic role in this election than they had previously. In addition, the two national TV programs that the party was allowed under electoral law[19] had greater MP orientation and direction. Introduced and orchestrated by George Reid, the presentation utilized an efficient format which projected SNP themes through individual MPs, within a framework of supportive public interviews and film. The programs were well produced and slickly presented, had an effective combination of fact and emotionalism, and quite obviously reflected the past professional skills and experience of George Reid. The dominant role of Reid in the campaign, as anchorman in television presentations and preeminent personality in multiconstituency walkabouts, in fact led to the charge by his Labour opponent "that they are trying to push [George Reid] like a packet of detergent" (Wapshott, 1974:8). Regardless of the charge, there is little doubt that the October campaign to a great extent represented the professional influence of Reid both as prime-mover and exemplar. Indeed, the impact of Reid's February tactics is well demonstrated by the fact that October saw both Labour and Conservative parties in his constituency adopt motorcade and limited walkabout tactics, though in the case of the Conservatives it is probable that, in terms of the somewhat mediocre efforts in this direction, the party might have been better disposed not to have bothered.

Apart from the limited, centralized direction, however, the overall structure of the SNP campaign was as in February, with the well-tried saturation techniques receiving local variation according to circumstances and the individuals involved, buttressed, as indicated, by efficient media projection and visiting delegations of party personalities. There is little doubt that in terms of campaign effort and organization the SNP endeavor was greater than in February. The results, as indicated earlier, must have proven to be something of a disappointment. While the Conservatives were the major losers of seats and votes to the SNP, perhaps the most significant feature of the election was the fact that in spite of massive campaign efforts by the SNP the Labour vote held relatively firm in the electorally vulnerable industrial heartland of central Scotland. The possibility that the SNP could pose a significant realignment in Scottish politics, therefore, diminished accordingly; but whether October 1974 represented a temporary setback to future hopes or an unassailable highpoint, remains largely unresolved.

V. CONCLUSIONS: REALIGNMENT POTENTIAL OF THE SNP

While evidence from a general survey of the 1974 elections is still wanting, some insight into the nature of the October situation may be gleaned from individual constituency surveys. In a study conducted in the Clackmannan and East Stirling constituency in the week following the October election, a fairly clear picture of the pattern of SNP support emerged (Hanby, 1975). Of those individuals who now supported the SNP but who voted for another party in

February, the clear bulk had switched votes from the Conservatives with only a very small proportion having switched from Labour. Of those voters who had supported another party before February but had changed to SNP allegiance at that election, the vast majority were previously Labour voters. Such results in a constituency where a Labour majority of 10,000 in 1970 had slipped to an SNP majority of 3,849 in February and to an SNP majority of 7,341 in October ought not to be surprising. What is surprising is the extent to which SNP support seems to have consolidated even over the short period from February to October 1974.

Clearly, most of the individuals who switched to the SNP in February and October were supportive of the view that inflation, unemployment, and housing were the problems of paramount importance to Scotland and that questions of the distribution of oil revenue and independence were of considerably less importance. Indeed, on the latter points only 15 percent of SNP supporters were in favor of complete Scottish independence, and roughly the same percentage favored total Scottish control of oil revenue.[20] However, by a ratio of about 2 to 1, Nationalist voters were more inclined than Labour voters to feel their party to be the most concerned about the problems of people living in the area. When voters responded to questions aimed at explaining such divergence, it became clear that even across parties there was some agreement that the SNP would do far more than any other party to obtain an economic fair deal for Scotland. In addition, just under 20 percent of the total sample related the quality of the SNP candidate to this belief. This figure went up to 45 percent when one looked at SNP supporters alone. A strong majority of the supporters of all parties believed that there should be greater emphasis on Scottish problems at Westminster. The majority of SNP supporters further indicated that the reasons for their transference of political allegiance, whether from Conservative or from Labour, was a desire to increase such emphasis and their belief that the SNP was the best vehicle for the transmission of such ideas. Of those individuals who switched to the SNP in February, 40 percent indicated that they felt such a change to be a temporary phenomenon; in fact, many suggested that their switch was more a desire to influence the dominant parties than any lasting commitment to the SNP and its aims. Of this group however, only half said that their October electoral decision continued to be a transient phenomenon. Indeed, just over 50 percent of October SNP voters indicated that they were unlikely to change their allegiance under any circumstances. It would seem apparent, then, that the period from February to October 1974 represented not just a quantitative increase in SNP support but also a considerable qualitative shift in the nature of this support.

While the SNP campaign themes seemed not to figure independently as actual reasons for SNP success, clearly they had played major roles in creating an image that had itself provided a strong predisposition in the electorate in terms of SNP allegiance; and events on the external political stage had similarly played a reinforcing role. The vigorous campaigning of the party had obviously provided an effective vehicle for the transmission of such an appeal. The net result seems to have been a considerable hardening of SNP support in October. While such a feature is undoubtedly important, the underlying figures hardly constitute a significant realignment in Scottish politics, since 38 percent of SNP support also indicated that there were circumstances under which they would revert to traditional party allegiances. What does seem particularly crucial is the fact that SNP support has been consolidated within sections of the community, such that the party will continue to have a significant support element in the electorate upon which to build for future electoral victories. The extent to which its future activities will be successful, therefore, seems dependent on its additional ability to hold loyal the transient component of its vote, and this in itself would seem to be very much at the mercy of external political considerations and the activities of the major parties.

While it is, of course, problematic to generalize on the basis of observations made in one constituency and while one awaits a more extensive survey before being able to generalize with any certainty, a considerable amount of evidence available from opinion polls illustrates that the underlying parameters of SNP support isolated in Clackmannan and East Stirling are found with varying degrees of intensity in several other Scottish constituencies.[21] One hesitatingly concludes that the dimensions of SNP allegiance expressed in this constituency would seem to be reflective of a general Scottish pattern. The coalition of small-town and limited rural supporters and nonunionized manual workers that characterizes SNP allegiance in Clackmannan (Hanby, 1975:22) is a combination that could provide the party with the necessary electoral base if it is meaningfully to create a realignment of Scottish political loyalties and ultimately threaten the hegemony of Labour and Conservatives in British politics.

One might therefore make certain tentative conclusions on the situation of the SNP at the culmination of the October 1974 election. There is little doubt that the party had achieved the necessary organizational base with which to mount effective electoral campaigns. By October 1974 its combination of vigorous campaigning and thematic appeals had created a sound electoral foundation that proved an impressive bulwark against the recharged efforts of the major parties to retrench their positions lost in February 1974. Indeed, the intensity of the conflict is indicated by the fact that SNP majorities slipped in a majority of the seats that they had held from February and that in several others their new victories were measured in leads of several hundred votes or less. The SNP victories of October are probably best viewed therefore as a "holding" action, a period of consolidation, both organizational and electoral, as an increasingly volatile Scottish electorate adjusted its identifications between the new appeals of a new party and the traditional allegiances of the old. Whether such a consolidation becomes the breakthrough that the major parties fear is a calculus of near infinite magnitude. Certainly there is no reason to assume that the SNP will allow its present organizational and electoral bases to atrophy to the extent allowed by the other parties prior to February 1974. Indeed, all available evidence points to the contrary. Continuing constituency advertising and media activities are testimony to the increasing electoral sensitivity of the SNP. The ongoing public debates over oil revenue and a Scottish Assembly will continue as before to provide political material that may benefit the party by contributing to the generally expressed image of Scotland with "second best" status within the United Kingdom. Yet is is also clear that the presence of all such features in the October campaign did not provide a major dislocation of electoral power in Scotland, though there was some significant consolidation of SNP electoral support. The crucial question therefore seems to be: Under what circumstances will the remaining transient support of the party undergo some identificatory metamorphosis and augment the party's present, permanent electoral core? [22]

In addition, on the basis of the evidence from Clackmannan and East Stirling, it is reasonable to assume that some potential SNP sympathizers continued to support Labour in October 1974 because of the tactical concessions on oil development and on devolution that the party made prior to the election. It is also reasonable to assume that those former Labour and Conservative supporters whose traditional allegiances to such parties had not been broken by their temporary support of the SNP in the two 1974 elections might consider reverting to such loyalties if such tactical concessions continued to be operative or, perhaps more obviously, continued to look credible. Indeed, it is clear from this study that a significant proportion of SNP supporters *are* possible "changers" in a future election and hence likely to switch back to usual party loyalties. The extent to which this will happen will probably be determined by the mutual interplay of "nationalist" type promises from all parties, as the major parties attempt to win back their lost support and the SNP continues to utilize every opportunity to gain from any weakness exhibited by its opponents.

One might argue, therefore, that, if the present Labour government shows any sings of reneging on its promise over a Scottish Assembly, then the impact on its electoral support will be catastrophic. The lesson of October 1974 might, in this light, be profitably seen as a reprieve for Labour domination of Scottish politics. To misunderstand such a feature and allow any weakening of commitment to previous promises would be to create exactly the scenario in which increasing electoral support would accrue to the SNP, with an immediate and lasting consolidation of its vote throughout the Scottish constituencies. The effect would be twofold. Transient SNP supporters with Labour identifications would begin permanently to identify with the SNP and reject their traditional loyalties. Consistent Labour supporters with SNP sympathies would likewise reject the old reasons for voting and augment a growing SNP vote. The overall impact would be to create a large body of the elctorate whose primary political loyalties were to the SNP, to the considerable and possibly lasting detriment of Labour party politics in Scotland and probably in Britain.

The lessons for the Conservatives are equally daunting. As the party tainted with the image of having "sold out" North Sea oil rights to the international oil companies, of having been publicly fractured over questions of a Scottish Assembly, and of having a party leader whose enthusiasm for devolution is known to be somewhat lacking, the Conservatives face a situation in which any further slippage of their vote to the SNP might eventually eradicate them as a major force from the face of Scottish politics.

The lessons, then, that one may draw from the political renaissance of the SNP are paradoxical. On the one hand, it is a salutary compliment to the democratic process that, in a political system hitherto dominated by two monolithic parties whose hegemony is buttressed by the additional vagaries of the electoral system, a small party may, in the space of 10 years, move from a position of eccentric social movement to one of potential power participant. On the other hand, a note of caution should govern such satisfaction. The growth of the SNP denotes a prime example of the speed with which a party, combining the twin pillars of emotive appeal and campaign professionalism and efficiency, may impact on the political process in circumstances where its traditional guardians have grown apathetic and complacent. The intensive retailing of SNP themes and imagery by the party campaign machinery together with their consequent swift success and influence on the population, should at the very least warn as to the possibilities for excess and manipulation inherent in the panoply of contemporary campaign practices, techniques, and modes of presentation that dominate present-day elections.

VI. POSTSCRIPT

The announcement in the Queen's speech opening Parliament on November 19, 1975, that the Labour government was intending to introduce legislation to create a Scottish Assembly was also accompanied by a strong implication that the political timetable was in fact unlikely to allow the passage of such legislation until at least the next session of Parliament in 1976, which would mean the creation of such an Assembly in 1977 at the earliest. Subsequent debate in the House of Commons, where the leaders of both major parties left a strong impression of their own doubts concerning the political advisability of devolution, turned into an angry shouting match as SNP members rose to proclaim a sellout in the middle of the leader of the Opposition's main speech. It seems quite clear that the main parties in Britain may not have fully realized the full implications of the SNP's present position in the electorate and seem determined to commit the one political action from which electorally the British political system may never recover. As the media reporting the day's events showed, the SNP is only too ready to maximize such opportunities to its ever-increasing advantage.

NOTES

1. The party's first national electoral success had been gained by its current president, Dr. R.D. McIntyre, in a Scottish by-election in April 1945. But he was subsequently defeated in the 1945 general election three months later, in the Labour landslide that brought Labour to power for the first time in a majority situation.

2. In the heavily industrial areas of Glasgow Pollock and Glasgow Govan, in 1967 and 1969 respectively, the party had achieved over a quarter of the vote cast, and in Govan it had actually displaced the Conservatives as the main challenger to Labour.

3. In the 1968 Scottish municipal elections the SNP garnered over one-third of the votes, but their support had slipped to about one-sixth by the 1970 local elections. In addition, SNP support in opinion polls in 1967 and 1968 was running at roughly 25 percent, but this too showed a significant decline by 1970.

4. In 1966, for example, the SNP won 5 percent of the Scottish votes but no seats. In 1970 it won just over 11 percent of the vote and one seat; in February 1974 and October 1974 the variance between votes received and seats won was even greater (see main text for details). In the period 1966-1974, therefore, the range of votes won by the party was from 5 to 30 percent, while the percent range of seats won (on a Scottish basis) was from 0 to 15 percent. In the same period, the range of votes won by Labour was from 50 to 36 percent, while the range of seats won was from 65 to 57 percent. Conservative magnitudes were reflective of the same pattern. (On the period up to 1970, see Kellas, 1973.)

5. In 1966 it had been noted, "We have shown that national consciousness exists to at least the same extent as class consciousness among Glaswegian electors and therefore, inferentially, among Scottish electors in general, and that national identifications are stronger than class identifications for a number of electors equal to those for whom class identifications are stronger (Budge and Irwin, 1966:133). This, perhaps the first meaningful analysis of the possibility of a nationalist strengthening in the electorate, made little impact on other commentators for whom traditional interpretations of British society were still convincing. "Voting in Britain is still largely class-voting. . . . By its nature the S.N.P. lacked a secure social base. It failed to make nationality a more important factor in electoral behaviour than class" (Bochel and Denver, 1972:315). As this paper shows, such complacent interpretations are rapidly losing their validity.

6. The bulk of the popular Scottish press, reinforced by the frenzied electioneering of the SNP opinion leaders, immediately began to prophesy the demise of the British two-party system and the imminent creation of an independent Scotland.

7. The November 1973 Govan by-election result had been greeted by the leaders of the major parties in Scotland as a "flash in the pan," and some journalists had extended such a comment to the overall situation of the SNP, particularly in the light of its volatile electoral position in the late 1960s.

8. Much of the rhetoric of the major British parties seems based on the presumption that it is through their political mistakes that the SNP has grown. The initial other-party reaction therefore led the major parties to reinforce their traditional appeals rather than to seek out SNP sympathizers on their own ground and attempt to win them over. With the consolidation of a secure social base, the SNP has indicated how seriously misguided and wrong-footed the strategies of the other parties were.

9. "Tartan Tories" was the most utilized gibe by nonsympathizers in the late 1960s and early 1970s when it was assumed that the bulk of SNP supporters were coming from former Conservatives who either were disenchanted with their own party or were voting strategically to force out entrenched Labour interests. In effect, the bulk of SNP supporters

over the two 1974 elections seem to have come from fundamentally anti-Conservative sections of the community (see Dyer, 1974:5).

10. One uses the notion of "committed supporters" advisedly with regard to the SNP of course, but in this usage "committed supporters" refers to that group of SNP followers who would be termed "members" in another context but for whom one is precluded from using such a term because SNP policy is guarded on its membership figures and because subsequent figures are only informed "guesstimates."

11. The question of party access to television broadcasts is one of the more vexing questions of a British campaign. Governed as it is by the dictates of convention and the formal constraints of the Committee on Political Broadcasting, the situation usually works quite well when solely concerning the major British parties, but it is clearly unsuited for settling minor-party broadcast requests. Indeed, in February the SNP was involved in a situation in which the TV broadcast scheduled to it was in fact rescheduled following a protest from the government that the timing of the SNP broadcast violated the standard allocation convention. It was only after court action by another minor party that the original schedule was adhered to. The fact that the SNP had no representatives on the Committee on Political Broadcasting, an all MP structure, clearly left it in a weak position, though, as will be seen, even having representatives after February still did not obviate the complaints of the SNP of feeling unfairly treated.

12. This constituency, held by the Labour party with large majorities since 1945, was one of a number in the Stirling region which were thought vulnerable to SNP threats. The Labour party organizations in this general area have perennially been torn with internal feuds and factionalism, complaints of nepotism, and charges of complacency and apathetic responses to the needs of the constituents. Though the Clackmannan and East Stirling Labour incumbent was considered a good constituency man in Parliament, the local organization that he headed was considered by his constituents, like those in neighboring constituencies, to be typical of Labour's "rotten boroughs in central Scotland." The social mixture of new suburban developments, decaying traditional industries, and decaying small towns that typified the constituency were considered likely sympathizers for the SNP cause. It is also the home of the author.

13. During the course of interviews of party workers during the campaign, such sentiments were voiced to the author by unidentified constituency workers in the small town of Alva, a decaying mill town with a significant new middle-class component living on its outskirts.

14. This is not to imply of course that the average candidate does not tour his constituency meeting people but rather to suggest that usually such behavior is *not* of the organized and structured nature that Reid's walkabouts were. The walkabouts in which the SNP engaged were creations qualitatively different in degree and design from traditional candidate behavior as represented by Reid's opponents in Clackmannan.

15. The slogan coined to launch the SNP campaign clearly laid the groundstones for SNP endeavor in every constituency. The extent to which this simple ploy was so successful is best measured by the fact that in three northern Scottish constituencies the Conservative party demanded investigations into the expenditure of the SNP on the grounds that no party could have run such an all-embracing and intense campaign without violating the law governing party campaign expenditure.

16. The SNP candidate was Dr. R.D. McIntyre, the party president who had won the 1945 by-election to give the party its first parliamentarian. Dr. McIntyre, a former provost of Stirling and an eminent physician, is a well-known and well-liked member of his community and, though so far unsuccessful in his general election campaigns, brings a degree of personal popularity and experience to the campaigns that seems to more than compensate for his increasing years. Indeed, over the last two general elections and one

by-election he has successively made inroads into the Labour majority, and it is probably true to say that his personal impact might have been more productive had his Labour opponent not been a prominent member of the Scottish Labour party (now a junior minister) and also a long-time advocate of devolution.

17. The months between the two elections were interspersed with periods of sharp exchanges of insults, with the SNP mainly the innocent party. The charges of "nazism," mentioned above, that filled many columns of Scottish newspapers in March, were superseded in April by a series of fairly specious comments made by the Labour Secretary of State for Scotland at the Scottish Trades Union Congress. In addition, Ross filled the weeks just prior to the election with charges that the SNP was the party of "littleness" and "there is an element of master racism, a rejection of other races . . . in the S.N.P." ("S.N.P. 'bases its proposals on racism'," 1974).

18. Such discussions among the two major parties in particular were dysfunctional for party solidarity. Indeed, Labour had to convene a special Scottish party conference in order to reverse the antidevolutionist stand taken by the Scottish party executive in June. In effect, the subsequent reversal of the executive's position left nothing but rancor and dissent within the ranks of the party.

19. In spite of the fact that its February election successes had enabled the SNP to have representation on the Committee on Political Broadcasting, the campaign was fractured in September by a furious row over the allocation of programs to the SNP, who claimed that the number of programs and their time slots were an insult to Scotland and a violation of the party's right to parity with the other national minor party, the Liberals. On a purely Scottish basis, it must be admitted, there seemed a basis to the SNP's claim, as it had consistently outpolled the Liberals, yet had less time allocated. On a national, British basis, of course, the Liberal vote was several times larger than that of the SNP. Because the allocation of number and placing of programs is done on the basis of British vote and not regional subdivisions, and because the major parties constitute a clear majority on the committee, it is not surprising that the SNP felt slighted. The standard of treatment that they received, however, was clearly in accord with the governing convention, but this does not mean that the present arrangements are at all satisfactory. As the case of the SNP shows, the present system takes little account of the special characteristics of minor parties.

20. A clear majority, however, were in favor of some form of devolution, at least to the extent that 70 percent of the sample found present governmental arrangements unsatisfactory, and an equivalent number wished Scotland to receive a more equitable share of oil revenue than was then being promised.

21. In particular, note the poll reported in the *Sunday Times* of November 9, 1975, that 30 percent of Labour voters in Scotland would switch their allegiance if Labour's plans for self-government were less than they desired and that, of the disaffected total, 20 percent indicated that the switch would be to the SNP. In addition, the poll also underlined the basic volatility of Labour opinion at present. While only 15 percent of the Labour supporters wanted all oil revenues to stay in Scotland (compared with 33 percent of SNP supporters) 35 percent of Labour voters wanted *most* of the oil revenue to be retained in Scotland (compared with 36 percent of SNP voters).

22. Obviously one uses "permanent" advisedly in the context of electoral politics, but it is used here to differentiate that sector of the Scottish community whose political identification or partisan self-image now lies with the SNP from that other section of the electorate whose votes may have supported the SNP in 1974 but whose underlying identification is with another party.

REFERENCES

BOCHEL, J.M., and DENVER, D.T. (1972). "The decline of the S.N.P.–An alternative view." Political Studies, 20(3):311-316.

BUDGE, I., and IRWIN, D. (1966). Scottish political behaviour. London: Longmans.

BUTLER, D., and KAVANAGH, D. (1975). The British general election of February 1974. London: Macmillan.

DYER, M. (1974). "Why Tory stronghold crumbled." Scotsman (Edinburgh), October 24, p. 6.

FAUX, R. (1975). "Scottish Nationalists prepare for devolution–III." The Times (London), October 27, p. 4.

HANBY, V. (1975). "The Scottish Nationalists: Threat or flash-in-the-pan." Unpublished manuscript, Department of Sociology, Stirling University, Scotland.

HANHAM, H.J. (1969). Scottish Nationalism. London: Faber.

KELLAS, J. (1971). "Scottish Nationalism." Pp. 450-455 in D. Butler and M. Pinto-Duschinsky (eds.), The British general election of 1970. London: Macmillan.

––– (1973). The Scottish political system. London: Cambridge University Press.

KERR, J. (1974). "The Nats bite harder." Guardian (Manchester), August 1, p. 8.

MacCORMICK, J.M. (1955). The flag in the wind. London: Victor Gollancz.

MACKIE, L. (1974). "S.N.P.s crack at Labour." Guardian (Manchester), October 2, p. 6.

McLEAN, I. (1970). "The rise and fall of the Scottish Nationalist party." Political Studies 18(3):357-372.

"S.N.P. 'bases its proposals on racism' " (1974). Guardian (Manchester), October 3, p. 8.

"S.N.P. campaign 'near to racism' " (1974). Scotsman (Edinburgh), March 16, p. 5.

WAPSHOTT, N. (1974). "Bitterness creeps into hot contest." Scotsman (Edinburgh), October 9.

WOLFE, W. (1973). Scotland lives. Edinburgh: Reprographia.

Chapter 9

WHAT TECHNOLOGY HAS NOT CHANGED: CONTINUITY AND LOCALISM IN BRITISH POLITICS

E. J. DIONNE

In discussing the impact of technology on the political processes of Western democracies, many writers are led to flights of Huxleian fantasy. Even Ben Bagdikian, a careful and insightful critic of the media, seemed to join the technological revolutionaries when he proclaimed that changes in communications technology "will be to politics what nuclear fission was to physical weapons, an increase in power so great that it constitutes a new condition for mankind" (quoted in Minow et al., 1973:166).

Without question, new developments in technology—especially in television and market research—have vastly altered the ways in which politics is conducted and in which governments go about the business of "informing" their citizens. But in the process of discussing these changes, many writers have often so emphasized the transformations in the nature of political conflict bred by technology that they have missed the more important continuities. For the most important fact is that radio, television, and market research have *not* fundamentally changed the *nature* of politics in Western democracies. They have changed the *methods* of politics, and even these have not changed so radically as many would contend.

Except for the heavy emphasis that has been placed on the effect of technology in recent discussions of politics, this would not be a surprising thesis. In a sense, it is not a thesis at all; it is a definition. Politics is about conflict—among individuals and groups, interests and ideas. Or, as Bernard Crick has said, following Aristotle:

> Politics arises, then . . . in organized states which recognize themselves to be an aggregate of many members, not a single tribe, religion, interest or tradition. Politics arises from accepting the fact of the simultaneous existence of different groups, hence different interests and different traditions, within a territorial state under common rule. [Crick, 1964:18]

It follows that if political campaigns and processes fail to be about the conflicts between these different interests and traditions, then they cease to be political at all.

Yet this is one of the key assumptions behind much of the writing on new political techniques. Analysts of this school argue that campaigns have become meaningless rituals in which all candidates are aiming at the same pool of voters and end up saying the same things—if they say anything at all (cf. McGinniss, 1969). Jeremy Larner's film *The Candidate* seemed to prove the point made years earlier by Daniel Boorstin in *The Image* (1961:249) that "in our daily lives the pseudo event seems always destined to dominate the natural facts." Butler and Rose (1960) uncovered the same tendency in British politics. "During the campaign" of 1959, they noted, "the term 'party image' was continually invoked, almost as if it represented a new magical force" (p. 17).[1]

Central to this view of politics is the decline of the ideology thesis, which in its various forms argued that voters were becoming less concerned with class-oriented ideological issues and more worried about party and individual performance in office. The more extreme political technocrats took this view even further and emphasized not even performance, but the image of performance. This notion was summed up neatly by a British political journalist with reference to the Conservative party's massive pre-election image-building campaign in 1959:

> I am sure people care much less about future programs just now than about choosing which side will give the better and friendlier service under roughly the present rules. Or to put it another way, which side has the nicest, most competent fellows. [Butler and Rose, 1960:19]

Under such circumstances, the linking of marketing techniques to politics is inevitable. Candidates *can* be sold like soap when, like Tide and Duz, there is little difference between them and when consumers (or voters) appear to be looking for roughly the same thing from each brand.

But what if this sort of consensus broke up? To this, the media advocates replied: it won't. In the first place, a rebirth of ideology seemed unlikely, especially in the late 1950s and early 1960s. Second, they argued that television itself would progressively deemphasize policy positions. Through television, argued Kurt and Gladys Lang (1968:210-211),

> The heterogeneity of views on complex policy matters can be factored down to simple alternatives. The search for "truth" becomes a search for "trust." Principles and methods become less important than "sincerity." Such a criterion can become all encompassing.

The end of ideology did not prove all encompassing, however, and just as television and marketing techniques had little to do with its decline, so could they do little to keep ideology from rising again. In retrospect, it is clear that the consensus which existed during the 1959 campaign in Britain, as well as the 1960 election in the United States, had very little to do with the new political technology and owed far more to social and economic conditions. So when truly divisive issues arose later in the decade in both countries (see, for example, Schneider, 1974), the polls and the media merely reflected the new divisions. However "cool" a medium it was, television could hardly undo the effect of riots, the Vietnam War, George Wallace, or the British miners' strike.

I. THE DECLINE OF PARTY ORGANIZATION AND LOCAL COMMUNITY

Needless to say, this extreme "apolitical" view of the effect of technology was rejected by many analysts. In 1960, for example, Butler and Rose (p. 34) criticized those who placed primary emphasis on image building:

> If a party's image and its achievements are greatly at variance, the image will collapse—for images are fragile as well as intangible. Unemployment,

> strikes, inflation and the threats of war cannot be concealed from the public. PR techniques could not have prevented great differences of opinion over Suez; they could only help heal the wounds the crisis created.

But even as they avoided this view, many have accepted several other far more plausible—but still highly debatable—notions concerning the interplay between the media and politics. These include the decline of party membership and organization in Britain (and of partisanship in the U.S.), the collapse of local community, and the nationalization of political campaigning. In their study of the February 1974 election in Britain, Butler and Kavanagh (1974:201) summarized these arguments:

> The developments in the mass media, opinion polling and public relations have by-passed electioneering at the local level. They have been exploited by national campaigners in a way that has undermined the constituency campaign. Party leaders are now able to communicate directly with voters *via* the mass media whereas in the 19th Century they relied largely on the candidates in the constituencies to convey their message to the electorate. This is of course linked to wider developments affecting the decline of community identification in an industrialized and urbanized society. Elections now turn on national events and issues, and voters choose between competing national parties rather than rival local candidates.

Butler and Kavanagh go on to document the decline in party membership, which is clearly the strongest part of their argument. Only the Labour party keeps figures on membership, and these show a steady decline, from 1,015,000 members in 1952 to 703,000 in 1972 (Butler and Kavanagh, 1974:201). More recent figures put membership down still further, at 691,889 (Forrester, 1975:695). This decline has made it difficult for even the more active local parties to stage strong constituency campaigns—and the result has been a steady drop in the number of voters who claim to have been contacted by party workers (Forrester, 1975:696).

Despite their decline, the local parties continue to wield considerable influence—often in the face of substantial opposition from the media—through their power to select their party's candidates (see Butler and Rose, 1960:22). As the recent move by the Newham Northeast Labour party to drop Overseas Development Minister Reg Prentice demonstrated, the actions of the constituency parties can be felt on the national level. But this residual power notwithstanding, the decline in the impact of the local party on the campaign is clear.

The other assumptions embodied in the Butler-Kavanagh view are far more questionable. To begin with, the degree to which local community identification has declined has been exaggerated. Studies of working calss neighborhoods in Britain indicate that forecasts of "the breakdown of 'traditional' forms of social solidarity" have not been borne out, even in the newer working class areas (Willmott, 1963:111; see also Jackson, 1972). And Frank Parkin contends that a working class voter who lives in a working class neighborhood is far more likely to support the Labour party than his comrade in a middle class area. This is so, Parkin says, because of the structural support that these neighborhoods offer for working class ideology and culture, which are subordinate to the dominant values of British society (Parkin, 1967, 1973).

It is also misleading to attribute the nationalization of politics in Britain primarily to the rise of the media. While acknowledging that "the individual constituency counts for less today than it did prior to the rise of the national morning press in the first years of the century," Donald Stokes has argued that "the change [toward nationalization] that took place in British politics in the latter half of the nineteenth century had more explicitly political origins." He also suggests that political factors, not the media, have been responsible for the slow but steady nationalization of American politics (1967:197-198).

Finally, as the following section will show, there was a marked resurgence of local factors during the 1974 British elections. In particular, the rise of Scottish Nationalism pointed to the remarkable degree to which local and regional viewpoints and loyalties have been maintained and strengthened despite the media and other forces pushing toward the homogenization of politics.

II. THE BRITISH ELECTIONS OF 1974: A LOOK AT THE CONSTITUENCIES

The Nuffield College studies of British elections traditionally included descriptions of the local election campaigns in selected constituencies. These were designed to give readers a sense of the flavor of the campaign and to show how the election was perceived by local candidates, campaign workers, and voters.

The 1974 studies do not include descriptions of local campaigns, and this is in part a reflection of the steady decline in the importance attributed to local factors in British elections. Needless to say, the decision to scrap these descriptions made a great deal of sense, in view of the near uniformity of party switching from constituency to constituency. In the introduction to their 1959 constituency reports, for example, Butler and Rose noted that "the results in each case closely matched the regional pattern" and asked: "Were party workers in fact performing a traditional ritual while the outcome was being decided by national forces?" (1960:147).

Yet in the election of February 1974—and to some degree in October—"swing," that privileged statistic in British psephology which measures change in vote from one party to another, worked rather badly.[2] In February, swings varied greatly from region to region, and the tiny two party swing of 0.6 percent to Labour told only a small part of the story of the election. "To the extent that swing is unable to summarize the big shifts in voting in 1974," wrote Michael Steed in his election postmortem (1974:313-314), "it has become less useful as a descriptive index." Clearly, the national, two-party perspective built into the concept of swing proved inadequate for 1974.

In an attempt to assess the degree to which local issues and local factors continue to influence British election results, an associate and I visited 20 constituencies during the February and October election campaigns.[3] In the course of the two campaigns, we interviewed some 200 people—voters, campaign workers, local journalists, elected officials, candidates, MPs, and their agents, and trade union leaders. We attempted to answer two questions: first, how do the national issues of the campaign translate down into the constitutencies? Second, what sorts of local factors and local issues have an impact on the electorate—if any?

The descriptions of the constituency campaigns which follow are necessarily impressionistic and do not claim to be representative. The constituency stories which follow here simply attempt to underline those areas in which politics has not changed radically. As such, they probably overdraw the local and constituency factors.[4] On the other hand, several of the examples do show the degree to which local parties *have* declined and the degree to which media and national strategy have correspondingly increased in importance.

IPSWICH

"Everybody in Ipswich took personal credit for our victory here in 1970," said an officer of the Ipswich Conservative Association during the February 1974 campaign. "They all claim to have brought 13 voters to the polls in the last half hour."

Whoever they were, these 13 voters were responsible for making Ernle Money the first Conservative Member of Parliament in 32 years. Money's 13-vote margin—the smallest of any in Britain's 630 districts—made Ipswich the focus of considerable national attention during the 1974 campaign.

If Ipswich was of interest as the most marginal seat in Britain, it was also a reasonable test for the parties. Both major party candidates, along with the Liberal, were satisfied with their party's leadership and were running campaigns closely in tune with national party strategy.

Money, who has lived in Ipswich most of his adult life, developed a reputation for reliable constituency service. During the campaign, he emphasized his ties to Ipswich and, for good measure, made a point of attending matches of Ipswich's successful football team.

The Labour candidate, Ken Weetch, a lanky economics professor at a nearby college, developed reasonable relations with the local Labour party and trade unions. This was crucial, for many Ipswich Labour supporters attributed their loss in 1970 to rank-and-file disaffection with the 1964-1970 Labour government and with former Labour MP Sir Dingle Foot, who, many Labour supporters argued, had not been a good constituency MP. "Last time, the trade union leaders split off from us because of 'In Place of Strife' (the Labour position paper, later withdrawn, which called for some restrictions on trade unions). This time, the union people are back and ready to work," said Andy Phelps, president of the Ipswich Labour association and head of a textile union local.

Two other candidates appeared on the Ipswich ballot. Mrs. Joan Knott, a 52-year-old housewife, believed that voters were disillusioned with what she called the "extremism" of both major parties. Dr. David Brown, who drew some 2,300 votes in 1970, ran again as the right-wing National Democratic party candidate. His platform was anti-Communist, antiabortion, anti-black immigration, and anti-Common Market.

Britain's decision to leave the Common Market should have been an important issue in Ipswich. Located 13 miles up the River Orwell from the North Sea, Ipswich had seen its port grow quickly as a result of new European trade fostered by Britain's EEC membership. "We in Ipswich are in the so-called Golden Triangle," said Money, "which means that of all places in Britain, we should benefit most from the Market. I was one of the few members to receive more letters in support than against." Weetch took the orthodox Labour line in opposing the terms of entry agreed to by the Conservatives. "The European Spirit is dead," he said. "Most of the cost of the Market is borne by poorer people."

Despite the importance of the EEC issue, all three leading candidates subordinated the Market to the problem of inflation. Money emphasized the fact that "inflation has gone up far less here than in any other European country in the last five years." Weetch simply attacked the government's record. He also stressed the housing shortage, which he blamed on the Conservatives' Housing Finance Act. And on the issue which was the cause of the election, the coal miners' strike, both candidates (and Mrs. Knott) also took the national party position. Money echoed the Conservative party's "Firmness with Fairness" theme, with Weetch responding that "the Conservative government has no idea what fairness is." He argued that the most important issue involved in the coal dispute was how to attract new men to the mines. Recalling his father's insistence that Weetch would never work in a mine, the Labour candidate said, "We need to attract new men and young men to an industry that devours men."

"Most people here don't even know what a coal mine looks like," said John Thompson, political reporter for the Ipswich *Evening Star*. But the class issues raised by the miners' strike went to the core of the Conservative-Labour division in Ipswich, as in the rest of Britain. These issues were dramatized at the two major parties' adoption meetings, when both parties officially named the candidates that they had chosen long before.

The Conservatives held their meeting on a Monday night in a red-carpeted room at the exclusive White Horse Hotel. Men in three-piece suits and women in fur exchanged pleasantries in the ballroom. Some went into the adjoining cocktail lounge, where hostess Fran Sheehan commented approvingly, "There's a difference between the parties. You might call it finesse. I don't know if it's class, education, or what."

About 130 Labour party members adopted Ken Weetch a night later in a room in the Ipswich Town Hall. Hard benches, drab yellow and green decor, and a faded painting depicting Ipswich's pastoral past greeted women in Marks and Spencer coats and men in work jackets.

Behind long tables at the Conservative meeting—attended by some 200 people—sat a large group of local notables including Lord Belsted, the young Under-Secretary of State for Northern Ireland. The meeting was dominated by a well-orchestrated set of speeches praising Money for his service to Ipswich. Money concluded his speech—largely a recitation of the Tory platform—with a patriotic appeal to "keep this country what it always has been: *Great* Britain."

Only five people sat behind the head table at the Labour meeting, including the candidate, his wife, and his agent. The candidate opened the meeting with the greeting "Comrade," a salutation that would be repeated 17 times by various speakers before the night ended. Most of the speeches were spontaneous, and the meeting ended with the passing of a collection basket borrowed from a local church and the singing of the Labour anthem "The Old Red Flag."

The differences in surroundings were symptomatic of the differences in ideology. Money pledged himself to a campaign which would avoid "union bashing," but spoke of the necessity of "not letting militants in the trade unions impose their views on the country." Weetch said that he came from the "moderate socialist center of the Labour Party," but went on to charge that Britain "is being ruled by an effete aristocracy and a grasping middle class." When it came to speeches from the floor, the first speaker at the Conservative meeting told Money, "I expect you to keep an eye on those Communists." As if to reply, the second speaker from the floor at the Labour meeting declared, "As far as I am concerned, a stockbroker under the bed is much worse than a Red under the bed."

In the February election, "the stockbrokers" narrowly beat "the Reds." But in October, Weetch won one of the victories which gave Harold Wilson his narrow parliamentary majority. In February, Mrs. Knott more than doubled the Liberals' 1970 vote, and dropped back only slightly in October. (Dr. Brown's vote fell substantially.)

The Ipswich results in both elections were right on the national form, and without question the returns were dependent on national, not local, issues. All three parties relied almost exclusively on the election materials, slogans, and ideas sent down from party headquarters in London, and none of the three local candidates had any serious disagreements with the national party positions. Both local parties made effective use of fairly large local organizations, and one could plausibly argue that Money's February victory resulted from his attention to and popularity in the constituency. But not even the most enthusiastic proponents of the political impact of technology would deny that local factors can swing at least 200-odd votes, Money's February margin. Moreover, despite Mrs. Knott's active personal campaign, her local Liberal party had little organizational strength. Yet she still managed 16 percent of the vote. The evidence is clear: Ipswich, the area in our sample most typical of marginal constituencies, was decided by national forces, including the media and the national party strategies, themselves partially determined by up-to-date market research.

And what of the class sentiment demonstrated at the two party meetings? Some of this sentiment is certainly part of the past, particularly in view of the high average age at both meetings. On the other hand, both meetings were a fair representation of the sort of people who are active in party affairs and thereby have substantial influence on party stragegy and ideology.[5] These people show no sign of having mellowed ideologically. In fact, if the sentiment of party activists has changed at all in recent years, it has changed on the side of greater ideological militancy. Whether the rising anti-partisan vote for third parties will move the parties and their members back toward the center remains to be seen. It must be said, however, that as long as both major parties continue to rely on class bases—and there are no signs of this changing—they will remain, at least rhetorically, quite far apart on the crucial issues of economic equality and trade union power.

EBBW VALE AND WESTON-SUPER-MARE

In some places, things never change. Wars, depressions, and new parties come and go, but party loyalty endureth forever.

In Ebbw Vale, in southeastern Wales, and Weston-Super-Mare, in southwestern England, the old patterns held up in 1974. In Ebbw Vale, the district once represented by Aneurin Bevan, the leader of the Labour party's left wing in the 1950s, aging steel workers and miners still challenge rebellious young people who say they are voting Tory, charging them with the question: "But don't you remember 1926, when the Tories sent troops into the Valley to break up the general strike?" A clerk in the public library, when asked where the Conservative party headquarters was located, replied, "I wouldn't think there'd be one here, and if there were, I wouldn't tell you where it is." In Weston, on the other hand, most people would not think of voting anything else but Conservative, and given the area's high income, there is no reason why anyone should.

In both districts, the incumbent MPs were so confident of victory that they spent most of their time campaigning for party candidates in other areas. Ebbw Vale's Michael Foot—the Labour Left's candidate for party leader in 1976—made a national tour in his capacity as a major Labour spokesman. Jerry Wiggin, Weston's Conservative member since March 1969, was off to Birmingham, Bristol, and North Devon campaigning for his Tory friends.

Party regularity is about all that Weston and Ebbw Vale have in common. Ebbw Vale is one of the poorest districts in the country, while Weston is a resort town surrounded by Conservative farming villages. Weston also includes a large number of retired people.

Ebbw Vale can be reached from the outside only by bus or car, and the main bus route from Newport winds 21 miles through the hills of south Wales, through coal mining areas and industrial towns. The British Steel factory, which employs 4,000 people, dominates the town's landscape and economy. (In 1975, the government decided to further wind down activity at the already sluggish plant. The action brought hundreds of demonstrators to Mr. Foot's door in London and might conceivably cause him problems in a future election.) Overall, the town is a cross between Appalachia and a rural Pittsburgh: rusted buildings, huge old wooden storehouses, stripped land, gigantic smoke stacks, steam pipes, housing projects broken up by small brick houses, multicolored oil drums, vast parking lots, and the occasional sheep walking across the street.

Jonathan Evans, the 24-year-old Conservative lawyer whom the Conservatives put up as their victim in 1974, knew what awaited him. Two and a half weeks before election day, he walked into Labour headquarters and told Labour agent Ron Evans, "You know I don't expect to win. I just wanted to stop by to say hello. It's a better campaign if we know each other." Evans wound up with 7.8 percent of the vote, an improvement on the vote of his predecessor, who received 7.1 percent in 1970.

In Weston, the situation was exactly reversed. Eton-and-Cambridge-educated Jerry Wiggin won by 20,000 votes in a 1969 by-election and was reelected in 1970 by a 19,000-vote majority. The last time that any other party won in the district was in 1923, when a Liberal squeaked by with a margin of 600 votes. George Witcher, the Conservatives' Weston agent who has been managing campaigns since 1946, admitted that Weston was not his toughest assignment. But he had put together a strong organization, a characteristic of the Conservative party—especially in those areas where it is unbeatable. His organization consisted primarily of middle-aged women who trooped down to the headquarters to engage in fellowship and to do their part to keep Weston from slipping to the Liberals, an unlikely event to be sure.

Foot carried Ebbw Vale by over 15,000 votes, while Wiggin took Weston by more than 13,000. In both constituencies, the Liberals came in second, and the major parties a poor third. (In Ebbw Vale, the Welsh Nationalist came in fourth, with 5.9 percent of the vote.) Weston's Philip Golding nearly doubled his Liberal party's vote, which rose to over 20,000. In Ebbw Vale, however, the Liberal could manage to pull his vote only up to 16.8 percent, a jump of a little over 2 percent.

Both Weston and Ebbw Vale underscore Frank Parkin's point that a community's local culture and value system are central to its concept of politics—and thus to its voting patterns. Particularly in isolated Ebbw Vale (where the first thing one sees getting off the bus is a newspaper rack for *Soviet Weekly*), the overwhelmingly dominant value system is very far indeed from that represented by the BBC, the national press, and other national institutions. But are these areas not atypical? In fact, they represent the vast majority of seats in Britain, where one party has been dominant for decades. To illustrate the extent to which this is true, one need only look at the results of the 1945 and 1959 elections. In 1945, Labour won over 60 percent of the seats, but the Conservatives held on to 213. In 1959, the Conservatives won a landslide victory, but Labour held 258 seats. Adding these two numbers together, one has accounted for 75 percent of the seats up in any election.

To be sure, Ebbw Vale and Weston are the last places one would go to understand political change. But they do demonstrate the remarkable degree to which huge segments of the British electorate have been impervious to the shifts which seem so obvious when viewed from the perspective of London or America.

GLASGOW'S GOVAN

> Your vote tomorrow will have nothing to do with the kind of government Britain will have.
>
> Margo MacDonald
> Scottish Nationalist candidate

"Minor parties can afford to make idealistic promises," said Peter Allison, the secretary of the Scottish Council of the Labour party. He was talking about the Scottish Nationalist party's plan to use North Sea oil revenues as the basis for an independent Scotland. In Scotland, where the Labour party has been strong ever since Scottish trade union leader Keir Hardy set the organization up, the separatist SNP has enjoyed huge success in breaking down old party loyalties. In October, the Nationalists passed the Conservatives in popular vote and ran second to Labour. "SNP gets much of its support from young people who haven't been in politics before," said Allison in his office in Keir Hardie House in Glasgow. "Though young people tend to feel strongly about ideals now, I think they'll find their way into the major parties eventually," he said.

Members of the Labour, Liberal, and Conservative parties all had different criticisms to level at the SNP. The SNP's views on oil were "selfish" said Edinburgh City Councillor and Liberal parliamentary candidate Nat Gordon; it was "too extremist on separation," said Allison; It was "economically naive," according to Conservative party spokesman David Walker. But all conceded that the SNP had "captured a mood," in Walker's words, a mood of protest against the major parties and of dissatisfaction with centralized political structures.

In Glasgow's Govan section, there is a lot to protest about. A blighted collection of empty lots, half-abandoned buildings, and decaying business districts, Govan is widely regarded as one of the worst slums in Europe. To make matters worse, the neighborhood has suffered from a tragic—if typical—failure of urban renewal. Govan had been promised large-scale redevelopment. But shortly after the bulldozers had cleared away many of the old dilapidated structures, the plans for new housing hit a snag in Westminster and were "temporarily" shelved. The neighborhood was left with more empty lots and with tenements which landlords have allowed to deteriorate further. Because of their strong sense of community,

Govanites are enraged over the destruction of their area. There is nothing but bitterness for the politicians who have turned their neighborhood into a new Dresden.

Like Ebbw Vale, Govan is not the sort of place one would usually visit to find out about political change. The workers at the Upper Clyde shipbuilders factory, as well as the rest of the district's blue-collar population, are firmly Labour and staunchly trade union. "You could put a donkey up in Govan," said a local pol quoting an old addage, "and if he had a Labour button on him, he'd win."

Scottish Nationalist Margo MacDonald disproved that theory in the November 1973 by-election. A 29-year-old housewife, she rocked the neighborhood with her rhetoric and her willingness to harrass the local council on behalf of angry tenants. She ran both her by-election and general election campaigns on local issues, stressing that neither party was doing anything about the housing problems in Govan. "Vote for yourselves, vote for Govan," she bellowed up to the families huddled together at the windows of the district's half-vacant tenements.

"I think she got this seat on a big emotional appeal," complained a local Conservative official, who labeled her campaign "American razzmatazz." Certainly the razzmatazz was there: the sound trucks equipped with tapes of a very effective campaign song, the buttons, the balloons, and the posters plastered all over the district. But MacDonald attributed her victory to the rise of nationalism, fed by a feeling that Labour as well as the Conservatives just did not care about Govan. "The problems of Govan just didn't happen in the last three years," she said. "Labour didn't do anything about them either." She added: "The Labour party is no longer a cause. Its only cause is the retention of power."

Some bitter Govan Labour party members complained privately that their party had actually helped the Nationalists by nominating City Councillor Harry Selby to oppose MacDonald. Selby is an affable man who has been fighting for socialism and the Labour party since age 16. But many Labourites felt that his diminutive appearance, his shyness on the campaign trail, and his preference for discussions of left-wing ideology over campaigning made him a pushover for MacDonald's flamboyant style. (As thousands of workers streamed by him at the end of the work day at Upper Clyde shipbuilders, Selby turned to us and began to analyze the political situation in Chile. "The problem with Allende is that he didn't have a

Lenin," Selby said. "The same thing would have happened to Kerensky if it hadn't been for Lenin.") These drawbacks might not have been fatal in the by-elections–indeed, they endeared him to many of his co-workers–had he not been burdened with the additional problem of being a local councillor. As such, he came to symbolize a group which had held power for years and had manifestly been able to do little for the community.

At Labour headquarters, Selby's agent, 67-year-old Joe McGloughlin, captured the spirit of the local Labour party. "I'm the agent, though you probably wouldn't have guessed it," he said. "I'm just doing it because I'm an old friend of Harry's. When he asked me, I said 'yes.' I must have been drunk. I'm too old for this sort of thing." In Govan, Labour was an aging, tired party, rapidly losing membership and support.

Selby did have some things running in his favor. As a local councillor, he had fought the Conservatives' Housing Finance Act–a Conservative measure which had raised rents for most Council House (public housing) tenants. In addition, he had given strong support to a "work-in" protest at Upper Clyde shipbuilders. Both acts helped him among Govan voters, who above all else oppose things as they are. But most of all, he was a Labour man in a district where, well, where even a donkey was supposed to win.

Selby finally did win–in February, by a scant 543-vote margin. The Conservative ran third, the Liberal a very bad fourth. In October, the campaign went along roughly the same lines, but with several important differences. First, Selby was the incumbent MP and, as such, had a chance to do some of the constituency work MacDonald had donw while she was in office. Second, Selby's self-confidence had improved dramatically–even his appearance had improved substantially!–and the Labour party was also more confident. In the meantime, the SNP, while gaining much momentum in the rest of Scotland, lost some of its organizational verve in Govan. Its headquarters, though still very busy, was not nearly so crowded. Many SNP supporters, it seemed, had resigned themselves to the fact the Labour party, once reestablished, was not likely to lose. That turned out to be a sound analysis: Selby was returned by a larger majority.

Still, MacDonald had an important impact on Govan. Her by-election victory was a feat in itself. But a poll by the Opinion Research Center in the district showed something even more important: that the voters agreed with her on the importance of local issues in a parliamentary election. When ORC asked Govan voters if they felt that local issues should be discussed in a general election campaign, 62 percent said "yes." The same question asked in the middle-class Pentlands constituency in Edinburgh drew a "yes" response of only 35 percent. When the 62 percent in Govan were asked which local issue they thought should be discussed, 45 percent said housing, far more than for any other issue. And while only 40 percent of those polled said they would support MacDonald (against 40 percent for Selby), 58 percent said that they would be pleased if she won—indicating clearly that they shared and admired her concern for local issues, even if many (for reasons of party loyalty) could not bring themselves to support her. Finally, *less than 1 percent* mentioned Scottish self-government—the motive force behind the SNP in the rest of Scotland and an issue which received far more media attention than Govan's housing problem—as an issue that they considered important in the campaign. Clearly, MacDonald's appeal on local issues, and not on the better publicized regional issues, won her the by-election and kept her in contention in February and October.

A Note on the Scottish Youth Vote

One cannot leave the subject of Scottish Nationalism without remarking on the fact that the party draws a large proportion of its support from the young, the group whose perceptions of politics have been most importantly influenced by the media. One hypothesis for explaining the SNP's (and also the Liberals') popularity among young people is that the young are far less class conscious than their parents and are thus more likely to oppose both of the major class-based parties. While many forces are at work in bringing about this lessening of class consciousness, television is surely an important one.

This theory of the SNP's youth appeal appears correct in one important respect: that the votes of the Nationalists and the Liberals owe less to any agreement with specific party policies than with the generalized mood of protest. One piece of evidence in support of this view is the fact that the Nationalists tended to do well where the Liberals did poorly, and the Liberals did well where the Nationalists did badly. They were, in other words, competing for the same votes.

Alienated voters selected whichever of the two seemed to have the best chance of winning. In Govan, for example, while MacDonald was rolling up over 40 percent of the vote, the Liberal won only 3.2 percent. In the Roxburgh, Selkirk, and Peebles constituency, on the other hand, popular Liberal party whip David Steel won with over 52 percent of the vote; the Nationalists could only manage 8 percent.

The question is: To what extent is the antipartisan, anticlass orientation among the young the result of television, which is supposed to be a "democratizing" and homogenizing force? This cannot be assessed here, but it is clear that television has had an impact in this direction. What remains curious, however, is that so much of this protest has found its expression in a movement which is nationalistic, anti-English (and the English are, for the most part, the people who run the media), and local and traditional in its search for cultural roots. None of these things would one expect from a generation trained on television. Whatever else it has done, television has not made people sufficiently homogeneous to render them immune to some very "old-fashioned" desires. The Nationalists have felt this way all along, and the two major parties have had to learn it.

LINCOLN

Left-wing Labour MPs like Harry Selby stand for all that Dick Taverne is against. The Member of Parliament from Lincoln, he took a strong stand for "moderation" in the Labour party—and in the process got himself unseated as the Lincoln Labour party's candidate. That Taverne continued to succeed as an independent until October 1974 indicates how important personality and local circumstances can be. On the other hand, his defeat in October demonstrated the difficulties that an independent can have in maintaining himself in the face of strong national political traditions.

The Common Market was the issue over which Taverne clashed with his local Labour party and which eventually led to his dismissal. A strong supporter of the EEC, Taverne joined 69 other Labour Members of Parliament in voting with the Conservatives in favor of Britain's entry. The local party, well to Taverne's left on most issues, used this vote as the basis (Taverne would say "excuse") for its decision to de-designate Taverne. Taverne promptly resigned his seat in order to challenge the party's decision by running in a special by-election as an independent "Democratic Labour" candidate. The election was a referendum on Taverne's position and that of his local party.

A great deal of national attention focused on the by-election, held in March 1973. This media attention enhanced his local image considerably. "His charisma was so fantastic that people ran up to him to touch him," said a Taverne campaigner. Taverne was also aided by public sympathy over what many thought was shoddy treatment by local and national Labour party figures, an impression bolstered by shrill attacks on Taverne by the Labour candidate in Lincoln. The fact that the Tory candidate was Jonathan Guinness, the outspoken national chairman of the right-wing Monday Club, precluded a strong Tory showing and strengthened Taverne's claim on the mantle of the "moderate." Finally, Taverne's 11 years in Parliament had given him a chance to perform the constituency services which always serve an incumbent well at election time. The combination of these factors resulted in a Taverne landslide. He received 58.6 percent of the vote and trounced his former Labour comrades' choice by a humiliating 13,000 votes.

"It was fun to make monkeys out of those guys," said Tony Elkington, an engineer who took leave from his job in marketing to manage both the by-election and the general election campaigns. Elkington was not interested in politics until Taverne drafted him.

Elkington conceded that the general election campaign was "less fun . . . than last time. It's a much more serious thing this time, with the country in such a mess." With Labour fielding a soft-spoken, 31-year-old woman who looked like Princess Anne and with the Tories picking a moderate, it seemed extremely unlikely that Taverne would be able to duplicate his stunning by-election majority. Most people thought Taverne would win by a reduced majority, but no one was quite certain who would end up making a monkey out of whom.

Margaret Jackson, the new Labour candidate, refused to attack Taverne and instead quietly canvassed the working class wards in an attempt to win back traditional Labour support. On leave from her job as a researcher at national Labour headquarters, Jackson ran her campaign on national issues. Similarly, the Conservative candidate, Peter Moran, a 37-year-old solicitor, asserted that "the by-election was a gesture, and now we're choosing a national government." Though Jackson and Moran were partially successful in making national issues the focus of the campaign, much of the voters' attention still focused on Taverne's battle with the Labour party. Even in February, however, Taverne had serious problems in maintaining the feelings of sympathy that he had won in the by-election. "All right, he made his point," said one woman at a doorstep. Others reacted with hostility. "He conned the district. We elected him, and he spent more time in Strasbourg than Westminster," said a man referring to Taverne's membership in the British delegation to the Common Market's European parliament. The frequent repetition of the charge angered Taverne, who saw it as another unfair attack on the Common Market. He considered it damaging enough, however, to resign from the European parliament after the election.

For Taverne, the February results in Lincoln were none too satisfying. His 13,000-vote by-election majority was reduced to 1,300. Jackson ran second. By October, Taverne's position had deteriorated still further, and Jackson defeated him by some 1,500 votes. Also going down to defeat in October was rebel Independent Labour MP Eddie Milne. Milne's disagreements with his party were not ideological–in fact, he was a left winger. His successful campaign in February was built on his charges of corruption against the Labour party in the northeast of England. Responding to what was regarded by virtually all observers as a courageous act, the voters had returned him in February. In October, however, he was unable to buck the trend to Labour.

What do these temporary victories show? In his analysis of the February results, Michael Steed (1974:335) wrote of the victories of Taverne, Milne, and other successful independent candidates:

> Although these were all exceptional cases, and it is noticeable that the majority of them were either in remote (and often insular) constituencies, or in towns which happen to be the right size to be the whole of a single constituency (hence facilitating communications and a natural sense of community), they do demonstrate that in special circumstances the British electorate is now more willing to vote for a person rather than a party.

Surely Steed is correct in the modesty of his claim, especially in view of the October results. Outside Scotland, the return of voters to the two major parties showed that an entrenched two-party system cannot be easily uprooted. Given eight months of minority government, many Labour voters in Taverne's Lincoln and Milne's Blyth constituencies decided that electing a national government was more important to them than registering a local protest. But what is noticeable in both cases is that the rebel MPs were defeated despite the enormous national publicity that they received. (This is especially true of Taverne.) Once again, Labour victories depended largely on the reassertion of *traditional* loyalties.

In short, the experiences of Taverne and Milne can be used to prove many (contradictory) things about localism and the media. It must be acknowledged that Taverne's by-election campaign was helped by the national media exposure that he received. But in neither case did any new campaign techniques have a decisive impact. In both victory and defeat, Taverne and Milne demonstrated the power of several political sentiments: dedication to the local man, admiration for a principled rebel, and loyalty to political party. Each of these sentiments goes back very far in the history of politics.

BRISTOL SOUTHEAST

Journalists from about 20 countries visited Bristol to see how the election was going there. They came to see if Dick Taverne's nemesis (perhaps his raison d'être) could hold onto his seat in Parliament. In social background and personal appeal, Bristol's Tony Benn is Britain's answer to John Lindsay. But when he appears on television, his remarks are to trade unionism what Bella Abzug's are to feminism. He is, finally, one of the most effective platform speakers in British politics.

Benn, who is only 48 but has spent the last quarter century in Parliament, is the personification of Labour's move leftward since its 1970 defeat. "The people who've failed in the last 30 years are the moderates," he says. "I should know. I was one of them," he continues, referring to his days as Harold Wilson's Minister of Technology in the 1966-1970 Government. "We tried as hard as we could, but we failed."

For a press which often delights in pillorying the left, Benn provides a convenient target. He was born Anthony Wedgwood Benn, the son of a Labour MP who was elevated to the House of Lords. Upon the death of his father in 1960, Benn found himself with an inherited title, Lord Stansgate—or, as Benn put it in his campaign literature, he found himself "saddled with a peerage I didn't want." He reluctantly resigned from the House of Commons, but launched an effort to make it legal for a recipient of a noble title to resign his honor (the receipt of which made membership in the House of Commons illegal). His efforts resulted in the Life Peerage Reform Act of 1963, which allowed peers to give up their titles—and Benn to return to the Commons.

Columnists and Conservative party speakers have enjoyed poking fun at Benn's role as a kind of "people's noble," but the constant attention that they have given him underlines the importance that Benn has assumed as a spokesman for the Labour left. This was true even before he became Minister of Industry in 1974. (He is now Energy Minister.) Benn was the man on the talk shows, the first Labour party leader to challenge the rationale for the Conservatives' three-day week during the first 1974 campaign, and one of the two or three Labour spokesmen most outspoken in his defense of the trade-union movement.

Despite his national notoriety, Benn, like Liberal leader Jeremy Thorpe, decided to stay home during the election period because redistricting had placed his seat in apparent jeopardy. In 1970, Benn was reelected by over 5,000 votes. But his district had been changed to include a large and strongly Conservative ward. In addition, two predominantly Labour sections had been replaced by a Labour ward with declining population and low turnout. "Statistically," said Steve Benn, the 22-year-old son of the candidate, "the district is almost a Tory marginal." (Some have argued that the extent to which the district was in fact made more Conservative was exaggerated by all sides for their own purposes.)

Four candidates contested Benn's seat: a Conservative, a Liberal, a candidate of the right-wing National Front, and a supporter of Dick Taverne who ran under the label Social Democrat. As for local issues, the most important was Concorde, the British-French version of SST. Bristol's economy is heavily dependent on the Filton Aircraft Company, which is in turn dependent upon Concorde. To end the Concorde project would be to put a serious dent into Bristol's economy. So all the candidates vied to be the most pro-Concorde candidate in the field.

The real distinguishing characteristic of the Bristol campaign, however, was Benn's personality and national stature. The television crews followed Benn and his family around as they canvassed in February, and, as usual, the Benns were unhappy with the treatment that they received from the media. "When you came up to a Labour person at the doorstep, the cameras just turned away," grumbled 21-year-old son Hilary. But Benn was more optimistic. "Here, people know me rather differently than they do nationally," he said. "I'm the local person who slugs away at local problems. People remember small favors," he says. "People tell me, 'You got my son his surgical boots' or 'You got my son out of jail'." He chuckles "More likely, it's 'You *tried* to get my son out of jail'."

He was to echo the same sentiments the next day at a press conference. "There are really two elections going on," he told reporters. "The electors' election in Bristol Southeast, and the election being run on Fleet Street by the press." The one he was interested in, he said, was the election in Bristol.

A mile away at his small, third-floor headquarters, Social Democrat James Robertson—who received much attention from the Fleet Street constituency—was echoing Taverne's proposals for a coalition government of the "moderates" in the Labour, Liberal, and Conservative parties. Robertson, a tall, articulate, immaculately groomed, former civil servant, characterized Benn as a divisive figure. In calling for his "alliance of moderates," Robertson suggested that Harold Wilson, Edward Heath, Anthony Barber (Heath's Chancellor of the Exchequer) and Tony Benn "should take a couple years' holiday." But despite Robertson's obvious attributes as "a good candidate" and despite the national press's emphasis on this fact, the Bristol Southeast campaign turned out to be a two-party contest. Benn's major opponent was Norman Reece, a respected member of the Bristol city council since 1955 and a local small businessman. Reece had stood against Benn in 1970 and had also been a candidate in a different constituency in the 1966 election. His theory about British elections is that "you can't keep an issue alive for more than four days." In the final days of the election, he hoped to turn voters' attention to Concorde and to his commitment to put the battle to save Concorde above all other concerns.

Reece's attempt to out-Concorde Benn did not work. Against all predictions, Benn won by an increased majority of 8,000. The Social Democrats received a shock in the form of only 1.2 percent of the votes; Robertson ran fifth, behind even the National Front. Benn had been right after all: the voters perceived him as their local Labour MP. Judging from the national polls, Benn had the active support of fewer than a quarter of Britain's electors. On the basis of this evidence, Benn should have won far less than his 47 percent, and

Robertson should have done far better. To the extent that the national publicity did have an impact on Bristol voters, then, it seemed to encourage them to feel the same sentiments toward Benn that Lincoln's voters felt toward Taverne. Even Steve Benn admitted the parallel. "It's a similar sort of feeling," he said. " 'We must be loyal to our guy'." Once again, the media's perceptions seemed quite different from those of the local voters.

III. POLITICAL TECHNOLOGY AND POLITICAL CHANGE

THE ARGUMENT SO FAR

Manifestly, no one of the above examples is in itself representative of the breadth of British politics. Moreover, even taken together, these constituency portraits present a limited and somewhat idiosyncratic view of the way in which British politics are conducted. Bearing this in mind, one can still safely conclude from these examples that:

(1) The new campaign technology—particularly television—has not changed British politics as much as many have claimed.

(2) Too great a focus on political change, and particularly on the changes bred by television, can lead us to overlook crucial continuities.

(3) A significant amount of the change that has taken place in British politics is best explained by nonmedia, nontechnological factors.

THE "FLOATING" VOTER

There remains at least one important aspect of the "technological argument" which has not been touched on so far, except in passing. Even if most people's political views have not changed radically, even if politics has stayed the same in most areas of Britain, and even if local factors continue to have a substantial influence on the political decisions of individuals and groups—even if all these things are true, what about the effect of the media on that important minority of "floating voters," who, by changing from one party to another, decide which way an election will go? Particularly in Britain, where the change of a small number of constituencies can decide which party will win an election, this voter has (for good reason) received an enormous amount of attention from both academic psephologists and political pollsters trying to win elections for parties and candidates. (See, for example, Butler and Stokes, 1974.)

V.O. Key's devastating description of "independent" voters derived from *The American Voter* studies remains the touchstone of most discussions of switchers. He wrote:

> This group of genuine "independents" is not an impressive lot. On the average, its level of information and sense of political involvement is slight, its level of political participation is not high, *its decision on how to vote is made late in the campaign,* and its sense of political efficacy is quite low. Moreover, the "independents" manifest a striking electoral volatility and, insofar as they vote, *tend to move in high degree toward the prevailing side.* [Key, 1966:92, emphasis added]

On the basis of this evidence, particularly Key's points on the switcher's tendency to make his decision at the last minute, usually toward the prevailing side, some have argued that the last-minute TV spot or news item can decide an election. The logic runs something like this: the most easily influenced voter decides elections. The media and market researchers have the greatest influence over him. Therefore, the media and market researchers decide elections. (See, for example, Nimmo, 1970:162, 163-199.)

Key has argued against the idea that American elections are decided purely on the basis of how this uninformed sort of switcher casts his ballot. The election of 1952, he noted (1966:92), was decided by Democrats who chose to back Eisenhower for reasons directly related to the issues which concerned them. The same sort of argument can be applied to the 1964 and 1972 elections. And although the closeness of the vote in 1968 would indicate that last-minute switchers decided the election, it is worth remembering that Nixon's victory came about not because he managed to win over thousands of last-minute changers, but because he managed to hold on to a small part of the huge advantage he enjoyed when the campaign began. Moreover, the 1968 totals reflected a massive swing against the Democrats, not simply a trickle of confused souls from one side to the other. Finally, much of the switching that did go on in 1968 was among Wallace voters, and polling evidence indicates that Wallace defectors were "rational" in their choices. Wallace's former supporters who were trade-union members, Democrats, and the poor—in general, those who were closer to Humphrey's positions1 on economic issues—tended to back the Democratic nominee. Wallace defectors who were wealthy, Republican, or nonmembers of trade unions—generally, those whose views were close to Nixon's—backed the Republicans (Lipset and Raab, 1973:395-398).

In Britain, it might be argued, switchers are a smaller group, have more influence, and represent the hard core of the "uninformed" electorate. Yet the evidence from the polls done for the Labour party by Robert Worcester of Market and Opinion Research International indicates that a very large chunk of these voters are "pragmatic" and decide on the basis of such bread and butter issues as wages and salaries, housing, poverty, and unemployment (Butler and Kavanagh, 1974:92-93). To be sure, last-minute media campaigns have an impact on this group, and the polls which identify their concerns obviously lead party leaders to discuss these themes. But to argue from this that the media or the polls are *the* decisive factors in getting these people to decide is surely misleading. Finally, the swing voter is surely not a new political phenomenon. Politicians have always aimed persuasion at the persuadable. Only the precision with which we can identify the concerns of the persuadables has changed. This is a significant—but far from revolutionary—shift.

CENTRISM AND THE FLOATING VOTER

A number of political scientists have criticized the focus on the "floating voter" and the related theories that parties must appeal to the political center because (a) that is where the floaters are and (b) that is where most of the rest of the voters are too. Richard Hamilton has argued that "the 'end of radical politics' in many countries may well be the result of self-fulfilling prophecies." Leaders of the parties of the Left, he says, "believing the people will no longer respond to liberal or leftist issues, now stress other concerns. The newly moderate leaders lose elections (because many voters no longer see them as standing for the issues that interest them)." In the wake of defeat, the moderate leaders attribute their loss to extremism and call for still more moderation (Goldthorpe et al., 1969:192).

Hamilton gets at part of the key problem now confronting students of American and British politics, particularly those interested in the role played by polling and the media. In general, the voters can make sense of the political system when they see that the major parties are taking clear stands and *when these stands are on issues that are of interest to them* (Verba and Nie, 1972:111-113). It is the second half of this sentence which helps to explain the apparent anomoly of so many voters who say at one and the same time that they no longer see any major differences between the two parties *and* that the parties are becoming "too extreme." (This problem is particularly acute in Britain, but it is also present in the United States.)

On the one hand, the vast majority of voters in both countries continue to believe that there are identifiable differences between the beliefs and (more importantly) the *interests* of various groups in society. While most voters do not have a full-blown model of the class structure, they do know how various schemes effect their interests relative to those of other groups. Or, as Verba and Nie (1972:113) put it, "What we are suggesting is that on matters of the politics of everyday life, citizens know what they want." Whatever else has changed in British or American politics, voters still want political parties to stand up for their own interests—and these voters know that these interests can be in conflict with those of other groups. Insofar as politicians fail to speak clearly—and differently—on these conflicts, they will be viewed as becoming more alike.

But while critics of the "decline of ideology" thesis are well advised in their attacks on a purely "centrist" politics of conflict avoidance, many of these same critics err in vastly overemphasizing the degree to which "ideological" differences which are salient to party activists are also important to the rank and file. For example, while the terms "left and right" and "conservative and liberal" are de riguer for those who devote a lot of time to politics, they are simply not important to most voters in Britain or the U.S. (Butler and Stokes, 1974:323-331; Verba and Nie, 1972:109). And this is not just a rhetorical point. Attached to these terms are a series of "litmus paper" tests which divide parties bitterly over issues which are often very remote from voter concerns. These issues are usually expressed in terms of moral choices, and sometimes, as in the case of Vietnam or racial equality, the questions actually are moral. But these moral tests are often extended to issues and strategies which are best considered—and are so considered by the great mass of voters—not in relation to some abstract "morality," but in terms of results, which of course can be measured as progress toward some desired moral goal. A good case in point is the issue of nationalization in Britain. Arguably, many voters oppose nationalization simply because they accept the dominant ideology of capitalism. But much of the opposition stems from the fact that many voters fail to grasp either the moral or the strategic arguments put forth by the Labour left. This is the case because must of the left's rhetoric on the issue involves not so much argument as the presentation of a moral imperative. Despite some clarification of the Labour argument for nationalization over the last few years, voters continue to wonder what kind of differences nationalization will make *for them.* The task for those who would nationalize is not to get voters to believe in nationalization as an abstract principle. Rather, it is to show what nationalization would do to foster greater equality, efficiency, or democracy. If those who favor nationalization cannot make this case, they will be viewed as extremists—and rightly so.

The second task in restoring confidence in the electoral system, then, is to avoid the sort of misplaced moralizing of which voters are naturally distrustful and which makes issues ever more remote from day-to-day concerns (Novak, 1973).

POLITICAL TECHNOLOGY AND POLITICAL CHOICE

What has political technology not changed? What have been the negative effects of the misconceptions concerning the role of political technology? Finally, what useful role might political technology play in the future?

Turning to the first two questions, we have seen that serious conflicts of interest persist and that these have not been attenuated by political technology. Moreover, we have seen that voters themselves have not changed that much and that they are still responsive to traditional appeals based on interest. Students of the media and of market research have persuaded candidates that image is more important than substance, that voters are no longer interested in getting different viewpoints from the parties, and that elections are decided largely by swing voters who do not know very much. In doing so, they have led us into a situation in which political choices are progressively less meaningful. As a result, an electorate which is far more intelligent than the politicians and technocrats think it is, begins to lose interest in democratic politics.

Second, we have seen that local factors and local concerns remain important to voters. Indeed, Lutbeg has found that, as issues become more local and more specific, voters' views become clearer and more consistent (cited in Verba and Nie, 1972:113). The widespread belief that the desires for local autonomy and for the preservation of local tradition are relics of the past could make both politics and the media ever more remote from citizens' real concerns.

With the new campaign spending limits in the United States, our politics are likely to resemble the British style a bit more closely. The spending limits will have the effect of reducing the role played by television advertising and could reduce the role of polling as well. The laws will also put a higher premium on political activism —campaigns will become more people intensive. (See Schlesinger, 1975; Polk, 1975.) In light of this, what role is campaign technology likely to play in the future?

Thus far, political technology has not changed politics as radically as many thought it would because many expected (and some even hoped) that the technologicization of politics would discourage diversity and reduce disagreement—in short, would foster a uniformity which is the antithesis of politics.[6] In the] future, we will probably get more by expexting less. For example, given the growing importance of political activism and given the tendency of activists to talk in a language and about issues remote from voter concerns, opinion polls could be used to inform them just how often their conceptions of the issues are at variance with those of the electorate. The point is not to use polls to "tell the voters what they want to hear," but to discuss issues in such a way that the central concerns of campaigns will relate more closely to the central concerns of the voters. With the reduction of television advertising, television could begin to play an even greater informational role, especially if cable television systems are organized in such a way as to foster more broadly based local participation.

When viewed as a way of *fostering* diversity and clarifying the bases of *dis*agreement, the new developments in political technology could begin to serve their real function: to democratize, not to end, politics.

NOTES

1. David Butler (1955:49) quotes an editorial from *The Times* suggesting a cutback in media time for candidates as a way of preventing image from dominating substance, and

manner from dominating content. Butler criticized the fears of those who, like the Langs, felt that television would reduce the content of politics.

2. Steed defines "swing" as follows: "Swing is an index of several types of movement expressed in terms of their net effect on the two major parties, as if all changes were in one direction from one main party to the other. Even in straight fights, the net figure also covers movement to and from abstention and changes in the composition of the electorate. In more complex contests, movements to and from third parties are compressed within the single statistic of swing" (1974:314).

3. My debt to Bud Sheppard, with whom I traveled during both elections, is very great indeed. He and I worked together on an earlier version of this paper, and Bud will recognize many of the ideas and descriptions here as his own, or as mutual concoctions. He will also disagree with many things here, and he bears no responsibility for whatever is wrong. I should also like to thank Dr. William Schneider and Frederick D. Weil, both of whom should also remain blameless.

4. Bernard Crick wrote of the lawyer's use of evidence: "The evidence is shaped according to his own and his client's self-interest; he does not throw a packet of facts on the table and invite judges to sort it out themselves. He, like any politician, attempts to prejudice the issue." He goes on to say: "The student of government should indeed attempt to be more dispassionate than the advocate or politician; but he will not succeed in becoming passionless unless he becomes quite irrelevant to the life of a free society" (1964:102).

5. The degree of influence which party activists have–and should have–is source of bitter debate in Britain and America, especially in the Labour and Democratic parties. For a critique of the role played by left activists, see Lipset, 1975:163-165, for the United States, and Taverne, 1974, for Britain. It should be noted that while the left and right "extremes" enjoy considerable influence as a result of their high degree of political participation, they surely do not have a monopoly on political activism. The "center" also enjoys considerable representation among the ranks of activists, especially when one includes trade union leaders, fund raisers, and office-holders.

6. In a useful study, which is wise in its caution, Edward Chester suggests that television and radio "have changed rather than revolutionized politics" (1969:309).

REFERENCES

BAGDIKIAN, B.H. (1971). The information machine. New York: Harper and Row.

BOORSTIN, D. (1961). The image: A guide to pseudo events in America. New York: Harper and Row.

BUTLER, D.E. (1955). The British general election of 1955. New York: St. Martin's.

BUTLER, D.E., and ROSE, R. (1960). The British general election of 1959. New York: St. Martin's.

BUTLER, D.E., and KAVANAGH, D. (1974). The British general election of February 1974. London: Macmillan.

BUTLER, D.E., and STOKES, D. (1974). Political change in Britain (2nd ed.). London: Macmillan.

CHESTER, E. (1969). Radio, television and American politics. New York: Sheed and Ward.

CRICK, B. (1964). In defense of politics. London: Penguin.

FORESTER, T. (1975). "Labour's local parties." New Society (25 September):695-696.

GOLDTHORPE, J.; LOCKWOOD, D.; BECHHOFFER, F.; and PLATT, J. (1969). The affluent worker in the class structure. Cambridge: Cambridge University Press.

JACKSON, B. (1972). Working class community. London: Penguin.

KEY, V.O. (1966). The responsible electorate. New York: Vintage.

LANG, K., and LANG, G. (1968). Politics and television. Chicago: Quadrangle.

LIPSET, S.M. (1975). "The paradox of American politics." Public Interest, No. 41(Fall).

LIPSET, S.M., and RAAB, E. (1973). The politics of unreason. New York: Harper Torchbooks.

McGINNISS, J. (1969). The selling of the president, 1968. New York: Trident.

NIMMO, D. (1970). The political persuaders. Englewood Cliffs, N.J.: Prentice-Hall.

NOVAK, M. (1973). Choosing our king. New York: Macmillan.

PARKIN, F. (1967). "Working class Conservatives." British Journal of Sociology, 18(3):278-290.

--- (1973). Class inequality and political order. London: Paladin.

POLK, J.R. (1975). "The new rules of money in politics." Working Papers for a New Society (Fall):31-36.

SCHLESINGER, S. (1975). "Parties to reform." Working Papers for a New Society (Fall):22-28.

SCHNEIDER, W. (1974). "Public opinion: The beginning of ideology?" Foreign Policy (Winter):88-120.

STEED, M. (1974). "The results analysed." Appendix 2 in D.E. Butler and D. Kavanagh (eds.), The British general election of February 1974. London: Macmillan.

STOKES, D. (1967). "Parties and the nationalization of electoral forces." In W.N. Chambers and W.D. Burnham (eds.), The American party system. New York: Oxford University Press.

TAVERNE, D. (1974). The future of the left. London: Jonathan Cape.

VERBA, S., and NIE, N.H. (1972). Participation in America. New York: Harper and Row.

WILLMOTT, P. (1963). The evolution of a community: A study of Dagenham after forty years. London: Routledge and Kegan Paul.

CONTRIBUTORS

JEWEL BELLUSH is Professor of Political Science at Hunter College of the City University of New York. Her work has been largely in the area of urban politics and includes *Race and Politics in New York City* and *Urban Renewal: People, Politics, and Planning.*

WILLIAM J.D. BOYD is Assistant Director of the National Municipal League. His research has concentrated on various aspects of electoral reform including reapportionment and changes in the Electoral College.

ALASTAIR DAVIDSON is Senior Lecturer in Politics at Monash University, Melbourne, Australia. He has published numerous articles on the Communist party in Italy as well as a recent biography of Gramsci.

PAUL A. DAWSON is Associate Professor of Government at Oberlin College and has been the editor and author of a number of works examining modern political practices. He has also taught at the University of Wisconsin, Madison.

E.J. DIONNE is currently writing for the Sunday Department of the *New York Times.* Previously he spent a good deal of time in Great Britain studying British electoral politics.

JOEL L. FLEISHMAN is Vice Chancellor for Education and Research in Public Policy, Director of the Institute of Policy Sciences and Public Affairs, and Professor of Law at Duke University. His previous articles on public financing have appeared in a number of law journals.

ALFRED GROSSER is Director of Research at the Fondation Nationale des Sciences Politiques and Professor at the Institute d'Etudes Politiques, University of Paris. His recent books include *The Federal Republic of Germany, La politique exterieure de la Ve Republique,* and *La politique en France* (with François Goguel).

VICTOR J. HANBY is Lecturer in Political Sociology, University of Sterling, Scotland. A former Fulbright Scholar, he is editor of *The American Indian: A Social and Political Evaluation* and author of several articles on European political parties which have appeared in American and European journals.

LOUIS MAISEL is Assistant Professor of Government, Colby College, and editor of the series of which this book is a part. He is coeditor of *The Future of Political Parties* and has published a number of articles on American state and national parties.

ANTHONY SMITH is Research Fellow at St. Anthony's College, Oxford. A BBC television producer for ten years, he has written on European politics for many periodicals and is the author of *The Shadow in the Cave.*

JAMES E. ZINSER is Associate Professor of Economics at Oberlin College. While his primary interest is Latin American economics, he has dealt with economic modeling of political campaigns in earlier research reported in the *Public Opinion Quarterly.* He has also taught at the University of Oregon and held research positions in Buenos Aires.

NOTES

NOTES

NOTES

NOTES

NOTES

NOTES